HD
70   Dreyfack, Raymond
.J3   Making it in management,
D73   the Japanese way.
1982
DATE DUE

SEP 19 1983			
NOV 15 1983			
NOV 29 1983			
MAY 12 1984			
DEC 9 1980			

DEMCO

MAKING IT IN MANAGEMENT— THE JAPANESE WAY

by

Raymond Dreyfack

FARNSWORTH PUBLISHING COMPANY, INC.
Rockville Centre, New York 11570

© 1982, Raymond Dreyfack.
All rights reserved.
Published by Farnsworth Publishing Co., Inc.
Rockville Centre, New York 11570.
Library of Congress Catalog Card No. 82-5175.
ISBN 0-87863-006-6.
Manufactured in the United States of America.
No part of this book may be reproduced
without the written permission of the publisher.

Library of Congress Cataloging in Publication Data
Dreyfack, Raymond, 1919-
    Making it in management, the Japanese way.

    Includes index.
    1. Industrial management—Japan. 2. Industrial
management—United States. 3. Industrial productivity—
Japan. 4. Industrial productivity—United States.
I. Title.
HD70.J3D73   658'.00952   82-5175
ISBN 0-87863-006-6   AACR2

Dedication

for Tess

THANK YOU

My thanks to the following corporations: Atlantic Richfield, Dana, Delta Airlines, Digital Equipment, General Motors, Hewlett-Packard, IBM, Proctor & Gamble, Texas Instruments, 3M, and to management consultants Leonard J. Smith and Roy W. Walters, for the helpful information and insights provided. Plus others too numerous to mention.

My special thanks to Matsushita Electric and Panasonic Companies—and specifically to Ken Kurahashi, Mitsumasa Aoyama, Yuji Inokumo, Yancy Y. Fukagawa, Ken K. Shimba, and Kappei Morishita—for their time, cooperation and patience. And my special thanks to Michael R. Losey of Sperry New Holland, Michael R. Simmons of Butler Manufacturing Co., and Myron Emanuel of Towers, Perrin, Forster & Crosby for sharing the results of their Japanese visits and studies with me and my readers.

And my very special thanks to Konosuke Matsushita, elder statesman of Japanese enterprise, for the inspiration he provided as I researched and wrote this book.

Raymond Dreyfack
Fair Lawn, New Jersey

PREFACE

Digested and considered objectively, this book will help you to make your company more competitive and, equally important, give you a fresh new perspective on your managerial style and effectiveness.

The U.S. is in a new kind of economic bind. We have been in "hard times" before, but this time is different. For long years in the past, hard times or not, America ranked as the world's leading and most productive supplier of high quality merchandise, the world's leading exporter, the world's leading competitor. We no longer can claim this distinction.

Today the U.S. is faced with declining sales and growing unemployment in several key industries—automobile, TV, textiles, watches, office machines, shipbuilding, and others—because consumers are opting for foreign products, most notably from Japan. The auto industry is the classic example with Detroit one of the nation's hardest hit cities, and with Big Three losses in recent years well into the billions. With more than 20% of America's working population engaged directly or indirectly in the production, sale or servicing of cars, we are, to state the case bluntly, in one hell of a bind. And the problem is rapidly spreading to other industries as well.

What can we do about it? Automation? Of course. Automation helps, and we are applying it to the hilt wherever we can. But automation helps foreign competitors as well, and probably helps the Japanese more than it helps us because automation creates far fewer labor-management problems in Japan than it does in the U.S.

Trade restrictions? Those in favor argue that a curb on imports would stem the flood of foreign products into this country and thus bolster the sale of American products. But restricted trade was bad news two centuries ago and it's bad news today. For one thing, it would reduce exports as well because foreign nations would retaliate. For another, it would penalize the American consumer who would be compelled to pay the jacked-up prices of Detroit and other manufacturers. For a third, and most important, we would jeopardize foreign relations with now friendly countries. Nations that trade freely with each other are far more likely to remain peaceful.

Nor is this all we are up against. Coincidental with faltering U.S. productivity, product quality problems, and the onslaught of foreign competition, we are experiencing a new "rights consciousness" among American workers. Mitchell Prize Award writer Professor James O'Toole of UCLA's Center for Futures Research, states the situation simply enough: "Wanting more for less is not a problem if the engine of economic growth is running in fine tune. But the engine has started to knock."

The U.S. economy today is ill equipped to boost the level of compensation and benefits to worker expectations while it attempts to cope with the flood of high quality imports from a country like Japan whose rate of productivity growth is at the top of the scale while U.S. productivity growth is close to the bottom.

So where do we go from here? The evidence has been mounting rapidly in recent years that the chief ingredient in the remarkable success formula for leading Japanese industrial corporations is *managerial effectiveness*. The evidence is equally convincing that the chief ingredient in the poor worker productivity and product quality decline in the U.S. is the failure of American management methods to respond satisfactorily to employee needs and desires.

No place is this contention more persuasively demonstrated than in Japan's Matsushita Electric Industrial Co., Ltd., one of the world's most successful and best managed corporations. In no individual is the contention more persuasively demonstrated than in the person of Matsushita Electric's founder and longtime chief executive, Konosuke Matsushita who today, at age 88, still functions as an advisor to the company. Konosuke Matsushita's style and philosophy of management is neither esoteric nor sophisticated. No computer will be needed to unravel its complexities. His techniques and principles are simple enough for a high school graduate of average intelligence to understand, appreciate and—most important—*apply*. Their beauty is that they work. They work in Japan and, as this book will prove, in the U.S. as well.

There are some who maintain that Japanese style management cannot work in America because of the differences in culture and lifestyle between the two countries. This claim is false and will be proven false in this book. Japanese style management does work in America. It works with American workers and when administered by American managers. Several convincing case histories will be presented to demonstrate *how* Japanese style management works in America and *why* it works. In fact, the evidence will reveal that in some corporations Japanese style management— *imported in large measure from the U.S.*—was working in America long before it was introduced to Japan.

While it is true that we can't superimpose Japanese strategies and techniques on U.S. corporations—nor would we want to—the fact remains that human beings are human beings the world over, with the same basic needs and desires. If these needs are satisfied, workers will respond positively. If workers are embittered and frustrated, they will balk, whether the workers are Japanese, European, or American.

This book, reinforced with and inspired by the wisdom of the greatest manager of them all, Konosuke Matsushita, will attempt to demonstrate what needs to be done to ensure managerial effectiveness, turn around U.S. worker productivity, restore America's high quality reputation in the marketplace, and reassert American economic leadership throughout the world.

Raymond Dreyfack

CONTENTS

1. The Foundation: A Philosophy Of Management 7
2. The Japanese Edge 25
3. The Japanese Way 49
4. The American Imperative 79
5. People 105
6. We-Power 125
7. The Workplace 149
8. Beyond The Bottom Line 173
9. Perspective 197
10. The Japanese Productivity Edge 219
11. The Look Alikes 241
12. Making It Happen 287
    References 329
    Index 337

1.

THE FOUNDATION: A PHILOSOPHY OF MANAGEMENT

> *The most important factor in management is sometimes overlooked; without an appropriate management philosophy, personnel, technology and capital cannot be used to their full potential.*
> —*Konosuke Matsushita*

The Man

Konosuke Matsushita is a living legend in Japan and is on his way to becoming a worldwide legend. In a nation sometimes criticized for followership or me-tooism, he is an entrepreneur in the truest sense of the word.

A frail 88 as these words are written—he has long been sickly—his words and thoughts possess the robust health and strength of a powerful giant. The son of a poor rice dealer, he could serve as a model for a Horatio Alger epic. Forced to quit school and get a job at an early age when his father lost the family savings and home, he was apprenticed to an Osaka merchant polishing porcelain all day with a grim future before him. He was subsequently apprenticed to a bicycle shop owner, then went to work for an electric power company.

In 1918 at age 23 he had an idea. Although electricity had come to Japan, bicyclists still rode the streets at night lighting their way with wax candles. Matsushita saw the need for a bicycle lamp, developed one, and practically browbeat dealers into stocking it after their unfortunate experience with a prior lamp that had proved defective. To convince them his lamp would burn at least 30 hours, he left a "demo" in each shop.

From these humble beginnings Matsushita Electric, manned by a contingent of three, was born. When the bicycle lamps started moving, Matsushita couldn't produce enough of them. Today Matsushita Electric Industrial Co., Inc. is the world's largest consumer electronic group with over 130,000 employees worldwide, 71 manufacturing and sales companies, and employees or representation in over 130 countries. It produces more than 10,000 products from flashlight batteries to computerized traffic control systems and in 1980 enjoyed sales of $13.7 billion.

In his "spare time" Matsushita founded a publishing house which, in addition to books and other publications, produces *PHP,* Japan's biggest selling magazine with a circulation of 1.2 million. He started a philanthropic institute also called PHP, which stands for Peace and Happiness through Prosperity, and has seen PHP Clubs spring up all over Japan where people come to study, meditate and exchange ideas.

In 1973 Matsushita traded his title of Chairman for Executive Advisor, but is as active as ever since his retirement. Japan's most sought-after lecturer, in 1980 he started his own graduate school, the Matsushita School of Government and

Management, for the avowed purpose of molding Japanese leaders for the 21st century. In student and newspaper polls Matsushita is consistently voted one of the world's most admired and respected men. Today he is more popular and better known in Japan than Reggie Jackson is in the United States. A thumping success by anyone's standards.

In November 1981, Matsushita Electric Industrial Co. donated $1 million to Harvard Business School to create a "Chair of Leadership" in Konosuke Matsushita's name.

The Role of Philosophy in Business

Picture this situation. A marketing executive in a U.S. company gives an assistant an assignment. A competitor has been making inroads in an important market segment. The aide's task is to come up with a cooperative advertising program for the area that will help the company regain its lost market share.

A couple of days later the young man returns to his boss with the program. The executive reviews it and winces. "How did you ever dream up this hare-brained idea?" The assistant is crestfallen. He feels defeated, his self-confidence and morale shaken. His boss reassigns the project. "This time, use your head."

Case No. 2. In a multiplant manufacturing company a division's profits keep shrinking in direct ratio to its increasing sales volume. The situation persists over a period of several months. The Chief Executive Officer at headquarters finally hands down a mandate: "Pinpoint the problem, or else." A bright young financial whiz is dispatched to the scene armed with hatchet and scythe. Ambitious and resolute, he surveys the situation. The cause of the deterioration becomes clear to him in a matter of days, or so he believes. It's a sloppy operation. Errors proliferate like moisture-fed fungus. Absenteeism and lateness exceed industry records. To state that morale was low would have been to admit it existed. The axman sets his mind to the task. He sees what has to be done. Employees in the plant are getting away with mayhem. The operation is loose and undisciplined. The division needs a strong, steady hand and a head focused on profits.

Strategy number one is to sift through the records and fire 10 percent of the division's least-productive workers. This should get the message across. It does. Within hours pure chaos erupts. Within weeks the plant is shut down.

One more example. Manager X, employed as purchasing vice president of a parts distributing company, is under pressure from his boss, who is under pressure from the CEO, to cut costs in order to boost bottom line performance. With this dictate in mind, he calls an important supplier and informs him that his prices are too high. "If you want to continue doing business with us, you'll have to give us a better discount."

"But Jim, we're at rock bottom already. If we cut our prices any further, we'll wind up in a hole."

The VP knows this is true but is adamant nonetheless. The supplier, dependent on the customer, feels he has no choice but to go along, for the present at least.

No one is saying these situations couldn't be duplicated in Japan. But they are much less likely to occur there than in this country. In the U.S., for many companies, shabby and

The Foundation: A Philosophy Of Management

inconsiderate treatment of employees, suppliers, and customers is more or less standard operating procedure. In Japan it runs against the cultural grain of the country. For the Japanese company with a proper philosophy of management, incidents such as those outlined above would be rare.

Take case number one. The Japanese manager, confronted with what he believed to be an unacceptable advertising program, would have in all probability said something like, "That shows good thinking and an interesting approach. But we should consider some alternative strategies as well. It will be interesting to see what you can come up with." He would then respectfully bow the aide out of his office. The aide would get the message, but in a "face-saving" way that would preserve his self-esteem, and certainly wouldn't provoke bitterness.

Similarly, in the second example, the human consideration would be uppermost in the well managed Japanese company. (No claim will ever be made that *every* Japanese company is well managed!) In the situation at hand, the premise would be that people, being human, are less than perfect. This is natural and expected. Shown the error of their ways in a kind, sensitive and humane manner, if indeed error is indicated, employees are only too happy to make the changes and corrections called for. After all, this is not only in the organization's best interests but in the best interests of the individual as well. Thus the rampaging indiscriminate ax wielder would be unpopular in Japanese management circles, whereas in the U.S. he is too often glorified as a hero. In the Japanese company where management is regarded as an art and its philosophies held sacrosanct, the assumption, until proven otherwise, is that where employee performance is found wanting, the manager and not the employee is at fault.

The third case indicates that the organization's underlying philosophy and standards of fair play are shaky. Philosophically, the successful Japanese manager believes that for the corporation to make progress and grow, its products and activities must result not only in a fair profit, but must be beneficial to the community in which it functions, to employees, customers, suppliers and all others with a stake in the enterprise, and to society as a whole. Making a profit at the expense of another's ruination or loss is looked upon as self-defeating and wrong. Thus it is unlikely that the supplier squeeze described would occur in the well-managed Japanese company.

No one would deny that large corporations make a major and profound impact on the economy of the modern industrialized nation. In balance, and based on what appears to be mushrooming evidence, proportionately speaking, a much greater percentage of large U.S. companies are operating counterproductively than large Japanese companies *because they are being managed without the direction and guidance of an underlying philosophy of management.* This is one natural advantage Japan has over the U.S. Much of the Japanese philosophy of management is built into the Japanese culture; it represents a philosophy of living as well. It represents most of all a philosophy of the individual's worth and of working and dealing with people.

In America the large corporation is in essence a vast and complex processing system that evolves over the years. More often than not its growth is generated by the numbers of products or services sold and the accompanying actions and transactions, rather than founded on a philosophically based growth plan. Each employee is slotted into his niche with little if any understanding of what the organization is, how it works, or why it is needed. This knowledge is not required for the individual to perform his daily task. He thus becomes deep-seatedly ingrained from a functional standpoint and inherently change-resistant, since he reflects a methodology divorced from ideals and principles habitually formed over years. He may be given pep talks to condition him for today's accelerating change. But this doesn't prepare him to cope with the change. You can't alter overnight habitual work and thought patterns that took years to develop. So the real barrier to growth and success lies not in natural apathy or low morale but in the ethos of organization itself, in the patterns developed and hardened; basically, in the way people think about themselves and their jobs.

The handicap is not insurmountable. But one thing becomes clear from a comparison between successful Japanese management and less-than-successful U.S. management: that for human attitudes and self-perceptions to be constructively modified, the process must be grounded in a proper growth-oriented *and profit-oriented* philosophy of management. Perhaps herein lies the greatest barrier of all to U.S. productivity—the lack of realization and awareness that a people-focused philosophy of management is not only decent, fair and compassionate, but that it is profitable as well. This may be the most important lesson we have to learn from Japan. Certainly it is the cornerstone of the Matsushita organization's success.

The Matsushita Credo

In the early years, the 1920s and '30s, as his business prospered and grew, Konosuke Matsushita began to wonder if good management wasn't something more than simple common sense. Although it's important to use your head, he reasoned, he questioned the *meaning* behind a business enterprise and wondered if there weren't higher goals involved than the accumulation of wealth. He talked about this with many people and out of his discussions and thinking a management philosophy started to emerge. He recalls, "My employees also were influenced by my philosophy and discovered a purpose for their employment in our company. In other words, you might say that a soul had been put in the company's management. From that time onward, I was surprised at the rapid development of our business."

Throughout the years, Japan lived through many periods of political unrest and economic upheaval, and finally its stunning World War II defeat. Many changes were made in the business thinking and climate. On more than one occasion the company had to face extremely difficult times, revise and adjust operating strategies and techniques. But through it all the company's underlying management philosophy held strong and remained intact.

Matsushita Electric continued to prosper and grow. "Only with a proper management philosophy," asserts its founder, "is sound business development possible."

He goes on to say, "The starting point of a true management philosophy lies in the laws of society and rules of nature. Though a management outlook which grows out of this philosophy may differ somewhat in application depending on the condition of the times, I think it may be said that its foundations are unchanging. In other words, a management philosophy established on what is right in terms of essential human qualities and nature is something which prevails through the past, present and future—both in Japan and in other countries."

What follows are highlighted excerpts from Konosuke Matsushita's philosophy of management as it applies to both business and life, since the two interact on a day to day basis. (From selected writings, *PHP Magazine.*)

On the Natural Laws. "When you talk about particular natural resources there are limits; some resources eventually may be used up. However, I think replacements will be discovered or produced as the result of advances in human knowledge . . . ."

"In some respects, even ordinary people can lead the sort of lives that past kings and nobles would not have dreamed possible. This prosperity results from the bounty of nature and the make-up of human beings functioning within the laws of nature and society . . . ."

"Human life, as well as the encompassing vastness of nature and the universe, has untapped resources of evolutionary potential; we must conduct enterprise activities with an awareness of these resources. Regardless of any particular situation, it is extremely important to understand and act in accordance with the principle of untapped creativity. A clear understanding of the laws of man and nature is the only foundation upon which to build truly strong management."

On Human Relationships. "Management is conducted by human beings, and the manager in charge is himself a human being. Employees, good customers and contacts are all human beings. That is to say, management is an activity carried out with the cooperation of human beings toward human happiness . . . ."

"My own management philosophy is based on my personal understanding of humanity. Stated briefly, it is that human beings stand at the pinnacle of existence as the lords of all things. In accordance with the natural laws that all things in nature are infinitely productive and progressive, humans can make the most of their lives, and also can make unlimited progress in their community by utilizing all things of the universe . . . ."

"The mission of a company is to manufacture good quality products after developing the potential of people with the ability to fulfill the company's mission . . . my experiences in business have convinced me that developing the true potential of employees and managers is an essential principle of business management. How can a manager develop the potential of others? I believe that the answer lies in the company's basic thoughts on two other important questions: 'What is the purpose of this company?' and 'How should this company be managed to fulfill its mission to society?' . . ."

"Without a fundamental philosophy of management, it will be difficult to promote self-development throughout the company. Therefore, as a manager, if you want good people, you must have a strong sense of mission and a proper understanding of the reasons and purpose of management . . . ."

"A management philosophy is worthless if it exists only on paper. To be truly effective, management must exist in the hearts and minds of each and every employee . . . ."

On the Manager's Role in Society. "Some people think that the purpose of an enterprise is to make a profit. Indeed, profit is indispensable for conducting proper enterprise activities . . . . However, profit in itself is not the ultimate goal of an enterprise. More basic is the effort to improve human life through enterprise management. Profit becomes important and necessary only to better pursue this basic mission. Enterprise management is essentially a public, not a private matter: an enterprise is a function of society . . . ."

"I have always asked myself whether the activities of the company which I founded and have managed are beneficial for people. 'If this company were to disappear now, would it be any loss to society? If the existence of the company has no positive meaning for society, I may as well dissolve it.' . . ."

"Since all enterprise activities are either directly or indirectly conducted toward the public, knowing what the public thinks and does is very important for managers. If you view the public as irresponsible and untrustworthy, your management will be likewise. If you consider the public is right, however, your management will be in response to public needs . . . ."

"There are times when management ideas are misunderstood and misconstrued. At such times, while working to clear up the misunderstandings, it is important to let the public know about your company's philosophy, achievements and products in order to avoid further misunderstandings.

For this purpose, public relations activities and advertising are important . . . ."

". . . each manager should become concerned about politics, and appropriate requests should be made to politicians for applying proper corporate or managerial knowledge to practical economic policies. Such an attitude is extremely important; it is more important today than at any time. When I advise that each business manager should make requests to politicians, people immediately think that these requests are for special government favors for the company or business as a whole. However, actions taken with such intentions are undesirable; they fail to understand that the government is a sharing of managers' special expertise with politicians for the betterment of society. If such requests are made in the proper manner and are incorporated in practical politics, the results will be desirable politics and successful corporate efforts to achieve the social mission of the company. . . ."

On Harmony and Cooperation. "Good labor-management relations depend upon management's recognition of the meaning and value of labor unions. On the basis of this recognition, management should strive for co-existence and co-prosperity with labor. In other words, the management should believe that the existence of the labor union is important and valuable . . . ."

"Labor unions have made important improvements in the life of workers, and they have enriched national life and society as well. If workers were not represented by labor unions, or someone to speak in their interests, I am afraid that the management would 'benignly neglect' their interests. . . . For this reason, I urge readers to keep in mind that labor unions are important because their existence, reasonable actions, and sound growth contribute both to individual enterprises and to society . . . ."

"It is not inconceivable that everything in this universe is in harmony, despite seemingly incessant oppositions. Everything possesses and asserts a unique characteristic: this is what I mean by 'opposition.' The sun and moon are opposed to each other; the mountains and rivers are in opposition; and men assert a uniqueness opposed to women. But the world is not simply opposition; harmony exists over seemingly incessant oppositions to establish order in nature and in society . . . management and labor must temper their opposition with harmony for their shared goal of contributing to society . . . ."

"I believe that the enterprise and labor unions share identical interests in contributing to society. Without the growth of the enterprise, a perpetual improvement of employees' welfare (which labor unions also try to achieve) would be impossible. And without improvements in employees' welfare, their willingness to work would wane, labor productivity would drop, and the growth of the enterprise would be impossible . . . . Therefore, I believe it is beneficial to both management and labor to cooperate and harmonize with each other when their interests are identical, and oppose each other when their interests differ. Enterprise executives must first believe in the idea of harmony over opposition, and then try to foster labor-management relations by sincerely educating the labor union and employees to appreciate the benefits of cooperation . . . ."

"The most desirable relationship is when both parties have equal power. Power of domination breeds a sense of arrogance and self-righteousness which, in turn, causes the subordinate party to react with defiance or defeatism . . . . Equality in labor-management relations might be compared to a car with opposing wheels of different sizes. If one wheel is bigger than another, the car cannot move smoothly. Opposing wheels must be exactly the same size . . . ."

On Organizational Growth. "One of the important things that make steady growth possible is what I would like to call 'dam management' . . . . management should have reserves and spares. As regards production machinery, for example, a manager should not rely upon all equipment operating at 100% capacity to realize a profit. A company should be making a profit even if its equipment is operating normally at 80 to 90% capacity with a 10 to 20% reserve capacity . . . ."

"Regarding capital, when you start a business that requires one billion yen, one billion yen is not enough. If something happens and more capital is needed, you will be unable to deal with the situation immediately. Therefore, you should prepare 1.1 or 1.2 billion yen. This extra capital can be called a 'capital dam' . . . ."

"Dam management means to have 10 to 20% of reserves and spares prepared beforehand, based on appropriate and accurate forecasts of how many products will be needed. The most important dam in management is a 'mental dam.' In other words, a manager should understand that it is necessary to have a dam in every aspect of management . . . ."

On Profits and Prosperity. ". . . any enterprise which abandons its real mission and, instead, makes the pursuit of profit its sole objective is impossible to defend . . . . Profit is simply the reward an enterprise receives for successful performance of its mission. Obviously management which isn't making a profit is not making a large enough contribution to society: it is not fulfilling its primary mission . . . . As long as an enterprise's social responsibility is to earn an appropriate profit and return part of this profit to society, a deficit proves that the enterpise is not performing its major responsibility. Such a situation cannot be allowed to continue . . . ."

"In order for an enterprise to contribute to the productive and progressive activities inherent in human life, it must constantly enrich its own productive and progressive activities. Investments must constantly be made for research and development, as well as for new plant facilities, to meet the expanding needs of the public. Such investments obviously require capital . . . through the steady accumulations of profit . . . ."

"True growth, development and prosperity of an enterprise are only possible when contingent on mutual prosperity for society . . . ."

"Co-existence and co-prosperity in all enterprise relations, therefore, are the only way to ensure long-term enterprise development . . . ."

"Sometimes I would observe suppliers' operations and I would suggest improvements to ensure reasonable profits after price reductions. In this way, even when I requested that suppliers lower their prices, suppliers were reassured that I had carefully considered their interests. While it is important to be concerned about appropriate profits for suppliers, a manager must ensure that the dealers who supervise the sales of enterprise products also benefit. Sales and merchandising must be coordinated in such a way that consumers are able to purchase products at reasonable prices. Such policies conform to a state of co-existence and co-prosperity where everyone in contact with enterprise operations benefits . . . ."

"Co-existence and co-prosperity means that the manager must carefully consider the other party's position and need to make a profit. To think of the other party's profit may seem a little difficult at first, but the profits of those people who depend on the enterprise are just as important as the enterprise's own profits . . . ."

On Knowledge and Its Uses. "I think that when things go well, fortune is smiling on me, and when things go badly, becomes larger, the manager can judge the problems of the whole company, but with individual jobs, his (people) will have the responsibility for making their own judgments themselves. In this way, the wisdom of many employees will be used more effectively. . . . the manager should seek the ideas and wisdom of other people without forgetting his position. . . . By doing so, the talents and ideas of every employee, including the manager, will be fully utilized."

On the "Untrapped Mind." "Among all the important qualities essential for management, I believe the most fundamental of all is the *sunao* spirit . . . for without it, a manager will never succeed in actualizing the company's endless growth. The sunao spirit refers to an untrapped mind. A person with this spirit sees things as they are, without special bias, emotionalism, or preconceived ideas . . . ."

"The wisdom of employees will not reach the manager who is convinced that his position makes him aloof from others' opinions and advice. Such a manager . . . will conduct the company's business by relying only on limited information and knowledge. This type of management insularity often causes business failure . . . ."

"The sunao spirit is the fundamental spiritual attitude that the manager must have to be successful at management. Developing and advancing the sunao spirit is extremely important for everyone—managers and nonmanagers alike. Without it, one can neither enjoy genuine success in management nor genuine happiness in life."

The Philosophical Edge

The company that functions without a well-conceived and defined management philosophy is like a car without a steering wheel, its managers like blindfolded drivers.

that I am to blame. In short, I attribute my successes to good luck, and I blame myself for my failures. When something goes well and a manager thinks that the result is due to personal management skills, he or she is apt to become arrogant and careless and thus will invite future failure. Success is the result of learning from many little mistakes, yet trifling errors of management can lead to very big mistakes if arrogance and carelessness blind the manager to small personality faults . . . ."

"When something has gone wrong and you think that you were unfortunate, then you cannot make the best use of the experience of failure. But, if you think that you are responsible for your failures, then by reflecting upon your actions you won't make the same mistakes again. In other words, failure is the mother of success . . . ."

"Since only high-quality products sell well during a recession, the proper management of a company during this period provides the opportunity for new product research and development. 'Good times are good but bad times are better' should become a firm maxim of management during economic hard times. . . ."

"It is impossible for the employees of a (large) enterprise to meet each time a problem arises. What is important, however, is not meetings, but the manager's willingness to ask for help and advice. Realizing the importance of conducting management on the basis of the wisdom of many people, the manager usually should do his best to listen to as many employees as possible and create an environment in which they can express their opinions freely and frankly. If the manager is always receptive to employees' thoughts, his judgment will reflect their wisdom and suggestions even when he must make an independent judgment if something unexpected happens . . . ."

"As for the whole company, the wisdom of each employee will be reflected in management. When the company

Konosuke Matsushita's philosophy has been guiding him and his company for more than six decades, in good times and bad, and working better each year. Its most significant aspect might well be its universality. Cultural differences notwithstanding, the Matsushita Credo is as practically and profitably applicable in the U.S. or anywhere else in the world as it is in Japan. The reason is as clear as it is simple. The philosophy has been tailored and refined to serve the needs of employees and suppliers, dealers and consumers, the society within the organization, and the society without. And as any psychologist will confirm, the basic needs of human beings are much the same whatever the continent, country or industry.

A proper philosophy of management is critical to the success of any company large or small, commercial or industrial, because it spells out the rules of the game by which success is achieved and sustained. In business, tough problems and thorny decisions arise every day, and invariably human beings are deeply affected. What to do? What is wrong; what is right? What will succeed; what will fail? With an established, clearly-stated philosophy to guide his thoughts and actions, a manager need only relate the issue in question to the guideline that applies to obtain the direction and purpose required.

A proper philosophy of management lends a deeper perspective and meaning to one's job and one's life. It permits the spirit sun to shine through the clouds of confusion and doubt.

2.

THE JAPANESE EDGE

> *Society is constantly changing and evolving, so that the company must, for steady growth, not only adapt itself to social changes but also take measures in anticipation of change.*
> —*Konosuke Matsushita*

A strange phenomenon is in progress.

As these words are written, two books on *The New York Times* Best Seller list for nonfiction, "The Art of Japanese Management" by Richard Tanner Pascale and Anthony G. Athos, and "Theory Z" by William Ouchi, attempt to tell America why Japanese companies are so successful and what they can do about it. Each week new articles on the subject appear in U.S. general and business publications. Increasing numbers of executives are flocking to seminars to learn what Japan is doing right that they should be doing. Institutions, associations, and consulting firms are sponsoring studies of Japanese management. The lecture circuits are thriving. More and more groups of Americans are touring Japan—and they're not simply tourists. They are business people and managers seeking the Holy Grail of Success, determined to find out how Japan is doing it.

Why all this fascination and preoccupation with the art of management as it is practiced in Japan? Why all the admiration for and envy of the Japanese practitioner? Are we on the wavecrest of another surging fad which next year will dry up on the beach? Is the Japanese manager as smart and resourceful as we deem him to be? The answers to these last two questions in succession are, "Indeed not!" and "He certainly is!" And to the student of business and management who takes the time and effort to delve into the subject, the reasons are clear.

In a nutshell, observes Rutherford, N.J., educator and management consultant Leonard J. Smith, "The Japanese long have been hard, lean and hungry, whereas we in the U.S. have become lazy and fat."

Shichiro Yasukawa, president of Tokyo's Nippon Credit Bank, agrees with this view: "Japan has extremely limited land and limited resources, but a very large population. With these conditions, Japan had to catch up with the West, and we had to work very hard to accomplish our goals."

But there's more to it than that. Not only are the Japanese working harder, they're working smarter as well.

Doing More with Less

A problem with some U.S. executives is typified by the attitude of a Chief Executive Officer I recently interviewed who, despite mounting evidence to the contrary, still believes American managers are the smartest kids on the block.

We were discussing the automobile industry, the classic example that proves how much we can learn from Japan. "Look at the inroads being made in the American market."

He sloughed this off easily. "Sure, look how much less the cost of labor is in Japan than the U.S."

That's true. Japanese labor costs are lower. But, rebuts Berkley, Mich., management consultant James E. Harbour, who did a study on the subject, that difference is largely offset by overseas transportation costs. The main key to the Japanese advantage is better management, more efficient operations. My friend was unable to see this or preferred not to see it. But U.S. auto experts agree. Management is our biggest problem of all, concedes Chrysler's vice president for quality and productivity, George F. Butts.

The blunt reality is that the Japanese productivity growth rate is gradually and consistently gaining on this country and the rest of the world. According to "Joint Economic Report" statistics from 1950 to 1978, Japan's average annual productivity increase was a robust 7.0% in contrast to the U.S.'s bottom rung showing of 1.8%, lower even than the 2.3% scored by the United Kingdom. France, Germany and Italy achieved average rates of 4.3%, 4.6% and 4.5% respectively.

If the current trend continues, Japan's gross national product, today third in the world, will be number one by the end of the century. This despite the fact that Japan is resource-poor and one of the most crowded countries on earth.

Japan's manufacturing productivity is well ahead of its overall productivity, 13% in 1979, and 9% in 1980. Considering the investment binge Japanese industry has been on for the past two or three years, though it did slow somewhat in 1980, many forecasters predict that Japan will thrust even further ahead in the technology-intensive industries it already dominates.

Autos, Electronics, and Then Some!

It has been well publicized that Japanese companies have been vaulting ahead at a prodigious rate in a handful of industries like automobiles, steel and electronics, although steel is now bogged down because of the energy crunch. But in this industry alone, Japanese investment rocketed from $356 million in the period from 1951 to 1955 to over $13 billion in the five years from 1971 to 1975. And in 1976, the Japanese cost of steel production advantage over the United States was $120 a ton as opposed to a U.S. advantage of $8 a ton in 1956.

Are these industries unusual? Are special factors at work? Perhaps. But the most special factor of all is the worker and how he is managed, and it applies not only to the industries cited above but to a growing rundown of others as well.

Despite Japan's agreement to cut car shipments to the U.S. 7.7% in 1981, the Department of Commerce predicts that the trade deficit between the two countries will grow to record proportions. According to Editor James M. Barry of *Dealerscope,* published in Boston, the home-appliance industry in this country is facing a foreign-competition crisis that is worse than Detroit's because foreign manufacturers are building modern plants here in the U.S. to avoid transportation costs that would eat into narrow profit margins.

Out of 11 major foreign competitors in the appliance field, six are Japanese; Matsushita, Sharp, Sanyo, Toshiba, Mitsubishi and Hitachi. States Nobuhiro Arimoto, a senior vice president of Sanyo, government regulation, union problems, and other hazards notwithstanding, his company can produce goods in America and maintain "Japanese quality."

IBM long has dominated the computer industry and still does and, as one of this country's best managed companies, fights hard and well for every inch of market share. But the battle has never been tougher. Notes consultant Leonard J. Smith, "Aside from IBM, Hitachi and Fujitsu are the world's only producers of integrated computers today." There is little doubt, adds *Business Week,* that "the hottest breath on IBM's neck comes from across the Pacific," and a Japanese-based computer analyst predicts a near-term rise of the worldwide computer market share from today's 10% to 30%.

A similar story is told in the sporting arms industry. "Like our cars," says Shoichiro Nemoto, technical director of the Japan Sporting Arms and Ammunition Manufacturers Association, "Japanese guns have gained a reputation for being well-made and cost-efficient." Today almost every major American make of sporting firearm is made under license in Japanese factories. Japan sold almost $40-million worth of firearms to the United States last year, making it America's top supplier of high-quality arms.

In 1960 Harley-Davidson Motor Co., Inc., had a near monopoly in the American motorcycle market. At that time it was selling about 10,000 bikes a year. Today, with sales around the 50,000 mark, the company sells about 5% of the million bikes sold. You can hazard a guess as to where over 90% of the U.S. market has flown.

"From virtually no U.S. sales two years ago, the Japanese are currently shipping half of all (computer printers) selling for less than $1,000," states *Business Week,* and their share will hit 75% of all units shipped by the end of the year, according to *Dataquest.* The under-$1,000 market will be worth $200-million this year (1981), and will grow to $950-million by 1985, the California market researcher estimates."

And so the story goes to include machine tools, cameras, semiconductors and, the latest item on the list, robots. U.S.

manufacturers are steaming ahead at full speed in this fast-growing industry which is expected to exceed $5-billion by 1985, and at present 90% of the CAD (computer-aided design) systems sold in Japan are produced in America. But that's only part of the story. According to *The Economist,* Japan has about 70% of all the thousands of robots installed thus far in the world, which puts yet another fine hone on the Japanese edge. The magazine's survey of Japanese industry adds, "Japanese companies now appear to be ahead in the next important step: joining machine tools together into automated metal-working factories. In April (1981), Murata Kikai, a company making textile machinery and machine tools in central Japan, started a new system connecting half a dozen big machine tools with 'robotrailers.' Small bleeping automatic trucks, of the kind already used in automatic warehouses in America, shuffle between machine tools picking up and leaving heavy parts to be worked on. Computers decide when each part should leave the automatic warehouse, and its timetable for arriving at each machine tool. The factory will soon work 20 hours a day, machining up to 1,500 parts automatically."

Activating the Edge

In researching the material for this book I talked and/or corresponded with a couple of dozen U.S. executives and consultants who visited Japan, toured Japanese plants, and asked innumerable questions of their gracious hosts—and no one I have ever met knows how to be gracious the way a Japanese can. If there is one thing on which the "tourists" agree it is that by and large the Japanese manager understands what he is doing and is doing it right.

For one thing, he is a consummate student. An extremely important aspect of his managerial life is his training, and it continues throughout his career. The Japanese manager's objective is to learn as much as he possibly can about the best way to do his job, and he seeks this goal with tiger-like determination. As a young man—the manager is almost always a man—he learns from his peers and superiors; the mentor system is a part of the culture. As he advances up the management ladder, he learns from lectures and seminars, published materials, and from experts both at home and abroad. He regards knowledge not as power, for power has no place in his culture, but as an obligation to society and his corporate family, for it is knowledge that refines procedures and produces improvement.

A Rather Ordinary Miracle

Words one often hears linked to the success of Japanese manufacturing companies are "secret" and "miracle." Actually, from the Japanese point of view, it is a rather ordinary miracle.

At a certain point the thoughtful outsider examining the whys and wherefores of it all is apt to come up with the revelation that if there's a secret at all it boils down to the basics of management which the Japanese emphasize doggedly, determinedly, and perhaps even a little religiously. One American plant manager told me, "The main difference between us and them is that we all too often pay lip service to the basics; they take them literally and seriously."

On top of that, the Japanese are tough and they persevere. Steve Kaufman, managing director of MacMillan Jardine, a division of Canada's MacMillan Bloedel Limited based in Japan, cites an example: "If you asked a North American to clean a room he would sweep out the middle and pick up the obvious dirt under the tables. The Japanese employee would move the tables and chairs, thoroughly clean them as well as the floor, clean the light bulbs, wipe down the walls and dust the ledges. You could be sure when he was finished that the whole room would be clean. The Japanese take the same thorough and persevering approach to the way they manage the business."

In the late '50s, adds MacMillan Bloedel's director of personnel planning and development, L.R. Armstrong, who recently returned from an executive's tour of Japan, the notion that motorcycles could be mass-produced and mass-marketed in the United States was met with ridicule or derision. The marketing manager who came up with the idea was laughed out of the top executive suite. No American company would touch it.

Honda moved in and, as mentioned earlier, the Japanese now have more than 90% of the U.S. market. The reason is simple.

In the wry words of a Harley-Davidson executive: "Nobody told them it couldn't be done."

Few nations have gone to such pains as Japan to seek out and apply the tried-and-true economic best from other societies, and most of all from the U.S. What inevitably evolved is optimum efficiency in the form of high productivity and a low fat operating diet. This explains why Toyota, for example, is able to build its cars with about one-third the manhours it takes to build cars in Detroit.

What, specifically, are the main ingredients of the Japanese recipe used to bake that rich and succulent pie of success so admired by the rest of the world? They will be discussed in, hopefully, applicable detail in the chapters to come. But here by way of introduction is a capsulized rundown.

Long-term Perspective

Industrialist Charles Kettering once said, "I expect to spend the rest of my life in the future, so I want to be reasonably sure of what kind of future it's going to be. This is my reason for planning."

Japanese managers take this rationale seriously. American managers would like to take it seriously but are prevented from doing so by the system.

The foundation of Japan's futuristic society is the thrift of its citizens. During 1980, Japanese citizens saved proportionately three times as much of their incomes as U.S. citizens. Thus the banks can rely on a steady flow of funds and the continuing ability to provide business with the capital it needs to expand facilities, remain modern and productive. This ties in neatly with the Japanese economy where a substantial portion of industry is owned by the banks, and a relatively small portion owned by private individuals, corporations and institutions, although this may change before long.

Long-term growth is in the bank's best interests as well as the company's best interests. On top of that, it is in society's best interests. Under the Japanese system, executives feel a moral obligation to provide for employees and their families on a long-term basis and take every action possible to ensure their continuing security.

No such executive sense of responsibility exists in the typical U.S. company large or small. Here managers are under running pressure to produce instant profits by shareholders who provide the major portion of industrial financing. American enterprise is a constant contest to win stockholder favor. Executive career growth often hinges on quarterly profit performance. Scarcely a week goes by without a story appearing in the press about one corporation or other that has come upon hard times because of its failure to invest adequately in product research and development, or to modernize its plant because the expenditures would have eaten into current profits.

U.S. industry is largely geared to profits today and let the future take care of itself. The Japanese executive will sacrifice the current period's income if he deems it to be in the best interests of long-term growth and strength.

The Prosperity Compact

American free enterprise is often referred to as an adversary system. If a company comes up with an ingenious new system to boost productivity, often its first consideration will be, "What kind of flak will we get from the union?" or, "What concessions will we have to give to get labor to go along with this?"

Free enterprise is rarely free to pursue profits and prosperity as its managerial wisdom sees fit, with much justification under our system, but the reality exists.

That's one part of the problem. The other part deals with the government. I spoke with a friend recently who for several years owned a small manufacturing company in the Midwest. He reached the point where in utter exasperation he sold his business and is now in real estate in Fort Lauderdale, Fla., where he has neither unions nor the government to contend with to any appreciable extent. "The labor situation was rough at times," he concedes, "but what really got to me was the government regulation. That and the paperwork I had to fill out in connection with it. In my book the so-called 'adversary system' refers as much to government as it does to labor."

Japan has labor unions too, and a fair amount of government regulation of industry. But it is not an adversary system. Unions are organized mainly by individual companies rather than on an industry basis which, at first blush, would lead any union member worth his salt to mutter, "Company unions! A lot of good they do labor!" The cynicism is well founded given the U.S. experience. But, as we shall see, although the Japanese system couldn't be labeled free of exploitation, the environment for anti-company, anti-management unionism doesn't exist. Notes Takeo Sagawa, president of Sharp Electronics Corp.'s U.S. facility in Paramus, N.J., the logical conclusion is that unless the company grows and remains profitable, union employees cannot expect to win better conditions and benefits. Getting this concept across isn't easy in the U.S.

Another point to consider, observes Michael R. Losey, Vice President for Personnel of Sperry Corp.'s New Holland,

Pa., division, is that keeping in mind that the company in Japan is looked upon as part of one's family, a strike against the company is viewed as counter-productive and a sign of failure of the process. "For instance," he adds, "after one recent long strike, the entire Board of Directors of one (Japanese) company apologized and resigned." Mr. Losey returned in late November 1980 from a study mission to Japan sponsored by the Technology Transfer Institute, a consulting firm headquartered in Tokyo, with offices in New York, Los Angeles, London and Singapore.

Following World War II, the Japanese organized the "Indicative Planning Process," which in effect is a co-operative arrangement between government and industry with economic development the mutual goal. Under this setup, which has worked out very well, a consensus is reached between the industry and government ministry involved with regard to industry capabilities and the role of government in helping corporations achieve profit objectives in a way that is beneficial to society—a far cry from America's complex and mind bogglingly cumbersome regulatory system.

A Strong Accent on Quality

What price quality? The 19th century French author Alfred de Musset wrote: "Perfection does not exist; to understand it is the triumph of human intelligence; to expect to possess it is the most dangerous kind of madness."

The Japanese do not buy this philosophy. Harvard Business School Prof. Robert H. Hayes quotes a Japanese scholar in a *Harvard Business Review* article: "If you do an economic analysis, you will usually find that it is advantageous to reduce your defect rate from 10% to 5%. If you repeat that analysis, it may or may not make sense to reduce it further to 1%. The Japanese, however, will reduce it. Having accomplished this, they will attempt to reduce to 0.1%. And then to 0.01%. You might claim that this obsession is costly, that it makes no economic sense. They are heedless. They will not be satisfied with less than perfection."

It seems clear at this point that, despite the high cost of achieving quality to the nth degree, the net result for the Japanese has been a resounding profit. Millions of consumers in the U.S. and abroad today are buying cars, TV sets, cameras, home appliances and other items stamped MADE IN JAPAN, not only because the price is right but because the product's performance is superior to units made elsewhere. The day when Japanese-produced goods were branded second-rate and shoddy is no more than a dim and hazy memory.

Japan's quick and steady crescendo to a position of world superiority marks an ironic note on the quality scale. One of the country's foremost folk heroes is U.S. statistician W. Edwards Deming who, more than three decades ago, introduced the values of quality control to Japanese industry. Today it is a top priority among employees, with awards in Deming's name eagerly sought.

In America's current race to emulate Japanese management methods, considerable publicity is being accorded the "quality circle" concept (actually a misnomer in the opinion of Myron Emanuel, director of Business Communication Programs for the management consulting firm of Towers, Perrin, Forster & Crosby, who recently led a research mission to Japan). The QC groups were originally formed with quality production in mind, but have since been broadened to cover all aspects of plant and office life. Groups are voluntary, but in every plant Emanuel visited, almost all workers participated. Circles usually run from five to seven members who work together in a coordinated effort to make improvements and solve problems.

Clearly, Japan's onetime reputation for shoddy merchandise had a profound effect on the extremely image-sensitive Japanese who over the past 30 years have been working aggressively to live it down. They have succeeded in this objective to the extent that today, so far as the typical worker is concerned, "zero defects" means quite literally just that, however unachievable the actual goal may be. The Japanese mentality carries quality-plus targeting to all aspects of industrial life. Employee hiring standards constitute a good case in point.

In the U.S., employees are often carelessly hired on a crash basis with the thought in mind that if they don't work out they will never pass their probationary period and become part of the permanent payroll. If they do pass probation and their performance subsequently slips, although it's problematical in some cases, they can usually be fired. The Japanese manager or supervisor doesn't reason this way. Workers hired into Japanese industry are employed with the long term, usually a working lifetime, in mind. Thus employment candidates are carefully screened. Tough entrance examinations and long periods of evaluation are often involved. Nor is a job applicant customarily hired by a single supervisor or personnel specialist. Key managers usually get into the act so that the final hiring decision is arrived at by consensus. It makes sense that if superior quality is the organizational goal, it stands the best chance of being attained by top calibre people.

Of course, the larger and more richly endowed the corporation, the better positioned it will be to skim the cream off the top.

We, Not Them

Bill Stephens, Atlantic Richfield Co.'s Employee Communications manager, recently joined the march of U.S. executives to the "Land of the Rising Sun." One of his insights: "From childhood, Japanese learn the value of group life. Cramped onto a small island, living in crowded, close-knit family circumstances with little privacy, the Japanese learn group values as a matter of survival. In Japanese companies, groups, not individuals, compete. And with strong peer and family pressure to succeed, the Japanese already are motivated by the time they enter the work force."

One hallmark of a strong and healthy organization is that employees identify themselves with the company and its objectives. If there's a deadline to be met it's "our" deadline. If something must be done it's a task "we" have to accomplish. Under the adversary system it's a "we" against "them" arrangement, "we" referring to the company or management, "them" to the workers, one group pitted against the other.

In Japan, to oppose one's company would be like opposing one's family. It happens, of course. But by and large group unity is established and sustained, in big companies particularly.

In large measure the partnership concept extends to all of society as well. Exorbitant, inappropriate profits, for example, are looked upon as a more heinous sin in Japan than the U.S. because they place individual greed ahead of the common (societal) good. As a key member of the partnership circle, the customer's needs and preferences are held in the highest regard and, completing the circle, the same thing applies to the supplier.

If the customer experiences a problem with the product or service, it is regarded as the company's problem, not from an economic standpoint alone, but as a moral obligation as well. Industrial customers send managers and technologists to supplier plants in an effort to improve operations to make the relationship more profitable for all parties concerned.

One Japanese manager recalled, "A supplier ran into technical difficulties producing a part that was needed for a motor assembly and had to increase the price. In the United States the customer would have quickly shopped the market in an effort to get the work done for less money. In Japan we are more patient. The relationship between people who transact business together takes on a deeper meaning. We worked with the supplier's people in an effort to solve the problem. It may cost extra money in the near term, but works out to everyone's advantage in the end. There is a greater feeling of trust, and we work more harmoniously."

In short, the Japanese economy consists of six friendly and courteous partners—the company, government, union, supplier, customer, and ultimate consumer—whose needs interact and interrelate, and whose objectives in the main part are mutual.

People-Sensitive Management

A Japanese manager, discussing his company's fundamental management and labor relations principles with Myron Emanuel, characterized them as "our sacred treasures." The first, he said, is life-long, guaranteed employment for all employees. Mr. Emanuel states: "While this pertains specifically to employees of the approximately 1,000 large firms in Japan, it is also practiced to a great extent by many medium-sized and small firms. The implications of this are enormous."

Think about it. Consider the twin pressures and anxieties experienced by virtually every American who works for a living. For one thing, one's livelihood is always in question; there is always the possibility of being fired or laid off for one reason or other. On top of that, career growth usually depends on a strange mix of individual performance, politics, and shrewd maneuvering, plus any number of conflicting ingredients. What it too often boils down to is running insecurity, resentment and bitterness because of unfair treatment, real or imagined.

As if this weren't enough—and for millions of U.S. workers this is the most sour ingredient of all—there's the interminable boredom of repetitious jobs that are the same day after day and week after week. In Japan all of these problems, if not totally eliminated are, at least, greatly alleviated.

Lifetime employment removes the heavy anxiety of job insecurity. Progressive wage increases and promotions based largely on age and seniority remove the bitterness and low self-esteem experienced when one is bypassed in favor of others. Job rotation, the frequent shifting of employees from one task to another, helps to break the monotony of perpetual repetition.

What it adds up to is people-sensitive management, and this is just a piece of it. Basic to the Japanese family spirit and philosophy is the personal responsibility the manager feels for his people and the sense of obligation each member of the work group feels for all other members. In such an environment constructive criticism tends to supplant disparagement. Cooperation and mutual assistance are in everybody's best personal interest. Realistically, no utopia exists. But the philosophical foundation for harmony and peace of mind is inherent to the system, and human frailties notwithstanding it works.

Apart from the human and humane considerations involved, there is the practical and hard-nosed aspect as well. Employing a person for life as opposed to a probable temporary stint, and training and developing him to perform a variety of functions to the utmost of his ability, gives the company a tremendous economic stake in his future.

Notes Emanuel: "It is Japanese industrial practice to hire just once a year, in April, when students graduate from the secondary schools and colleges. Recruiting is substantial and fierce, with every effort made to attract the brightest and best graduates. Grades count heavily, but successful candidates must pass a company test as well."

The point is clear. The company's investment in each recruit is heavy from the standpoint of screening and employment and throughout his career in terms of training and development. In the face of this giant expenditure, grooming employees for responsible jobs, and giving them the education, guidance and coaching required to build and hone their expertise, in a climate that encourages bitterness, friction and disloyalty doesn't make sense to the essentially logical and pragmatic Japanese mentality.

As Sharp's Takeo Sagawa sums up the case, "Since both workers and managers have made up their minds to work for a company for many years, they do not consider their employer simply as a labor purchaser or salary payer. For everyone, the company becomes part of one's body and soul."

Investment Binge

Western executives unwilling to concede Japan's managerial advantage like to explain the nation's "competitive edge" as a natural byproduct of postwar plant rebuilding, often with U.S. aid, to replace bombed-out factories. The trouble with this rationale is that too many years have gone by since the postwar building boom, so that any edge dating back to that time is no longer very significant. In the past decade or more Japan has been investing heavily—except in selected industries such as petrochemicals and paper, marked as disadvantageous by government and management coplanners because they are oil guzzlers or for some other reason—with the future in mind.

One educated assessment by Japan watchers is that twice the annual industrial investment rate of the '70s will be spent through this current decade, about half of it to replace worn or obsolete equipment installed in the late '60s and early '70s. In short, understanding and appreciating the productivity benefits of plant modernization, the Japanese are taking whatever steps are necessary to optimize the competitive edge, often at the expense of current profits.

Plant modernization extends to management strategies as well as equipment. Cooperative, or matrix management, assumes a meeting of minds among line and staff managers prior to the setting and implementation of production and marketing plans. This is difficult to achieve in America's rank-and-status-based business climate, but is a natural offshoot of Japanese group orientation where consensus decision making is standard operating procedure. Here design engineers, production managers and marketing executives bend over backwards to understand and make realistic provisions for one another's problems and needs. What carries weight is objective-based practicalities and not political clout. The result is often machine loading, manpower planning, and production scheduling more realistically geared to reasonable and achievable standards, with breakdowns, foul-ups and delays minimized.

An American manager, transferred to his company's Japanese plant in the consumer products industry, tells about "production that is somewhat slower-paced, yet yields an appreciable increase in productivity. Machines last longer here," he adds, "because we don't beat hell out of them. Conscientious preventive maintenance costs money, but saves a lot over the long pull."

In the U.S., he recalls, upgrading PM was a perpetual battle because "the emphasis was always on now."

Consensus Decision Making

Michael Dorota, president and Chief Executive Officer of Apex Electronics, Inc., a manufacturer of television ray guns and other components, described a recent purchase of an expensive machine from a company forced out of business. Mr. Dorota, impressed with the unit, discussed its qualities and feasibility of purchase with his chief engineer who agreed with his judgment and within two days the purchase was made.

This occurrence would have been unlikely were a Japanese instead of an American company involved. Prior to giving the go-ahead signal to buy the machine, the worker slated to operate it would be given a demonstration of the unit and consulted, along with the other members of his work group and its supervisor. The production manager would be brought into the act and his opinion voiced plus that of one or more engineers. Eventually, assuming that all opinions were favorable, a recommendation would be made to a vice president or plant manager that the piece of equipment be purchased.

If it were a second-hand machine offered at a bargain price, by the time consensus agreement was reached, the opportunity to buy might have been lost. If the machine were needed in a hurry—rarely the case, because in Japan advance planning is long range and thorough—the plant would have had to do without it. But you can be sure of one thing: There would be no resentment or disgruntlement because the decision to buy was contrary to an employee's wishes, or because he didn't think it made sense.

In Japan a decision isn't finalized as a rule until all parties involved agree it's the right decision to make. The process can be interminable at times and is exasperating to Americans who are accustomed to quick action. A manager transferred to Japan after 18 years' experience in supervision and management in U.S. plants, and then relocated to America after a 30-month stint, says he found this practice the most difficult of all to get used to and live with.

"For one thing," he explains, "a Japanese will rarely come out with a flat 'no.' It's regarded as discourteous. He will tell you he likes your idea, and if you're uninitiated you'll be optimistic, figuring the mechanics of final approval will be just a matter of time. Of the time you can be certain, much more so than you can of the approval, however encouraging the manager's voiced judgment. After waiting six times as long as you felt it was humanly possible for the matter to be considered and resolved, the ultimate response may be a polite and regretful, but unequivocal turndown, because consensus agreement couldn't be reached."

Clearly, given the current working environment, making consensus decisions succeed in most U.S. companies would be difficult if not impossible. Managerial attitudes would militate against it. Middle management thinking for the most part is geared to the question: "What's best for me? What's best for my operation?" Too often the decision process turns into a contest, the objective being to win, rather than resolve the issue in the way that is best for the company.

The Japanese are the first to concede the disadvantages of consensus decision making. On the one hand, it encourages an inbred environment. On the other, it is usually a painfully tedious and time consuming procedure. But for the Japanese, at least, the pluses appear to outweigh the minuses. The system is sensitive to the importance of respecting the egos and feelings of all parties concerned. It brings multi-disciplined thinking to bear on the problem being considered, avoids rash, superficial and impulsive judgments. Most important, it provides the assurance that once consensus agreement is reached all parties involved will be strongly behind the decision.

Lean and Hard Body-building

Among Japanese industrials the corporate body is typically lean and hard and growing that way.

One notable difference between large U.S. and Japanese companies is the proportion of flab at the top in relation to the amount of muscle at action and implementation posts.

America has far more staffers per capita than Japan; Japan has many more doers. Where the Japanese company has five channels of management between, let us say, an engineering function and the top, an American company will have eight or nine.

For the classic case in point we need only turn once again to the automobile industry. If a foreman at Toyota has a problem, he can take it directly to the plant manager. If a foreman at GM or Ford has a problem he would like to bring to the plant manager's attention, he must wade through channels, and channels, and channels. In the end he'll probably figure that it isn't worth the effort.

New Jersey management consultant Roy W. Walters, whose firm bearing his name helps clients boost productivity by redesigning jobs and the workplace, observes, "We have far too many layers of management. On top of that, we have a superabundance of expediters, senior technicians, etc. The interesting work is assigned to them. What remains is dull and boring routine. It's no wonder workers are frustrated and disenchanted."

The U.S. has 20 times as many lawyers per capita as Japan, seven times the number of accountants, while Japan has five times as many engineers. While we are hectically auditing performance and honesty and settling disputes, Japan is concocting new ways to make products better and cheaper.

Although the Japanese invest heavily in research and development and the modernization of equipment and facilities, they are tightfisted when it comes to such frills as fancy offices and lavish building construction. One Japanese manager told me, "The main function of a building is to keep the rain out."

A study conducted by Sanford C. Bernstein & Co. estimates the "total cost advantage" of Toyota over Ford and GM at $1,350 per car. Other estimates run higher than this. States *Business Week:* "The studies of Japanese auto makers say Detroit could whittle away at its problem simply by streamlining the way it runs its plants. Japan's 'just in time' inventory system, for one, saves Toyota about $61 per car, compared with Detroit's routine method of stockpiling lots of spare parts, according to the Bernstein study." Another study puts the difference at $94.00.

Notes Harvard's Robert B. Hayes: "In factories I saw, the sense of order also resulted from an almost total absence of inventory on the plant floor. Raw materials were doled out in small batches only as needed. In many cases, vendors maintained stores of materials and purchased parts that the company 'called off' periodically. Suppliers often made three or four deliveries a day to avoid excess stock in the plant."

That's just a piece of the penny-pinching pie. The Japanese are on an unending search for new ways to save time and chop costs. Hayes calls to mind a specific press change procedure that takes an American auto company six hours, Volvo and a German car maker four hours, and Toyota 12 minutes.

Many American companies, accustomed for decades to market supremacy and taking product acceptance for granted, have grown lazy and complacent. Compounding this we have the productivity lag produced in the main by the underutilization of manpower and sluggishness caused by a general insensitivity to the needs and feelings of workers. So the flab tends to multiply.

Given the cultural differences between the U.S. and Japan, the worst mistake a corporation could make, consultant Roy W. Walters believes, would be to attempt to superimpose Japanese management on an American company. There are too many complex factors involved. But that doesn't say we cannot give close examination to what Japan is doing successfully and how it is doing it, adapt the best applicable techniques and strategies, and put them to work in our behalf—just as Japan has been doing for years so far as the rest of the world is concerned.

Finally, in outlining above the principal ingredients of Japanese success, U.S. weaknesses were necessarily highlighted in contrast. But as the final chapter of this book will make clear, taking the two economies in balance, the *potential* advantages are weighted in favor of America for a number of very strong reasons. It is simply a matter of making the most of our pluses, something we demonstrably can do and in some cases that will be cited, already are doing. In closing, as subsequent chapters will prove, the greatest potential of all lies in redefining and restructuring the way we communicate with and respond to our people, and the way we develop and utilize the treasure trove of their available talents.

3.

THE JAPANESE WAY

> *As a manager, I have consistently carried out a policy of management based on the wisdom of many people.*
> —Konosuke Matsushita

Managements have gone to remarkable extents in an effort to improve worker productivity and thereby boost corporate profits.

Take "Diminishing Productivity Theory and Evaluation," a proposition which states "that when any varying factor, such as labor or machine efficiency, is increased through application to any fixed factor, such as the materials or equipment used in production, the variable-factor output will eventually decrease."

Or the "Third-Dimensional Theory," a "technique intended to combine the two basic types of managerial behavior—*task-oriented* behavior (T.O.) and *human relations-oriented* behavior (R.O.)—in correct proportions to achieve the greatest overall effectiveness of the manager in cost reduction or other business problems."

A comprehensive and well documented book, "Cost Reduction From A to Z," by Lindley R. Higgins and Ruth W. Stidger, presents hundreds of such productivity-raising techniques and strategies. Investigating and experimenting with such theories, if you can find enough esoteric geniuses to understand and apply them, is certainly one road to travel in your quest for a corporate utopia. The Japanese offer an alternative—not that they aren't into sophisticated techniques too where they don't mess human relations. Stated as plainly as possible, it boils down to a mix of ordinary common sense combined with a keen inbred sensitivity to human feelings and needs.

What, specifically, are the Japanese doing that's so different from what we are doing here in America? Many things, some technical, some culturally based, some more sound economically. But if there is one over-riding advantage enjoyed by the large Japanese industrials, it stems from the way the people are treated and managed. In a nutshell, Japanese workers are self-motivated; American workers are not.

Certainly Japan has its share of abuses, finaglings, and human exploitation, plus a fair number of workers who are unhappy with the country's ultrapaternalistic system. But the majority of the Nipponese workers do the job they are paid to perform to the best of their ability. The majority of Americans earn a whole lot more and do a whole lot less. Why should this be? Equally important, what can we learn from the Japanese way of management that will help us achieve our ultimate goal of developing more productive and better motivated employees?

One thing we can assuredly learn from the Japanese is the value of clear and forthright communication and the establishment of a mutual trust relationship between labor and management. We can learn the value of simple, down-to-earth, fair human treatment as opposed to theorizing of the third-dimensional variety, and a return to the time-tested psychological basics of management as opposed to an overdependence on computer-controlled problem solving and decision making.

What follows is a sampling of industrial life in Japan, an on-the-scene look at business functions, situations and problems addressed the Japanese way. A special vote of thanks is owed, among others, to Michael R. Losey, of Sperry Corporation, for his willingness to share his insightful, and often penetrating, observations following his visit to several Japanese plants.

A second special acknowledgment goes to Atlantic Richfield Company's employee communications manager Bill Stephens for his helpful information and insights following an on-the-scene investigation of Japanese management methods.

Toshiba Corporation

Toshiba's Fukawa Works plant, about two hours from Tokyo, was completed in 1965. Covering 97,000 square meters, it produces 5,000 to 6,000 color TV sets per day and 200,000 tubes per month, making it Japan's—and possibly the world's—largest tube maker.

There is no way to distinguish supervisor or manager from rank-and-file worker. The thousands of employees in various manufacturing operations all wear identical brown jackets and sport "FF" buttons which refer to the plant's slogan, "Fresh Fukawa," signifying the innovative ideas that are sought.

According to production manager Iwane Shinoda, the plant is basically a self-managing facility. He sees his main task as that of developing a consciousness that helps employees to understand and fulfill their roles more effectively. A good deal of his time is devoted to reflection about how to achieve this objective.

The supervisor at Fukawa Works serves primarily as a facilitator, obtaining parts, filling in where needed, providing a variety of services. He is also responsible for on-the-job training. The new employee gets intensive instruction lasting several days. He is then turned over to his supervisor who assigns him a variety of tasks that start simple and grow progressively more difficult as he gains experience and self-confidence. Fellow employees work with him along with his supervisor on a day-to-day basis providing guidance and encouragement.

The objective, says Mr. Shinoda, is to develop a multi-skilled worker who can move from job to job, performing each with a high degree of efficiency. The continual job rotation, an important element in the system, contributes to the team and family feeling at the same time it helps to minimize the inevitable boredom that is a byproduct of repetitious routine.

Some tasks that might have been automated were performed manually to ensure an appropriate balance between work that is tolerable and work that is dull, mindless routine. Every 25 seconds or so a bell sounds as a signal to assembly line workers to trip a release mechanism which moves the unit to the next station. If the worker isn't ready, however, he or she has the option of holding up the release.

A prominently displayed electronic sign informs employees what the day's production goal is, how many units are already completed, and the number of units behind or ahead of the goal for each work group of about eight or ten people.

"If a group is behind," explained Shinoda, "all team members work together in an effort to catch up. If they are still behind schedule at the end of the shift, the deficiency would be added to the next day's requirement."

Most assembly workers at the Fukawa plant are women. They rarely look up from their work, but take periodic breaks for about five minutes of exercise to piped-in music. This also helps relieve the monotony of repetitive tasks at strategically selected intervals when workers feel themselves growing drowsy and hence inefficient.

Contests are effective work stimulators. The results of group competitions for quality, production and efficiency are posted on bulletin boards on a continuing basis. Winning teams get free coffee and, more important, badges of honor that are proudly displayed. Every so often employees are shown videotapes of team members working together which suggest ways to upgrade skills and boost performance.

Mr. Losey recalls coming upon one assembly line that was badly behind schedule. The production supervisor explained that a major problem had developed requiring a shutdown for a considerable period of time. Nonetheless, despite the fact that the shutdown was beyond the workers' control, the original goal was not adjusted. There is a loss of peer esteem when a group fails to meet its goal. It is not at all unusual, the supervisor said, under extraordinary circumstances to make up a 200 unit deficiency in a single day.

No incentive pay is handed out for exceeding one's goal. Where special recognition is accorded, it is geared to the boosting of individual and group self-esteem, primary consideration to the image-sensitive Japanese.

Quality control circles meet on a voluntary ad hoc basis, often for five minutes or so during the lunch hour or at the end of the work day in order not to interfere with production. Mr. Shinoda credited the United States with introducing the quality circle concept, which has been refined over the years.

In the period from 1970 to 1977 the strong emphasis was on "zero defect" performance, another U.S. adaptation. Quality control efforts today are concentrated in four key areas: product development, design, production, and inspection. Most suggestions that come out of quality circles, the manager added, are not full fledged ideas, but merely hints. At that point the skilled professionals—product design engineers, industrial engineers, etc.—take over to work on the concept and hone it down to usable form.

Employees often check their own work. In one assembly operation a procedure was developed where the worker inserts elements with one hand and checks them with the other, a quality circle idea. Although it seems basic, Shinoda explained, it contributed to an important quality improvement. The manager exhibited the plant's quality and efficiency charts which are kept scrupulously accurate and up to date. Between 1978 and 1980, the percentage of defects dropped from 1.79% to .31%. The current target projection was .25%.

The plant's 160 quality circles meet for about five minutes at a time, sometimes two or three times a day if required. Their main objective is to improve productivity, which Mr. Shinoda defines as the amount of time needed to complete an item.

Losey's study group arrived at the plant in the midst of a lunch hour union rally. Several hundred employees were assembled in a garden setting listening to a "union delegate" on top of a truck complain about the lack of progress in negotiating with management on the winter bonus issue. Management was being unreasonable, he insisted. A larger bonus was required. At the end of the tour Shinoda was asked about the demonstration. The manager explained it was part of a coordinated effort being made at all Toshiba plants that day. Its main purpose was to display solidarity.

What about the issue itself? Shinoda smiled. "It will be settled tomorrow."

Nissan Motor Co. Ltd.

Nissan workers are indeed "driven" as the Datsun (now Nissan) slogan claims. But with one of the most modern and highly automated plants in the world, there are fewer workers who need to feel driven than competitive producers would have to employ. Today, 35 assembly workers assisted by robots—or maybe it's the other way around—turn out 350 Nissan car bodies each eight-hour shift, seven times as many as Detroit carmakers.

The Nissan work day begins with a calisthenics warmup on the plant floor to get the juices flowing and employees in the proper frame of mind to shoot for new productivity records. The company is famed for its family spirit and personalized management approach. Even the robots are personalized with photos of Japanese movie stars pasted on them.

Nissan employs about 60,000 people, produced 2.6 million vehicles in fiscal 1980, almost half of which were exported, and had total sales of more than $13 billion. Its Murayana plant with 6,850 employees, over 90% of them male, produces approximately 30,000 cars and forklifts a month. The average employee is 36.5 years old and has 11.4 years of service. The operation is highly robotized.

Like other large manufacturers, Nissan recruits college graduates with general backgrounds and provides them with a broad range of business and job-related skills. It also grooms future plant workers in its own technical vocational school, and factory workers are continually trained in the skills they need for progression.

A college or high school graduate doesn't know where he will work, only that he is now a member of Nissan, a proud distinction in Japan. He can expect to work until he is 60, and because of his long-term employment knows that a strong emphasis will be placed on his personal development, that the company will assume responsibility for his welfare, and that he will hold many jobs during his career. Vocational school hires are trained specifically for assembly line work, and this is where they are placed to rotate from job to job within this general classification. At Murayana inplant training is developed by supervision with personnel department approval and goes on for years in a continuous upgrading procedure.

Compensation at Nissan generally increases at the following rate: Blue collar workers, at age 35, receive twice the salary paid to the 18-year-old high school graduate, three times this rate when he hits 55. The white collar employee doubles the 18-year-old rate when he reaches 35, and at 55 gets four times as much—on a progressive basis, of course. While seniority is traditionally the major wage determinant, the Japanese admit that in recent years merit increases as well have begun to creep into the system.

Job advancement follows a similar seniority pattern. The 31-year-old with nine years' service can expect to become a supervisior, at 38 a section head, and 10 years later a department head. Night shift workers earn a 40% premium over daytimers. A third shift is regarded as socially unacceptable due to transportation difficulties and family considerations.

Does a deadbeat employee unable or unwilling to do his job ever get fired? Only under the rarest of circumstances. Every possible alternative would be carefully explored, supervisors consulted, salvage experiments tried, and union agreement sought before this almost unthinkable last ditch action would be taken.

At Nissan as in other large industrial companies, a strong emphasis is placed on the value of quality circles. The reasoning is simple. Workers who assemble the vehicles are the ones who understand the job best, but they don't understand the design and engineering aspects. The engineers and designers are trained well for their jobs, but don't assemble the cars. Thus it is only natural that the two groups coordinate their efforts and thinking to put their total knowledge to most practical use.

When quality circles were introduced at Nissan in 1969 with 400 circles, employees participated only because the company suggested they do so. They didn't become enthusiastic, noted vice president and general personnel manager Hiroshi Urakawa, until they began to discover the "hidden" team and individual benefits, most notably the circles' usefulness in resolving job problems. The year the circles were introduced, the company received about 300 suggestions for change. In 1980, 18,000 suggestions for improvement were processed. Nor do the ideas necessarily relate to the upgrading of quality. They deal with cost reduction, human relationships, and encompass productivity improvements in general.

At Nissan, there are no white collar quality circles, but 99% of all production employees participate, and while white collar workers don't belong to the circles, they often act as advisors, particularly engineers and technologists.

Notes Sperry's Michael R. Losey: "To enable employees to make the most of their leisure time, complete recreational, cultural, and athletic facilities, such as employees' lodges and resort areas, baseball fields, gymnasiums, swimming pools, and classrooms for learning traditional Japanese arts are provided by the company. There is also a comprehensive system of employee benefits, including the latest in medical and hospital care, subsidized meals, and transportation allowances. In addition to housing facilities, such as family apartments and bachelor quarters, the company has a home loan program for employees."

After World War II, labor unions in Japan were officially recognized by law. Union organizers were radical and very militant. Small segments of the economy were often struck, sometimes affecting virtually all business activity. Plants were idled for months at a time. In the mid-1950s, after a series of disastrous strikes, the situation became sufficiently desperate to restructure the system. Agreement was reached by thoughtful Japanese leaders that unless a company could succeed in achieving reasonable profit objectives, neither labor nor management could benefit.

At this time Nissan, along with other large companies, responded affirmatively and responsibly to the societal need for labor-management harmony. A special union-management council was established. A key participant is the company's president. Although the union is not a decision making body, it is involved in company affairs, and employees are kept informed through meetings and by means of a special newsletter about the progress of labor-management activities. In 1956, at Nissan, the accumulation of prior labor agreements and practices was boiled down to a collective bargaining agreement. There have been no strikes at Nissan since the tumultuous days dating back to 1953.

Kubota, Ltd.

Kubota, founded in 1890 and incorporated in 1930, is Japan's largest manufacturer of agricultural equipment, operates 19 plants in Japan, and employs 18,000 people worldwide. 1980 sales were $2.3 billion, up 7.9% from 1979; net income of $78.5 million was up 1.9% over 1979.

Kubota's Tsukuba plant, completed in 1975 after three years of intensive planning, is the company's newest facility. It produces two- and four-wheel-drive "Sunshine" tractors. To start the plant operating, 40% of the workforce was transferred from other facilities to provide an acceptable base of experienced personnel. The plant works a single shift with selected machining operations conducted on a second shift. The average age of plant workers, predominantly male, is 26.5 years.

The overall industrial site covers approximately 341,000 square meters with a little more than a sixth of the space devoted to the physical plant. Management is especially proud that with only 450 plant employees, an annual production capacity of about 60,000 tractors is achievable. Tsukuba probably has the most automated and sophisticated assembly line operations of its type in the world.

Manual labor is reduced to one-sixth of its original amount. This has been made possible through full use of automated processing and assembly units linked by conveyors controlled through a central computer. Transfer machines are used extensively for automatic machining, measuring, assembly, quenching, and washing operations. One such machine, used for transmissions and engines, is 160 meters long. Scores of operations at Tsukuba are sequentially accommodated without human intervention. In fact, one could walk several hundred feet through the plant without encountering a person.

Housekeeping is impeccable. The entire plant is air conditioned, well-lighted, and with a surprisingly low level of noise. International gardens surrounding the plant are in themselves worth a tourist's visit.

Typically, Japanese frugality and space economy are apparent in the plant's operation. Almost all suppliers are located within a few miles of the plant and purchased parts are carried for no more than two days. Shipment of finished tractors is usually immediate, with very little provision for the storage of completed units. Seventy percent of the production requirement is geared to direct dealer orders, and 30% in response to market forecasts.

On the work floor itself there is no observable idleness. And there is a conspicuous absence of lift truck operators, supervisors, and quality control inspectors. The final inspection area provides for a total check of each unit. It is assumed that since employees are thoroughly trained and familiar with their jobs that they will perform satisfactorily.

Characteristically, highly visible electronic signs inform workers of their progress in relation to preestablished production goals. Management goes all out to demonstrate its interest and concern in employee problems and working conditions. Thus employee loyalty and dedication are taken for granted, the assumption being that if management cares, it is human nature for workers to care in response.

One sign of the caring is a continuing high level of quality performance. Prominently posted in the plant is the much-sought Deming Prize, Japan's ultimate quality award (after U.S. statistician W. Edwards Deming, who introduced quality control to the Japanese), won by Kubota in 1976 for its product excellence. To assure the quality of purchased parts, Kubota inspectors are sent to vendor plants where a special effort is made to upgrade performance and take advantage of the latest and most advanced technology.

Like Nissan, Kubota has its own vocational school where specialized production techniques are taught. New hires must attend this school for a year before being permitted to work in production. Following this there is a six-month stint of on-the-job training. Clearly, the justification for such intensive training lies in the life-long employment concept. Kubota management estimates that the training investment pays for itself within five or six years. There is no incentive pay system per se, but employees have an opportunity to earn a little bit extra if their performance is exceptional.

As in other Japanese companies, quality circles meet briefly and informally on a day-to-day basis, usually in response to plant problems. Unlike the U.S., where an employee's lunch hours are held sacred with any intrusion an unforgivable invasion of privacy, Japanese workers initiate QC lunchtime meetings themselves because they consider it to be in the company's best interest—and hence in their own best interest—to do so. It's a matter of improving working conditions and job satisfaction, and at the same time making productivity goals easier to achieve.

As one worker stated the case: "What person does not wish to make things better for himself?"

Sharp Corporation

Sharp is in its 69th year, employs 16,100 people, and in fiscal year 1980 had revenues of $2.3 billion. The average age of non-management workers is 28.4 years; the average age of all employees, including management personnel, is only 29.8 years. Of the 16,100 employees, almost 14,000 are male. The average annual earnings of a 30-year-old production worker, including wages and bonus, is about $14,220, plus extensive fringe benefits.

Sharp produces a wide line of high quality electronic items for home and business use. One of its plants outside of Osaka employs 2,000 people and manufactures large scale integrations (LSIs). Its theme is "Sensitivity and Creativity," with sensitivity relating to employees and creativity to products and marketing. This is typical of large Japanese industrials today. Criticized for not being sufficiently innovative, managements are bending over backwards to demonstrate that this is no longer so and, at the same time, taking steps to shore up this weakness if indeed one does exist.

Automated to the hilt, computer-aided design and production techniques often surpass human capabilities in certain aspects of the work, according to management. A spokesman explained, "This helps to cut costs and, at the same time, provides maximum reliability." A great many tasks, in fact, are simply checking followups to machine processing.

As a prime producer of videotape equipment, this medium is used throughout the plant for training purposes, communications, and the self-monitoring of performance. It also plays a key role in employee orientation on quality control.

Quality control takes on an extra dimension at Sharp because of the plant's need to be kept painstakingly clean, reminiscent of the "clean rooms" maintained by aerospace companies involved in the Apollo space program. Visitors were told that the manufacturing area must be kept 2,000 times cleaner than the average office, with special clothing, air showers, etc., required for production workers.

Sharp's quality control programs date back to 1949 when they were encouraged by the U.S. military for whom work was being done. A central reliability control group prepares QC manuals and provides help and guidance for the company's voluntary quality circles. At Sharp, each quality control group leader wears a special insignia, and each circle has its own slogan such as "Attach 80s," "Ace 80 Plan," "New Quality Approach," and "TQC" (for Total Quality Control).

Here, unlike many other Japanese plants, quality control circle meetings are usually conducted during working hours on an as-needed basis. They last longer, usually 30 to 40 minutes, and sometimes extend into non-working hours. Such meetings often take place once a week, during some periods less frequently. Quality circles are so successful at Sharp, they have been initiated at the company's U.S. manufacturing facility in Memphis, Tenn., a state that seems to have special appeal for Japanese electronics companies.

Sharp makes a special effort to disseminate the good ideas developed by quality circles to operations throughout the company. This is done through publication in quality control news bulletins, periodic meetings, and through the circles themselves.

At Sharp, as in most large Japanese plants, an overriding emphasis is placed on managerial sensitivity to employee needs and desires. Layoff, for example, is a virtual impossibility, not because the government mandates against it, or because union pressures discourage it, but because of the company's responsibility to provide ongoing job security. Steady employment is also economically feasible, slack periods or not. The extra cost is regained in terms of eliminated employee turnover, employee loyalty and commitment, and reduced training investment.

Toshiroh Sakata, a 26-year veteran, manages the administration division of Sharp's Tenri plant. A hundred people report to him, including four assistant managers, six chiefs, and 90 clerical employees with the classification of "foreman." Good human relations extend beyond the workplace, he says. Mr. Sakata attends employee weddings and makes hospital visits. This is what human relations is all about. Of the hundred employees working for him, he adds, "I know the hobby, sports interest, and health condition of each one."

Extensive clubhouse, athletic, and recreational facilities are available to employees on a year-round basis, along with dormitories and other housing assistance. Seventy-five percent of benefit costs are for insurance and pension-related fringes, along with subsidized housing and loans. In addition, all public transportation tabs are picked up by the company.

Although employee equality is a Japanese cultural by-product, a clear trend in the direction of individual merit awards is in progress. At Sharp, non-supervisory employees are eligible for 10 special awards. These range from the "Shop Grand Prize—Best All-Around Contribution," for which several million yen are awarded, to technical ability, special innovations, and prizes for assistance in safety programs and fire prevention. A minimum award would amount to about 5,000 yen ($25).

"Solidarity" is as important in Japanese plants as in Poland or with U.S. amalgamated clothing workers, but on a totally different dimension. Here the need is simply to display group cohesiveness. At Sharp, for example, many employees sported red armbands which read: "With determination—pursue our demands." This was in connection with the union's winter bonus negotiations. What about workers who neglected to wear their armbands? The answer was that, "They probably forgot and left them at home. Everyone is expected to play a role in the union activities."

A union bulletin board depicted a man and woman in a wedding ceremony with the blurb: "The best thing in life is a good agreement between the interests of labor and management." Alongside were announcements summarizing company profits and suggesting that management could certainly afford to meet "winter bonus demands." Another announcement urged the company to eliminate overtime, reduce working hours, and hire more people.

Although Japanese unions do not wield the power of U.S. unions, they are clearly taken seriously and given important roles in company decisions regarding conditions, compensation and benefits. And most managements stretch to the utmost to make fair and reasonable concessions. At Sharp, the winter bonus demand was for 6.2 months' compensation. The final negotiating teams settled for a figure of 5.95 months and everybody was happy—or at least reasonably so.

Kobe Steel

Kobe has been in business since 1905, employs 31,500 people, and has sales of more than $4 billion a year.

Nobutaka Kanehara, 42, a Kyoto University law school graduate, is the company's manager of labor relations. "My main job," he says, " is to motivate people." Despite Japan's fairly rigid system of wage increases and promotions based on seniority, Mr. Kanehara can reward an exceptional employee with a larger bonus and help him gain advancement a bit faster than the normal waiting period.

If an employee's performance is below standard, the manager becomes personally involved in his training. If he still fails to upgrade, he will probably be transferred to avoid loss of self-esteem.

The importance of training and development is stressed at Kobe as it is in most large Japanese companies. Classroom and on-the-job training emphasize not only job skills, but the conversion of recruits into "Kobe men," so that they will think like, and feel one with, management. "When young graduates first join the company they are sometimes egotistic," says Mr. Kanehara. "It's a manager's duty to educate them to the company philosophy, and occasionally remind them not to be arrogant."

Kobe's general manager is particularly proud of the company's safety record which, he believes, surpasses that of any other company in the world. The record held to date by Kobe is 19 million accident-free man-hours, three million more than the U.S. record.

Barring bankruptcy, lifetime employment is viewed by management as "an employer obligation." Thus, in place of layoff, employee transfers are relatively frequent. Lifetime employment, for all its advantages, is viewed by some as "an intimidating benefit." It would be costly for an employee to leave a company after putting in 10 or 15 years. It would almost invariably mean a loss in absolute wages because of the seniority status he would sacrifice, and by the time he reached 55 his earnings would be substantially less than his counterpart whose entire career was devoted to one employer. Long term employment, therefore, eliminates the turnover problem on a built-in basis. It also "traps" employees who, for one reason or other, might desire a change.

Characteristically, Kobe employment offers workers a host of social and recreational benefits. At the company's

Kakogawa plant, for example, almost a fourth of its 6,000-plus employees live in low-cost company-subsidized dormitories. A Kobe employee gets 20 paid vacation days per year plus 12 national holidays. In addition, days off are allowed for weddings and other special events as they occur.

Thrift is vigorously encouraged. The company sponsors its own saving plan which pays a higher than ordinary rate of interest. Employees also receive financial assistance in making home purchases. The interest charge on home purchase loans is about one-third the interest yield of the Kobe saving plan. Food service is subsidized, clothing costs on the job are fully paid by the company, complete medical, recreation and athletic facilities are provided, and a survivors' welfare pension of 20,000 yen monthly is allowed for one's spouse and each child under 18 years of age.

Quality control circles started modestly at Kobe as in most other companies, but expanded in scope after potential gains became evident. Today, a professional staff helps to guide and direct this activity, with managers and technologists getting in on the act to reap maximum application and productivity from the idea flow.

Tokai Bank, Ltd.

The sixth largest bank in Japan, Tokai has 228 branches, 24 of them overseas in New York, Los Angeles, and other big cities. It employs a total of 15,000 people.

Interestingly, Matsutani spent five years in the U.S. as president of the bank's Los Angeles branch. When he was transferred back to Japan, he was promoted to the high executive job of general manager of personnel administration despite his never having held a specific personnel post. This bears out the Japanese philosophy that an individual is hired for the organization and not for the job.

Reflecting on the most productive ideal, Matsutani said he believes the best system of management probably lies some place between what he knows of the U.S. and what exists in Japan.

Approximately 30% of his responsibility, he explained, is to find jobs for employees, usually in their late 40s, prior to their retirement. This is just the right age—when their financial expertise is at a peak and so in demand by some of the bank's customers, and they are not yet at the point where their age is a handicap. Males in Japan, Matsutani added, have a life expectancy of 73 (79 for females), so that post-retirement jobs can be extremely important. In most cases, retirees are in demand by smaller companies which pay lower wages and offer less fringe benefits. Since older people are revered and respected by the Japanese, the retired person in Japan is not "put out to pasture" to the extent that he would be in America.

Nonetheless, there is clearly an accent on youth in Japan. People are retired earlier to free up more jobs and better opportunities for the young. What's more, the instant success syndrome doesn't exist there as it does here. In the U.S., the typical bright young college graduate recruited by industry wants to "get into the action" as soon as he's hired and become a high priced key man overnight.

At Tokai the stress is placed on intensified, specialized, and diversified training. A new employee is given three to six months of on-the-job experience under close supervisory guidance, and is then rotated from section to section for further training and indoctrination. If he's a college graduate he is trained for about two years, then tested and, based on test results, selected for additional individualized training and development. This might include language training, special bank and management courses, possibly a stint in the U.S. or elsewhere.

Of all Japanese systems, Matsutani feels the one most likely to see change is the one that deals with wage and promotion boosts by seniority. He thinks this will be gradually modified to include greater credit for outstanding performance and profit contributions.

Today there are slightly more opportunities for women in Japanese companies than existed a decade or two ago. But progress in this area is slow. The problem, one Japanese explained, is that nine out of 10 women leave work before the age of 25 to raise families and keep house.

Tokai Bank is a notable pioneer of quality control circles in banking and white collar jobs. The program has been in existence several years and everyone through the assistant managerial level participates. Approximately 1,500 circles are operating in the Tokai Japanese branches. QC meetings are viewed as problem-solving vehicles and customarily take place for brief periods during lunch and break sessions.

Significantly, Tokai doesn't feel it would be effective to carry quality circle activity to branches outside of Japan. "They do not see how to adapt the system elsewhere," says Mr. Losey, "but are planning further research. This suggests pretty strongly," he adds, "that the quality control effort, its discipline, and the contribution of employees, is indeed reflective of the Japanese economy, environment and culture," although this has not been clearly resolved as yet and some U.S. experiments (Sharp in Tennessee, for example) seem to be working.

At Tokai, each quality control circle has a chief, and in each bank there is a committee of chiefs as well as a chairman who coordinates activities with other branches and helps to disseminate ideas. The chiefs are selected by the committee members and are usually young, non-officer bank personnel. Circles meet once or twice weekly, the chiefs once a month. Every six months a new theme is pinpointed for special attention. As the circles took on importance and increased in effectiveness, special plaques, letters of commendation, and the like were discontinued by way of recognition. The assumption is that the QC program itself improves working conditions, makes the employee's life easier, and helps eliminate frustration. Within the program one finds the reward.

Suntory, Ltd.

Suntory, Japan's oldest and largest liquor distiller, employs about 4,000 people. Its Katsura Brewery outside of Osaka produces 40 million gallons of beer annually. The plant started production in 1969 with 235 employees. Today its output is 2.8 times greater and it employs 268 workers. Much of the improvement has come through automation, a great deal more by way of management and employee efforts to boost productivity. Katsura is a shining model of the kind of Japanese efficiency and industrial progress that is attracting worldwide attention.

Quality control circles have been in existence from the plant's inception. They meet one or two hours a week, usually when the production line is shut down for changeover. If QC meetings are held before or after working hours, here, unlike most other companies, workers are paid for their time. Indicative of a new trend in Japan? Perhaps. Circles vary in size from as little as three members to as many as 34, depending on the organizational arrangement. This also indicates that, as is the case worldwide, Japanese companies are each unique in a special way and have individual personalities.

Each of Katsura's 18 groups has its own efficiency theme, ranging from how to reduce errors and the number of unwashed bottles to the development of ideas to upgrade the labeling system.

Yoshinobu Hamanaka, the plant's top ranking executive, is a strong advocate of employee equality. He dines in the same employee cafeteria as everyone else, wears the same uniform as the first-year worker, and involves himself in the personal lives of his people.

"Around here," he says, "the manager serves the workers. The manager is not a big shot. The worker is the big shot."

Shades of the famous Matsushita philosophy: Each November Hamanaka spends two days at Suntory headquarters where he and other high level executives learn the president's "vision" for the coming year. The 1981 theme, for example, related to ways and means whereby the corporation could make meaningful contributions to society. Hamanaka's task is to carry the vision, along with individual plant goals geared to its fulfillment, back to his own managers and supervisors who carry the message down the line to their people.

Another Japanese trend, in response to employee demands, is toward higher wages and bigger bonus payments which often amount to half a year's salary or more. At Suntory, the average wage for a 32-year-old production worker is 260,000 yen per month plus an annual bonus equal to eight months' wages. This comes to a yearly total, including a million yen allocated to benefit costs, of about 6,200,000 yen, about $29,500, much higher than is paid in most plants. Of the million yen benefit burden, approximately 60% is required by law. The most significant part of the remaining 40% applies to housing costs and long-term employee loans. In an interesting comparison, Mr. Losey used Sperry New Holland's $9.45 per hour base rate, including incentive pay and benefit burden, and came up with a rough estimate that his division pays about 13.8% less than Suntory.

This company's management confirms the growing trend that, despite a commitment to lifetime employment and wage levels based on seniority, more and more consideration is being given to merit. At Suntory, for example, an exceptionally talented and conscientious employee can advance to supervisor in five years instead of the customary 10. Hamanaka predicted that in the future a major challenge of industry will be to continue to motivate and inspire young workers who, as in the U.S. and throughout the world, are less loyal today than they have been in the past. Thus, he suggested there will be somewhat less reliance on the seniority system, and less acceptance of the existing order of things by more spirited and aggressive young people.

And Then Some

In balance it is clear that just as the U.S. is faced with a critical productivity challenge in the months ahead, the Japanese will be faced with a challenge of their own to sustain the productivity edge they currently enjoy. In short, Japan's society and economy are also in flux so far as the expectations and demands of its workers are concerned, and its youth in particular, so that its culturally-based advantages relating to such items as pride in achievement and team and family loyalty, may diminish somewhat in months to come. On the other hand, Japan can afford a bit of slack. Running well ahead of the pack as it is, the nation's *need* to address its challenge quickly and effectively is far less desperate than the need for America's swift and decisive response—not that the lack of need will cause the lean and hard Japanese to sit back and rest on their laurels.

The question every thoughtful U.S. executive who, having observed the Japanese productivity phenomenon, would like answered is: "What can we in America learn from the Nipponese way of management that might be applicable in this country despite the inbred cultural and societal differences between the two nations?" Here is a rundown of some of the changes we might think about in our effort to help regain the economic turf we have lost:

• *Work From a Groundbase of Employee Trust, Concern and Respect.* Japanese workers are absolutely convinced that when the company benefits, they benefit too. Japanese managers express humility, eschew pomposity and arrogance, don't "pull rank"; they dress like employees and socialize with subordinates. Thus a oneness is experienced among all workers regardless of level. They care about each other; they care about the organization. And they know the organization cares about them. At Sony plants, for example, working hours are made flexible to accommodate women whose familial responsibilities make it difficult for them to show up for work at the start of the regular 8 A.M. shift. Proof that Japanese employees respond to employer caring with caring of their own can be found in the comparative number of ideas turned in by Japanese and U.S. plants. General Motors, as an example, offers employees attractive sums for acceptable suggestions, far more so than Japanese companies. Yet Toyota's main plant at Nagoya receives more than nine ideas from each worker per year on the average, while GM receives less than one. And at Toyota more than twice the percentage of submitted ideas are implemented than at GM. The point makes itself. Show an employee trust, concern and respect and he'll measure up to the stature you endow him with.

• *Hike U.S. Quality to New Levels of Excellence.* It is ironic that Japan, which received its quality control education and indoctrination from the U.S., is now teaching this country and the rest of the world what quality refined to its most conscientious level is all about. Tokyo's Casio Computer Co. serves as a classic example. Its sales of calculators and watches, $27 million in 1970, rocketed to $697 in 1980 to make it the world's largest producer of digital watches. Good quality products at low prices are clearly responsible for the surge of acceptance and reported high marks from dealers. Casio's main stress is on strengthening and sustaining the company's quality image, more important even than its low-price reputation, a spokesperson reports. Today, with markets for digital watches and desk calculators at or near saturation, Casio is turning to personal computers and other electronic products with the same concentrated resolve. Time was not so many years ago when MADE IN THE U.S. signified absolute top-of-the-line quality. As the sire of quality control, we must go all out to restore an image of excellence in domestic markets and world-wide.

- *Build WE-Power Into U.S. Plants.* Corny, trite, regarded scornfully and cynically by most U.S. workers, the "one big happy family" concept works in Japan. When a Mitsubishi assembly line employee proclaims, "These are my people, they are like my brothers and sisters," he is totally sincere and conducts his working life accordingly. The family concept may well be the most powerful of all worker motivators. True, while it is culturally based in Japan, it could never persist and survive if management as well as rank-and-file personnel didn't believe in the precept and treat their people accordingly. Can the corporate family concept take hold in this country and gain acceptance without cynicism and doubt? Oh yes! it can and it has, as we will demonstrate in a subsequent chapter. But for the family concept to be credible and translatable to productive ends it must be honestly *felt,* and supported by actions and reactions that demonstrate this integrity.

- *Unchain Yourself From Short-Term "Performance" Goals.* Few U.S. giants have as many new products on the drawing boards as Matsushita Electric. The company pours untold millions into research and development each year. One of the minor secondary interests at Matsushita and other large Japanese industrials is today's, or next month's, "bottom line." "Care to take a tour to the future?" a Matsushita ad asks readers. The question is well taken, for it is on the future that Matsushita thinking is focused. "New products hit the domestic Japanese market with dizzying frequency," states *Time.* " . . . When Toyota last year introduced the world's first chip-operated voice synthesizer to warn drivers of low fuel and fluid levels in their cars, Nissan hustled out its competing version within weeks."

Can stockholder-pressured managements in this country abandon short-term preoccupations in favor of long-term achievement and growth? Indeed they can and, as we shall see, a handful of America's ultraprogressives are leading the way with stunning success. Not only are these organizations proving that futuremindedness is the only basically solid and productive managerial approach to take, but they are, in the process, keeping Wall Street in its place.

- *Maximize Employee Talents and Capabilities.* It may be hard for Westerners to understand, observes Sony Chairman Akio Morita, but one of the reasons the company is so successful in such a wide diversity of operations is the career paths it provides for its young middle managers. When a graduate is recruited, he explains, there is no telling where his talents and interests will take him. "My objective," he adds, "is to utilize each person's unique abilities to the utmost." Morita sees the managerial attitude toward employees as the biggest gulf between Japanese and American management. In the U.S., he notes, "you write a job specification for every position, and if a person does not fit the specification, you get rid of him and hire another one. Our way of doing things is different."

From the Japanese perspective, "Viva la difference!" Under the Japanese perception of career growth, the more the individual employee knows about the company, its goals, his job, and interacting activities, the better equipped he will be to think and perform productively. Here again as we shall see is a concept some U.S. companies are adapting with growing success and impressive results to the American way of industrial life.

- *Upgrade Employee Stability.* The employee who feels he may be here today and gone tomorrow cannot very well be expected to harbor feelings of goodwill and devoted loyalty toward his employer. According to Nippon Steel's president, Eishiro Saito, one of an executive's primary responsibilities is to help plan and design a stable and secure life for the company's employees and their families. To the Japanese manager's way of thinking, were he forced to lay off a worker it would be a disgrace and embarrassment, an indication of management failure. Without committing the error of attempting to superimpose Japan's system or the Japanese mentality on U.S. executives, some American companies are proving they can provide a far greater level of long range employment stability than the norm, and make the policy pay off in terms of profits and productivity as well as human revenues.

- *Don't Be Lulled by Reports of Japanese Weaknesses.* It is true as will be demonstrated in the final chapter of the book that U.S. companies enjoy many advantages over the Japanese, some of which are natural, and some built into the system. Yes, the Japanese do have serious weaknesses to overcome. Those too will be expanded upon. But don't make the mistake of permitting wishful reports of weaknesses by those who would like to brush off the Japanese success phenomenon as a freak occurrence or passing phase to lull you into believing Nipponese companies will one day soon cease to be the tough and relentless competitors they are today.

Typical of ascribed weaknesses is the allegation that Japanese managers are in the main noncreative conformists who come up with few innovations of their own. This is probably true to some extent. But progressive Japanese executives are acutely sensitive to the charge, and determined to upgrade personal and organizational images along this line. It is apparent in their advertising. Matsushita Electric, for example, is proud of the "international recognition" it has received for technical innovation. Its I-R100 Prize, as a case in point, is awarded annually to the world's 100 most outstanding achievements in technological development. And in 1980 the company won an Emmy for its Digital Video Processor. The company has not been backward in publicizing such accomplishments.

Another charge is that all Japanese industrials are stamped from the same mold. Untrue. While certain cultural characteristics and inbred beliefs may be common, each Japanese company, like each U.S. company, is a highly individualistic entity. Matsushita Electric, for example, although very Japanese is also very unique. Another good example is Japan's second largest petroleum refiner, Idemitsu Kosan. It is like no other company, in Japan or America. States *New York Times* writer Mike Tharp: "Idemitsu Kosan . . . does not operate like most Japanese companies: There is no labor union. There are no time clocks. There is no mandatory retirement age. There is no overtime pay. Married workers earn more than single workers doing the same job. Since it was founded by Sazo Idemitsu 70 years ago, the company has maintained a corporate style that is unusual by any standard."

The point is clear. That Japanese managerial weaknesses do exist is certain, though it is this writer's belief they are often overstated. What's more, historically within the past decade or two at least, the Japanese have demonstrated a capacity to convert weaknesses to strengths. They are fierce and determined competitors, and this isn't likely to change. The U.S. executive who either rests on his laurels or settles for status quoism in the hope that competitive inroads will somehow miraculously cease may be in for a sad and jolting awakening.

• *Work Together With Labor and Government Toward Common Goals.* This may well be the toughest challenge facing not only American industry, but all of society, today. A keynote of Japan's success has been the coordination that the key elements of free enterprise—management, labor, and government—has been able to achieve. In Japan, the Ministry of Finance and Bank of Japan assume roughly the functions of our Office of Management and Budget, Federal Reserve System, and Treasury Department, plus a number of government regulatory agencies. These institutions, manned by hardnosed bankers, understand the nation's financial needs and, equally important, what is required to sustain industry without hampering growth.

Japan's powerful Ministry of International Trade and Industry (MITI) is primarily concerned with measures and issues that will ensure the continuing competitiveness of Japanese industry, and figures prominently in the consensus system which has as its first and foremost objective economic and industrial good health. In the U.S., management often wonders whose side government and the regulatory agencies are on. And labor shares this concern.

In Japan, the unions, all 70,000 of them, while focused on obtaining improved wages and conditions for its members, are also consensus-minded, recognizing that an adversary system in general and strikes in particular can only hurt all parties involved. Most large industrials in Japan have avoided the ravages of labor war since the mid-50s thus far.

To the Japanese mentality, a strike is looked upon as a failure of labor and management to reach agreement, and is thus an embarrassment. Not that the nation has been strike-free. Far from it. But by way of contrast, in 1978 the U.S. lost an estimated 39 million workdays due to strike; Japan lost only 1.4 million workdays. Incorporated into product cost and price, the differential adds up to a bundle. To the Japanese worker, his employer is, with some exceptions of course, a source of comfort, support and security. To the U.S. worker, in far too many cases, the organization he works for is the enemy. When we succeed in equalizing these disparate attitudes, we will have come a long way toward parity with Japanese industry.

4.
THE AMERICAN IMPERATIVE

> *I think that the mission or principle of enterprise management consists in responding to the fulfilling of the desire to maintain and improve the quality of human life.*
> —*Konosuke Matsushita*

Gradually, dramatically, in a mood of cautiously restrained excitement, what has been referred to as "the new industrial relations" is taking root in America. Addressed by a variety of labels, the one that is most common and persistent is Quality of Working Life (or Work Life) (QWL). Its noble purpose is to restructure the labor-management condition from an adversary relationship to one of mutual striving and trust.

The premise is simple enough. Evidence is mounting rapidly that QWL programs, effectively planned, introduced and implemented in the corporate environment can serve the twin objectives of boosting job satisfaction and worker morale while they improve productivity.

The concept, which incorporates many of the elements of management which catapulted Japanese industry to its place of world leadership, is steadily gaining acceptance of and sponsorship by top level executives in major U.S. corporations.

Ben Fischer, director of labor studies at the School of Urban & Public Affairs, Carnegie-Mellon University, and former assistant to the president of the United Steelworkers of America, states the case bluntly enough: "Workers are unlikely to have high morale and constructive interests in improved performance while they are engaged in periodic or incessant combat."

One indication that QWL concepts, flourishing not only in Japan, but in most industrialized nations around the world, are finally taking hold in this country, was a September 1981 international quality of working life conference in Toronto, attended and spiritedly participated in by 200 union officials and 750 executives, the actual parties to the conflict that thoughtful managers are attempting to resolve. Previous meetings of this type were marked by meager attendance and strongly dominated by academics and theoreticians. This meeting meant business.

One of the more auspicious signs of the times is that QWL's growth in this country now appears to be certain. Clearly, industrial democracy already has spread to key segments of the economy. Detroit's auto makers are strongly pledged to the concept, and the world's largest employer, AT&T, with over a million employees, signed a contract with the Communications Workers of America, which incorporates major QWL elements. Programs are underway or on the drawing boards in a host of other industries as well, ranging from steel, rubber, paper and aerospace to electronics, food processing and glass. A handful of giant retailers, most notably the Atlantic & Pacific Tea Co., are also getting into the act.

On top of that, as we shall see later in the book, a significant body of America's most progressive—and profitable—corporations, long have had QWL programs effectively in force, although the QWL label is rarely if ever applied.

The Urgency of QWL Inroads

Today's young generation of office and plant workers, supervisors, and managers are as different from the generation of the 40s, 50s and 60s as actress Jane Fonda is from Jerry Falwell. Worker expectations and interests these days are immensely more self- and fun-oriented. Employees aren't easily motivated to dig in for hard times because they never really knew what hard times are all about. The prospect of hard times provokes little if any anxiety.

Daniel Yankelovich, whose firm of Yankelovich, Skelly & White surveyed 3,500 American families in 1980, found that 40% of today's labor force is made up of "new work-value" employees. These people like money for the leisure and upgraded lifestyle it can bring them, but the message they are hammering home to employers is that they are unwilling to substitute dollars for self-respect and job fulfillment.

What do young—and not-so-young—Americans in U.S. plants and offices actually want? In a nutshell, says Ben Fischer, as their income rises, concerns about other matters in general, and the quality of life at the workplace in particular, come to the fore. This labor relations expert stresses the importance that representatives and negotiators on both sides of the table understand each other's needs and objectives.

For one thing, American workers today will no longer accept the kind of regimentation their parents and grandparents automatically assumed came with the territory. For another, they insist on being treated as *thinking people,* not robots, or machine extensions. They want what is often broadly referred to as "a piece of the action," to become involved in the problem-solving and decision-making aspects of the job.

Notes *Los Angeles Times* labor writer Harry Bernstein: "Thomas J. Murrin, president of Westinghouse Electric Co.'s Public Systems Co., is convinced like so many other Americans these days, that bringing workers into the decision-making process is the single most significant explanation for the truly outstanding quality of goods and services produced in Japan." He goes on to say that "in the 1960s, plagued with a reputation for producing only low quality 'Made in Japan' products, the Japanese took the concept (of worker participation) and expanded it into a nationwide system of quality-control circles that now involves most Japanese workers. That, plus a practice of avoiding layoffs, has produced a company loyalty almost unheard of here."

The United Auto Workers' Irving Bluestone makes the observation that, "while (the U.S. worker's) rate of pay may dominate his relationship to his job, he can be responsive to the opportunity for playing an innovative, creative and imaginative role in the production process."

A frequently posed question is: "Would most American employees be more interested in making their time on the job more meaningful, or in minimizing the amount of time they spend on the job?"

Pondering this question, while provocative, is less productive than adopting a managerial attitude that responds to the challenge of making the job more interesting, fulfilling, and capable of building human self-esteem so that whatever time must be spent on the job will be palatable instead of frustrating. That in an eyecup is what QWL is all about.

What It Is, What It's Not

Since the automobile industry has been hardest hit of all industries by the Japanese productivity surge and the competitive edge it fostered, it's no surprise that Detroit's Big 3 display a very special interest and concern in the kind of managerial restructuring that promises to narrow the productivity gap. General Motors corporation, for one, has certainly risen to the call. It is firmly dedicated to the proposition that QWL programs offer American industry an unprecedented opportunity to regain its long-claimed status of worldwide economic leadership.

The gauntlet at GM has been taken up in particular by its department of Organizational Research and Development, headed by its director, D. L. Landen, and assistant director Harold C. Carlson. Both these men and their staffs have done a great deal of innovative and imaginative pioneering work in the structuring, implementation and study of QWL programs. The nation owes GM a debt of gratitude for its willingness to share with others what it has learned at considerable pain and expense. Lesson number one in making QWL—or any other corporate endeavor, for that matter—succeed, is the importance of having the effort backed by management at the very highest organizational level. Landen and Carlson are certainly getting this kind of essential support.

What is Quality of Work Life? "It is an organized way," states GM President James McDonald, "to allow employees to make more contributions to their individual success and to the success of the organization."

GM Vice President A.S. Warren adds: "Best organizations . . . tend to be characterized by good communications, openness, teamwork, talented people and accomplishing objectives. To put it very simply, the process of improving quality of work life involves taking steps to move the organization toward those positive characteristics."

Surely this is what Konosuke Matsushita talks about in espousing his philosophies of management. And it is what the Japanese way of management turns out to be all about when one delves into the whys and wherefores of the success of Japanese industrials.

QWL is most of all a philosophy of management. It is a means of pinpointing employee disenchantment and frustration, investigating and clarifying their causes and, finally, replacing adverse and negative employee feelings and perceptions with positive feelings and perceptions. In short, QWL's aim is to imbue in workers a desire to contribute to the combined advantage of corporation, individual and economy, to replace indifference with pride, and to feel a sense of identification with, and belonging to, the organizational group.

Two of QWL's strongest elements are employee participation and quality control circles, introduced conceptually, not as a superimposition of the Japanese system. It would be well to keep in mind at this point the previously stated contention that each corporation is an individual and unique entity. Thus, one cannot install a QWL program as one might a computer billing or payroll application. Each program must be custom tailored to the organization it is designed to serve.

In considering or initiating a quality of working life system, it is as important to understand what it is not as well as what it is to understand its result-based objectives.

- QWL is not designed solely to improve employee job satisfaction. Its purpose and intention is, through work improvement and participation techniques, to achieve increased returns for the individual, group, and organization.

- Though referred to as a program or combination of programs, QWL is not a sometime or temporary system. Once initiated and implemented successfully, it will become a working way of life or philosophy.

- It is not a technique. Although several techniques such as job rotation, job enrichment, work simplification and the like, may play a part in the overall restructuring, the basis of QWL is to involve employees in the design and development of their own work roles.

- QWL doesn't imply that the work will get harder or easier. The objective is to improve the job in a way that will optimize the worker's talents and capabilities and, at the same time, yield for him maximum reward and fulfillment.

- Although a major QWL goal is to allow the worker greater participation in the planning, problem solving, and decision making aspects of his job, QWL does not shift management responsibility from the company's supervisors and executives to its rank-and-file employees. It does, however, substantially change the uses of power, wherever possible replacing mandates with group consensus, guidance, and positive influences.

- The introduction of QWL is not a personnel department function. The concept is much broader and deeper than that. It includes the entire organization, with management and line personnel sharing responsibility for its successful implementation and continued well-being.

- It is not a scheme, fad or device. QWL is a permanent conceptual change in the relationship of managers and supervisors toward each other and toward line personnel, and a change in the relationship of all employees from top management down, to their jobs.

Basically, QWL is a new style of, or approach to, management. It is in many aspects a close approximation of managing the Japanese way. It might also be well to add that QWL is different things to different people. One of several companies experimenting with the concept, with generally favorable though not as yet dramatically exciting results, is Butler Manufacturing Company. Michael R. Simmons, Vice President-Corporate Personnel, offers the following observations with reference to "self-management" approaches made operational at the company's Story City, Iowa, plant:

"It is important to stress several things which Story City's nontraditional operation is *not*. It is not a 'country club' setting. The atmosphere is comfortable and worker satisfaction is important in line with the basic goal of product and profit. The Story City plant is not a democracy, although employees are allowed a high level of participation and their recommendations are encouraged and usually implemented. Butler's strong belief is that it makes good sense to give employees a voice in decisions which affect their jobs. And it is by no means a permissive atmosphere. Management does not regulate workers' every activity because it does not have to, with control exerted by everyone in the plant rather than those few in management capacity. In fact, those involved in the Story City operation believe this type of regulation to be more effective in the long run."

The Underlying Foundation Is Trust

James Ramsay Macdonald once said, "To be trusted is a greater compliment than to be loved."

If anything is the underpinning of a successful QWL program, this is it. C. Stuart Sullivan of Canada's Energy & Chemical Workers Union states the case simply enough: "If you have a relationship based on trust, you can get to the real issues a lot sooner."

Productivity is a handmaiden of trust. Management consultant Roy W. Walters, who applies missionary zeal to the restructuring of low-productivity offices and plants, pinpoints trust as the operational word in successful endeavors.

He decries the use of time clocks, for example, as an illustration of mistrust. Ninety-five percent of people at work, he believes, are capable of doing more than the job allows. "This conviction," he told the author, "is spawned out of 40 years of working experience, 25 in large companies, 15 in consulting. People can do more. Most people want to do more, even if they're not aware of it themselves."

The key, he insists, is to operate on a different trust level in the large, too impersonal, plant. He cites a client engagement where he was called in to deal with a serious tool loss problem. The general manager explained anxiously, "We tried everything. We created employee awareness of management concern with close monitoring techniques. People were checked as they clocked out of the plant. Nothing helped."

Walters persuaded management to try an experiment. He suggested that the general manager talk to employees, tell them he realized they have work at home and need tools to complete it. Invite them to feel free to borrow what they need and to return it when they're done.

Almost immediately, says Walters, the loss rate was chopped by 30%. "It's human nature," he adds, "to try to beat the system in a poor trust situation."

An important part of the consultant's work restructuring strategy, a key QWL success factor, and one of the strong roots of high productivity yield in Japan, is self-management. "Make every employee a manager in his or her own right," Walters urges. "I've seen it time and again. The message workers are trying to hammer across to executives is simply this: 'Let me manage what I do.' "

Self-management is the ultimate expression of trust.

The most dehumanizing premise upon which a work system can be structured is that the thinking part of the job is confined to supervisors and executives, that management is fortunate if it finds a work force capable of following simple instructions. Experiment after experiment these days is demonstrating the degree of creative and constructive thought workers are capable of if permitted to think for themselves in a trust-based environment.

"Traditional systems rely on hierarchical controls," notes Harvard Business School Prof. Richard E. Walton. "The innovative system is the opposite; therefore, it must rely on individual or team self-management."

The Japanese system relies on group self-management. QWL relies on self-management, period; in some cases group, in some cases individual.

Butler's Story City operation appears to be modeled after the Japanese system in this regard. Simmons explains that as the structure currently functions, all jobs in the plant fall under three broad, non-restrictive classifications:

- CRAFTSMEN: Tool and die makers and maintenance activities.

- TECHNICIANS: Workers involved in welding, setting up presses and lathes, and other work of the setup-and-run variety.

- OPERATORS: All other employees.

Each self-managed team consists of five to 12 employees who have collective responsibility for large segments of production. These teams are responsible for the following functional areas:

- Fabrication—Initial production of parts from steel coil and other raw materials.

- Machining—Production of finished machine parts such as fan blades, through precision balancing, etc.

- Welding—Welded assemblies.

- Painting—Operation of power coating paint system.

- Assembly—(12-14 teams organized by product type) Assembly into finished products, testing, and preparation for shipping and the like.

- Shipping and Receiving—Receiving of purchased materials, storage, warehousing and shipping of completed product.

- Engineering and Maintenance, Tool Making—Tool and die making, complex maintenance, and instruction in routine maintenance to maintenance workers.

- Production, Inventory Control and Purchasing.

- Accounting/Financial.

- Plant Manager (staff team).

The Story City organization, Simmons explains, includes a controller, engineering manager, production control, fabrication and assembly managers, and the plant manager. Four unit coordinators oversee the activities of the 20 to 22 shop teams on day and night shifts.

"Information gathered at seminars and lectures," Simmons adds, "books citing research into the field, actual visits to plants using many of these (QWL) approaches, and consultation. . . led to the evolution of a premise upon which the Story City plant design was based:

That participation by employees in all phases of the business would benefit both employees and the company in achieving the goals of productivity and profitability."

Employee Participation Groups at GM. The General Motors equivalent of Japanese quality control circles—a synonym for team participation—is called Employee Participation Groups (EPG), and is operational in several GM plants. "These small groups," the company reports, "are operating successfully to improve the work environment and to identify and resolve problems at the shop floor and office."

The company makes the following pertinent comments in regard to the system:

An Employee Participation Group usually consists of a group leader (usually supervisor) and eight to 12 hourly or salaried employees who meet regularly on a voluntary basis to identify, analyze and solve problems in their workplace. The EPG is an ongoing, structured element of quality of work life activities which is based on the premise that the employees closest to the materials, the process and the product are in the best position to develop effective solutions. Where the group consists of employees who are eligible to earn awards under the GM Suggestion Plan, the group is encouraged to submit its cost-saving ideas under the plan and share any awards equally among the members who submitted them.

Importantly, EPGs have been given the range to pool their interests and skills in solving a variety of problems. Product quality, communications, plant safety, absenteeism reduction, housekeeping and production problems are some of the subjects successfully handled by such work groups. They often start by improving their own communication and interaction skills. These skills build the needed trust and understanding for a continuing effort. As groups become cohesive teams, problem-solving skills usually continue to develop and improve. . . .

A two-part program was designed to assist GM locations in the preparation, development and implementation of employee participation groups, including:

- Orientation and Consulting Assistance—A videotape overview was produced based on interviews with managers, supervisors, union leaders and other employees at GM locations that are involved with the EPGs. Consulting support will be provided on request to help units determine their organizational readiness for establishing EPGs. The international UAW assisted in developing this support. In July 1980 all personnel directors worldwide were advised of the availability of the videotape and booklet containing the answers to the most frequently asked questions about EPGs. As a result, more than 80 GM units have requested this information.

- Comprehensive Training for Coordinators, and Follow-up Consulting—Training for local management and union EPG coordinators began in October (1980). This training focuses on problem solving skills for use by group leaders and members. The roles of a coordinator, a group leader and a steering committee are emphasized. The coordinators are given materials and are then responsible for training EPG leaders at their locations. During the implementation, assistance is provided as needed with QWL administrators and training supervisors so they can support the EPG process.

GM goes on to stress that "not every organization is ready to implement Employee Participation Groups.

Cooperation among various segments of an organization is a 'must' if EPGs are to function effectively. The Employee Participation Group concept has important implications for all levels of management, the union and employees, and unless all parties are ready and willing to accept and support the change, the approach has little chance of succeeding.

"Thus, an essential step in the process for units interested in EPGs is to make an assessment of readiness. This also is required prior to enrolling in coordinator training. The Organizational Research and Development Department consulting services are available to assist with this assessment."

Finding Out

It's one thing to know what QWL is all about. It is quite another to understand what quality of work life is from the perceptions of the men and women who man the desks, work benches and machines in your organization. Clearly, before you can boost job satisfaction sufficiently to prompt greater feelings of loyalty, and so motivate increased productivity, you must know specifically what frustrations employees seek to eliminate and which positive inputs they seek to improve. On top of that, if one's objective is to improve the quality of work life, a measure of some kind is needed to assess where we are now in order to ascertain whether or not the place we wind up six months, or a year, or five years after the QWL program gets under way represents true progress and, if so, how much progress.

With these aims in mind, GM created a QWL Survey designed to measure the attitudes, opinions and work climate of GM organizations from the employee's point of view. As Howard C. Carlson points out, "Quality of work life is essentially an individual concept." Thus, obtaining the individual employee's personal assessment of the workplace, what it is now from his point of view, and how he would like it to change, constitutes a vitally important foundation upon which to base work restructuring efforts.

The General Motors Survey measures 16 key dimensions of the quality of work life, along with three other factors which line up as follows:

1. Employee Commitment
2. Absence of Developing Apathy
3. On the Job Development and Utilization
4. Employee Involvement and Influence
5. Advancement Based on Merit
6. Career Goal Progress
7. Relations with Supervisor
8. Work Group Relations
9. Respect for the Individual
10. Confidence in Management's Understanding of My Concerns
11. Physical Working Environment
12. Economic Well-Being
13. Employee State of Mind
14. Absence of Undue Job Stress
15. Impact on Personal Life
16. Union-Management Relations

And the three additional factors:

- Attitude Towards Change
- Job Satisfaction
- Employee Motivation

Because of the increasing number of requests from companies all over the country and abroad, General Motors is now making the QWL Survey itself available through a commercial sales group, which is part of the company's Marketing Educational Services.

For further information contact:

> Richard Luther, Assistant Director
> External Sales, Marketing Educational Services
> General Motors Institute
> Flint, Mich. 48502
> (313) 762-9825

No Shortcuts. The plant's operational structure, Butler's Michael R. Simmons reported to the American Productivity Center, allows a great deal of job rotation, and stresses continual training and education. To illustrate, he follows a hypothetical employee from the time he or she is hired through the first 18 months on the job.

Pre-employment training consists of 10 three-hour evening classes, for a total of 30 hours. The first class is an orientation which offers the employee and spouse information about company history, benefits, etc. The following nine sessions deal with such topics as materials handling, safety, math, blueprint reading, assembly techniques, and electrical plumbing and wiring skills. The new hire then gets another 32 hours of training, starting with three days on the shop floor to become acquainted with the specific team area to which he will be assigned. An eight-hour orientation to production and inventory control, computer areas, and financial reporting concludes the formal training period. The employee is now ready for on-the-job training.

After 30 days on the job, the team conducts a group performance review, to identify the worker's strong and weak points. At the same time, he is encouraged to discuss personal concerns and needs with team members. A similar, but individual, performance review with the unit coordinator is held after four months. Two months later, the worker moves to a new team assignment in another shop area, following much the same procedure that is operational in many Japanese companies.

The shift takes place three times in 18 months so that by the end of this time the employee has skills in three of the five plant areas. Thus, not only is his work more interesting, but he is a more valuable worker who can take over a variety of assignments as conditions require.

"At the present time," Simmons concludes, "an estimated 80% of the Story City plant employees have the skill and experience to build from scratch, a complete Kan-Sun grain dryer that retails for $30,000."

The Roadblocks Don't Give Way Easily

Self-managed work teams succeed in Japan because employees, unions, corporate executives and government officials all believe in their sincerity and have faith in their value. A by-product of faith is coordination and a unified effort toward common objectives. QWL programs have a distance to go before a transition on the part of U.S. workers and their unions can be made from a state of wariness to one of unconditional acceptance. Labor officials in particular question the motives of large companies which profess to restructure the workplace along the lines currently being pioneered by General Motors, AT&T and a few others. It will take a combination of fulfilled promises and results to bring their thinking around, and this can only come with time.

But it now seems to be coming, however gradual the program's credibility gains may appear to be. Bethlehem Steel, General Foods, Shell, Procter & Gamble, Chrysler, Ford, Digital Equipment Corp., Xerox, Polaroid, Honeywell and Sperry are but a sampling of the corporate bandhopping giants whose recruitment ranks are rapidly mounting as the QWL movement shifts into full swing.

A strong resolve on the part of both labor and management leaders, founded on concerns about stagflation in general and Japanese industry inroads in particular, to restructure the U.S. economy along more productive lines will certainly help, and this is already in evidence. The United Auto Workers union has joined hands with Detroit's Big 3 in an effort to achieve QWL goals. The United Rubber Workers are also cooperating. The United Steelworkers are going along warily, recognizing the values to be derived from such positive results as worker skills upgrading and new surges of employee suggestions, but at the same time fearful of abdicating shop floor powers to management.

Like a snowball rolling downhill, increasing numbers of workers in a growing rundown of industries are demanding basic changes in the boss-employee relationship and a greater voice in running their jobs. Responsive union leaders have little choice but to echo these mandates. Many, including AFL-CIO's top brass, are still reluctant to publicly proclaim agreement with management, but on the other hand are as sensitive as corporate Chief Executives to the undisputed fact of economic life in America that, as one labor official states the case, "Labor warfare is a self-defeating macho exercise that can only bring down the warriors on both sides. It's a battle that no one can win."

Further evidence of QWL's growing labor support and acceptance is seen within the massive General Motors-Labor complex itself. Point one is that wide acknowledgment exists that in plants where the new structure is operative, employee grievances have been less hot-tempered than in the past, more coolly and rationally listened to and, what's more important, settled more rapidly, which adds up to quicker satisfaction for workers. Point two is that in every GM plant where QWL is in force, UAW leaders who have been pro-QWL and were instrumental in helping to win cooperation, have been reelected.

The UAW's Irv Bluestone summed up the new top labor awareness in 1978 when he said: "Quality of work life programs which are directed toward the human development of the workers, elevating human dignity and self-fulfillment require mutual, cooperative effort on the part of management and the union. That is why the first stage in the development of such programs should be devoted to creating a solid climate of mutual respect between the parties. It is important to understand that hard-line collective bargaining between the negotiating parties continues even while the quality of work life program is in effect. Experience indicates that normal collective bargaining and the introduction of quality of work life programs can exist and succeed side by side."

They can and will succeed side by side if management goes all out in its efforts to convince labor that its objective in advocating and sponsoring QWL is not to reduce worker rights or weaken the union's bargaining position, and if labor goes all out to convince management that, given a chance to work and think like a manager, the employee on the line can manage the everyday aspects of his job—and do it more productively than it has ever been done in the past.

No Instant Solutions

Several years ago a QWL-type experiment was conducted at General Foods Co.'s Gaines pet food plant in Topeka, Kan. Early response was high enthusiasm on the part of both workers and management. But after a couple of years the new system was abandoned. There were too many problems. Reviewed in perspective today, the author has been told by more than one manager currently involved in their companies' quality of work life programs that, whatever other causes may have contributed to the ultimate failure, one thing is certain: They didn't give the program much of a chance. Perhaps that is why GF is trying again at some of its plants.

GM work innovations toward humanization and democratization in several of its plants are being met with cautious optimism. A union official comments he is seeing "less hostility" than ever before. Workers talk about increased self-esteem, greater dignity, improved job interest and satisfaction. Butler Manufacturing Co.'s Simmons points to a 27% boost in productivity at its Story City plant, absenteeism appreciably lower than the industry average, safety record improvement, a drop in indirect labor costs and a significant increase in net margins, with product quality and shipping reliability improved.

But—and this *BUT* may be one of the biggest roadblocks of all—there are no quick and easy solutions. If there's one thing you can be certain of in the attempt to restructure your workplace along lines which stress trust over computer and/or human-based systems of tight control and close monitoring, it is that a successful transition will take time and will, in all likelihood, be a slow and painful process of trial and error and learning and unlearning and relearning.

Simmons spells out some of the problems:

- Self-management sometimes means more time is taken in decision-making. However, when decisions are made, they tend to be of equal or higher quality and are better implemented, due to increased employee commitment.

- Individual performance is downplayed in favor of the group. Some workers have trouble adjusting to this atmosphere which generally does not provide opportunity for one person's efforts to stand out.

- The self-managed work team concept is intolerable to the more autocratic management style. Choosing a manager who can work well in this climate could be difficult at times. Likewise, workers uncomfortable with increased autonomy and responsibility tend to suffer frustration.

- In some cases it may be hard for traditionally indoctrinated staff people to go along with ideas and proposals initiated by self-managed employees.

- First-level supervisors are sometimes unable to see a clearly defined role for themselves under the new structure. Even if they understand the role, the emphasis on participative problem solving and deferment of issues to teams of workers can be frustrating.

- Office and clerical employees may feel neglected. This was, and continues to be, a fairly serious problem at Story City. Office workers are organized into teams like everyone else. Yet they often fail to display the same degree of acceptance as their shop floor counterparts, possibly because they view the new structure as a breakdown of the traditional class distinctions between office and factory. Some office personnel may feel the new system somehow diminishes their status.

- Not all workers lend themselves well to the new approach. In Story City's fabrication area, for instance, employees are tied to machine pace and geographically separated from each other so that less interaction occurs as in the assembly area, as an example. The nature of work to be done appears to be a significant factor to consider in designing a nontraditional work system. Extra effort may be needed to increase participative opportunities in jobs where a dearth of these exist.

On one point most economosociologists, B school academicians, and other students of management appear to agree: In this undertaking, there are few if any simple answers and no overnight nice guys. QWL practitioners echo this sentiment. Stating the harsh reality of the situation, Gene Kofka, AT&T's director of work relationships, says, "The worst enemy that quality of work life has is the impatience for quick and finite results. . . . You measure the success of these things in years. Our management is willing to wait."

Even in Japan with its homogeneous population and other societally based advantages, refining the industrial democracy to the point of operational effectiveness took several years and a great deal of patience. The Japanese are better noted for patience than we are. Perhaps one of the primary challenges facing the U.S. economy is that of proving to ourselves and the rest of the world that we too are willing to wait for the new mold to jell properly and willing to settle for bite-sized portions of progress at a time.

Where Do You Go From Here?

Obviously, only large companies can afford to invest significant human financial resources in ambitious work restructuring programs, however rich the basket of fruit may prove to be in the end. But the human basics dealing with trust, dignity and self-esteem apply to all people whether employed by giant AT&T or the neighborhood gas station. So that even if the small or medium company is in no position to pioneer QWL, it can certainly learn from the giants and apply tested principles and strategies on a bit-by-bit basis.

The question is: Where does one start?

Clearly, with the educational process. What follows is a rundown of field-tested recommendations to follow and pitfalls to avoid in setting up a QWL program—whatever label you choose to apply to it.

- Contact one or more of the industrial giants that already have at least two or three years' experience with such techniques as quality circles and participative management. Accumulate as much literature and documentation as you can. After studying the material and attending some lectures and/or seminars, visit two or three plants where QWL programs are in force armed with a list of the questions that trouble you most.

- Consider a management consultant if you can afford one. And if you do, make sure you select one with extensive experience in the specific area in which you are interested. What you want is a hard-nosed practitioner, not a spellbinder.

- It's worth saying again: Enter into the enterprise without an expectation of instant success or overnight miracles.

- Get everybody you can into the act, employees at all levels, supervisors and managers. And keep in mind that if top management isn't sold on QWL, it will stand little chance of success. Nor is being "sold" enough of itself. You will need top management commitment and support for the program to work.

- Make it clear to all employees and their labor representatives that your purpose is not simply to improve worker productivity. You will have to prove to employees at all levels that they will stand to gain in a significant way by cooperating with the system. Show them how their jobs will be made less problematical and more interesting. Explain to them how they will acquire added skills which will increase their marketplace value. Convince them that through QWL they will have an opportunity to have more to say about their day-to-day jobs, and explain how this will help to build their self-esteem. Persuade your people that they will be given a fair share of the added profit that results from adopted ideas dreamed up by their group.

- Bend over backwards to prove that QWL will not in any way weaken the union's or workers' collective bargaining powers and privileges.

- Establish that formally organized work teams, and not management, will be responsible for work quality and productivity within designated areas.

- Make sure it is clearly understood by all that the standards of product and performance quality will be high, that QWL is designed to upgrade quality and not relax it.

- Demonstrate how jobs will be rotated within sections, departments and work groups in an effort to improve individual skills and simultaneously reduce boredom.

- Explain that under QWL, supervisors will function more as teachers and guides than "bosses." Management-worker class distinctions will be substantially reduced.

- Work teams will be given an important voice in designing work rules and policies, determining individual assignments, and will be responsible for getting the job done on schedule. Where disciplinary problems exist, these will in general be worked out by the team.

- Point out that a continuous and ongoing program of training and development will be in force.

- Stress the importance of continuing communication and feedback through group and plant meetings and interaction with management.

- Carefully evaluate the organization's culture and environment before attempting to introduce significant work innovation to make sure employees are ready to deal with the change in a clear and positive way. A carefully planned pre-introductory stage is often essential to prepare people for the transition and convince them to the maximum degree possible of management's sincerity and forthrightness.

- Keep in mind that QWL doesn't become an actuality once it is "installed." It cannot be mandated, only molded over a period of time so that, based on experience and the unique characteristics of the organization, it will evolve, develop and adjust to the environment.

- Don't sell short the value and importance of the preliminary survey questionnaire. As GM's Howard C. Carlson points out: "Measurement or research should be used as a source of developmental information regarding both the organization and individuals and as an action-seeking QWL strategy in itself."

- Don't bite off too large a chunk at the outset. Ideally, select a segregated division or operation of a couple of hundred to a thousand or so employees for the initial QWL experiment. This will probably be essentially a learning experience until enough knowledge has been acquired and refinements made to introduce the work restructuring to other parts of the company, a unit at a time. Start by offering each unit the *opportunity* to learn about and consider QWL. For the program to succeed, the people with a stake in the program must be intrigued by the concept and desirous of trying it.

- A dedicated, high level manager, preferably with QWL training and experience, and reporting to a top executive officer of the company, should be selected to plan, launch and administer the effort. His organization or group must make available to the rest of the company the training materials, education, and guidance required to clarify the program and satisfy any questions, reservations or doubts in the minds of future participants.

- Don't forget that the word "system" or "program" is applied to QWL solely as a semantic convenience. In effect, QWL properly and successfully introduced and implemented, will become a philosophy of management, an industrial way of life that will, in a great many aspects, resemble the Japanese style of management that already has proved so successful.

5.

PEOPLE

> *When my company was still small, I often told employees that when customers asked, "What does your company make?" they should answer, "Matsushita Electric is making men. We also make electrical appliances, but our company makes men first."*
>
> —Konosuke Matsushita

As was noted in chapter two, a variety of factors work together to make the Japanese economy work and give Japanese companies the competitive edge they currently enjoy throughout the world. To recap, these range from the long-term corporate perspective, the labor, government and management prosperity compact, and pure dedication to product excellence, to consensus decision making, the teamwork or family approach, and the lean and hard, delayered organizational structure. But one factor stands out from all the rest and may be as important as all the rest put together. It is the factor that makes all the above cited factors possible.

That factor is sensitivity to people in general and employees in particular.

The organizational thrust in America these days is toward more *productivity*—more mileage per person, more return on the dollar, increased output for each nickel invested instead of higher selling prices. The bitter foe is inflation and high interest rates. An endless number of techniques and programs have been dreamed up with the goddess productivity in mind. But mounting evidence proves, in Japan and this country as well, that simply treating people like people will outperform every scheme ever devised for boosting output per person and will help avoid the indifference and sloth that result in profit erosion.

The sociologist Saul D. Alinsky stated the matter bluntly enough: "The world is deluged with panaceas, formulas, proposed laws, machineries, ways out, and myriads of solutions. It is significant that every one of these . . . deals with . . . the structure of society, but none concerns the substance itself—the people. This despite the eternal truth of the democratic faith that the solution always lies with the people."

If Matsushita's philosophy of management were to be summed up in a nutshell, this is what it would come to. It is the foundation of his thinking. It is the basis of his company's prodigious success.

If there is a weakness in this rationale it lies in its utter simplicity. No sophisticated expertise or advanced degree is required to interpret its meaning. Your average high school dropout will understand just how it works. Yet it is as pure in its truth as the design of a snowflake.

Expectations

I talked recently with the frustrated Chief Executive Officer of a small to medium-size manufacturing company. For the past several weeks he and his attorney and top aides had been engaged in hard negotiations with the union. The contract was about to run out and a strike was threatening. Management already had yielded more than it had ever intended, but settlement still was not in the offing. The CEO, an old friend, poured out his heart to me. His final words: "What the hell do they want?"

It's a question being posed more and more these days, by sociologists, psychologists, behavioral specialists and hard-nosed executives. It's a question being soul-searched extensively by QWL advocates and would-be Japanese emulators.

"What the hell do they want?"

"What will it take to convert indifferent employees to loyal employees? What must we give them?"

A great deal more than they ever received in the past. That much is certain. Are their demands unreasonable? Unjust? Most scholars who have studied the problem think not. Money is an important piece of the pie. Most people who work for a living want to live better; they want more leisure, more culture, better housing, a greater return from their daily investment of time. But this is by no means unique to the U.S. It is the condition in Japan and throughout Europe as well. And what workers want extends far beyond money. Human expectations have been gradually upgrading all over the world in recent years, thanks in large part to TV and the communications and information explosion.

The United Auto Workers' Irving Bluestone, in a talk at the General Motors-sponsored 1980 Executive Conference on the Quality of Work Life, made wry reference to two of the work rules published on April 5, 1872, by the owner and chief executive officer of the Mount Cory Carriage and Wagon Works:

- An employee who smokes Spanish cigars, uses liquor in any form, gets shaved at a barber shop or frequents public halls, will give good reason to suspect his worth, intentions, integrity and honesty.

- The employee who has performed his labors faithfully and without fault for a period of five years in my service, and who has been thrifty and attentive to his religious duties, and is looked upon by his fellow men as a substantial and law abiding citizen, will be given an increase of five cents per day in his pay, providing that just returns and profits from the business permit it.

Clearly, we have come a long way in the past 11 decades or so. Yet despite the progress, worker expectations continue to rise. And interestingly enough, the corporations today which are most successful and most profitable—in Japan and the U.S.—are the ones that come closest to fulfilling worker expectations and desires. Surely this must say something to the toughminded manager who believes that every inch given toward employee satisfaction places bottom line results on the chopping block. And it must say something to the business person who stubbornly maintains with economist Milton Friedman that the only business of business is business.

The simple fact of economic life is that, true to human nature, if you don't give the people who work for you the satisfaction they require, they won't give you satisfaction in return. In short, they won't give a damn. If you demonstrate that you honestly and genuinely care about your people's welfare, good health and security, true to human nature, they will show they care in response. The managements of most large Japanese industrial companies seem to understand and appreciate these basic realities, and respond to them in the way they handle and deal with their people. In this country, sad to say, many high level executives still take the autocratic unyielding approach where every freedom or advantage granted the workforce is looked upon as another drop of blood wrung out of the corporate body. The ancient biblical adage, "Give and ye shall receive," never enters their minds.

The Business of Business. The business of business is people. People buy and use products, do the work that changes raw materials into usable merchandise. People sell products, pack and move them, stock them on shelves or in bins or in warehouses. People rake in the profits from the sale of products and bank the money or spend it. People are what every aspect of business is all about.

This condition is as obvious and unalterable as the rising sun in the morning. Yet scarcely a week passes by without a new horror story hitting the media about a corporation in trouble because of people mismanaged, mishandled, mistreated.

Rutherford, N.J., management consultant and educator Leonard J. Smith tells the tale of a Chief Executive who called on him for help in coping with a serious sabotage problem.

"What kind of sabotage?"

"Damaged merchandise. Busted equipment. Warehousemen ramming lift trucks into cartons and cases. Desks and tables with holes gouged in them."

Smith investigated the situation, conducted off-the-record interviews with employees. Typical of the comments he heard voiced:

"There was a big layoff last month. Know when the poor slobs found out about it? The last working day before Christmas."

"They use closed circuit TV around here. You don't even have privacy in the locker room."

"If you get too many raises in this plant your job is in jeopardy. They go out of their way to find a cheaper replacement."

That reflects the general attitude, Smith says. The sabotage in particular was caused by a news leak that automatic merchandise handling equipment was being installed that would produce a massive layoff. The employees weren't even consulted.

"I rarely turn down an engagement," Smith added. "But I had to tell this guy I couldn't help him unless he was willing to restructure his philosophy of management. He wasn't."

A recent business article lead runs as follows: "Transplanting a winning corporate culture to a sleepy company is not easy, as William Hartman, chairman of Interpace Corp., may have discovered."

The piece goes on to describe Hartman's practice of modeling his managerial style after that of famed ITT autocrat Harold S. Geneen, making excessive demands on his people while, according to a former vice president, "he was not willing to spend time to develop them." Others describe him as demanding and difficult, an executive whose single-minded focus on financial dicta and bottom-line concerns make him give short shrift to human concerns. A typical move: the callous axing and replacement of 35 members of a 51-member management team.

Is it any wonder his once successful and dynamic company is now shrinking instead of growing? Someone should inform Hartman that the heyday of the autocratic chief executive who rides roughshod over people is rapidly fading into the past.

Another classic example of dehumanized management is troubled Adolph Coors Co., the beer maker which, in the words of a *Business Week* writer, "has gone flat." Coors, which has been described as America's most "un-Japanese company," has a long history of labor unrest. Notes the *Business Week* piece: "A lingering boycott by union members, homosexuals, racial minorities, and women continues to take its toll."

Operations of this kind encourage the so-called "adversary relationship" between labor and management at its best—or worst. They also pinpoint most eloquently the primary reason Japanese management—friendly to and protective of its people—has gained the managerial edge it currently enjoys. The reason is as simple as the Golden Rule itself. A friendly and beneficent attitude toward employees, once a sign of magnanimity, is today evidence of pragmatic management and, the human and humane aspects aside, a managerial stance that pays off.

Reminiscent of Paddy Chayevsky's award-winning televison drama, "Network," insensitively treated employees are sick and tired of being mismanaged and they aren't going to take it any more. Even if they don't yell their frustration out of windows as was done in the film, workers at all levels are hammering the message across.

In his Mitchell Prize Award paper, UCLA Prof. James O'Toole refers to "the entitlements consciousness" currently developing on the American work scene. He presents a checklist of "new demands for purely *social* employee entitlements." These include:

- The right to "blow the whistle" on illegal and unethical employer practice.

- The right to privacy (e.g., confidentiality of personnel files).

- The right to conscientious objection to unethical orders.

- The right to freedom in outside activities (e.g., political activities).

- The right to sexual freedom (e.g., homosexual rights).

- The right to freedom from sexual harassment by superiors.

- The right to individual choice of appearance (e.g., for men to wear long hair and hippy beads in a bank teller's cage).

- The right to vote on plant relocations.

- The right to participate in all decisions directly affecting one's job.

- The right to self-actualization on the job (i.e., the right to develop one's full productive potential).

- The right to adequate leisure time (e.g., adequate time to spend with one's family).

- The right to reject a cross-country transfer.

- The right of all employees to full access to information about corporate activities.

Costly Thrift

On the face of it, when business gets slow and a company lays off three workers earning $200 each per week, it saves $600 plus the related fringe benefits. But the reality of the matter isn't as simple as the arithmetic.

The large Japanese industrial under the same set of circumstances, and many small companies as well, would bend over backwards and then some to avoid layoffs, business reverses or not. It would find other work for idled employees to do, cleanup or refurbishing tasks, for example. It might adjust the hours of the rest of the work force to take up the slack. Layoff or discharge would be an absolute last resort, an admission of failure and an acute embarrassment to management.

So the Japanese company would pay out the $600 plus fringes, but it would gain a whole lot more in return by taking the long range in view. Observes Towers, Perrin, Forster & Crosby's Myron Emanuel: "This supportive climate reinforced by the guarantee of no layoffs, has led to an extraordinary outpouring of employee ideas and suggestions for cost-savings—and exemplary two-way communications."

Layoff, or discharge, aside from the economic consequences, is a dehumanizing and humiliating experience. It is unnerving to face one's family and friends and inform them you are no longer needed by your employer. Being employed on the job and knowing you are likely to be sacked should a downturn occur or a product line be discontinued could only promulgate feelings of insecurity and anxiety, which in turn trigger ill will and hostility. Harboring this attitude, who cares if the job assignment takes an hour or two longer than it should, or if corporate assets are damaged, or if the work is efficient or not?

In contrast, consider the Japanese enterprise in trouble. Should recession strike, instead of firing workers, management would take action to pare down everyone's semi-annual bonus or, if absolutely necessary, levy pay cuts for all right down the line, top brass included. Individuals aren't singled out to bear the brunt of a business reverse. The sacrifice is made on a group or family basis. Trouble, like prosperity, is shared. It may require a payout in hard yen, but the long-run return in loyalty, and the productivity loyalty fosters, is well worth the price.

Approximately one-third of Japan's work force enjoys guaranteed employment for life. This usually means retirement from a large industrial at about age 55. But here too the people factor comes to the fore. The retiree in Japan isn't looked upon as a castoff as so often occurs in this country. In his 50s, the Japanese employee is at the peak of his skills, savvy and earnings. On top of that, it is inherent to the culture that age be revered. The manager in his late 40s and early 50s is much in demand by the smaller companies which pay lower salaries and offer less fringe benefits. Thus, reemployment follows the natural course and is anything but a stepdown in status. The Japanese retiree isn't left to face a future of wall climbing and accelerated aging as is so frequently the lot of the U.S. industry discard.

Discussing this subject with a Japanese manager, the man smiled gently and tolerantly and explained, "In my country, the old man is *la creme de la creme.*"

In Japan, retiring employees receive generous lump-sum settlements, and about 75% are rehired by smaller companies immediately, most often suppliers or contractors with whom the original employer has been doing business for years.

As was pointed out earlier, it would be folly to attempt to superimpose one nation's system or culture on another society, and no one is suggesting that U.S. employers abruptly revise their employment structure eliminating layoffs and firings. But it is worth noting that in the best managed and most profitable American companies, terminations are far less frequent than in their less successful counterparts, and occur only in extreme situations. The rationale is as dollars-and-cents practical as it is humanitarian. As a rule, the worker who believes his employer has his best interests and future well-being in mind, is a whole lot more productive than the worried and insecure employee who thinks of his boss as an adversary.

Programmed Dehumanization

In a New England insurance company the vacation schedule was plotted largely by a computer. A periodic printout predicting workload expectations for the days ahead determined the size of the work force that would be required on a week-by-week, month-by-month basis. One June day Marie, a long-standing, loyal, and reliable statistician, asked her department head if one of the two vacation weeks she was entitled to could be the last week of July. Her sister, she explained, would be visiting her at this time. The busy manager, hardly concealing his annoyance at the request, which he felt should have gone through channels in the accustomed routine, consulted his latest computer run-off.

"I'm sorry," he replied, "that's one of our peak summer weeks. A full staff will be needed."

"But," the employee persisted, "my sister . . . ."

"I'm sorry." Her boss cut her off brusquely. "There's not a thing I can do about it. We have to go by the printouts."

He went by the printouts; Marie simply went. She handed in her resignation a few weeks later after finding another job that was scheduled to start after her sister's departure. Marie hadn't seen her sister and family who lived in California for almost six years. The last week in July was the only time her sister could visit, and nothing in the world—not even a computer—was going to stop her from taking the week off. Her boss was not only deprived of her presence during that crucial week but had to go to the time and expense of hiring and training a new employee to take over an important and complicated job.

When managerial behavior gets programmed along with electronic equipment—as is bound to happen when human needs don't hold top priority in an organization—the result is most often disruptive.

Had Marie been a Japanese employee, in all likelihood, not only would her boss have arranged the requested vacation week for her, but in addition would have urged Marie to bring her sister into the plant to meet the rest of "the family."

Inevitably, the word "programmed" conjures up visions of churning computers and spinning reels of magnetic tape. The electronic brain has been touted by maker and user alike as the biggest boon to business since the invention of the wheel. Nor would any student of management deny the computer's productivity-boosting potential. Thanks to its invention we are able to grind out more transactions, more documents, and more information as an aid to decision making far more swiftly and efficiently than ever before.

But computers, for all their remarkable capabilities, don't have hearts and they don't have brains. You can't beat them when it comes to processing numbers. But when you permit a preoccupation with numbers to take precedence over a consideration for human beings, you are asking for trouble. If this happens the danger exists that the monster will devour itself.

General Motors today, possibly the nation's foremost Quality of Work Life advocate along with Ma Bell, learned this lesson the hard way. Marshall McLuhan described GM's Lordstown operation of several years back as a classic example. Billed at the time as the world's most automated plant, he pointed out, efficiency was refined there to the dimensions of a flea's hind leg. It was a programmed miracle, said McLuhan, a paragon of technoscientific management. Only one thing went wrong. The operation collapsed because people wouldn't work there.

Technology, he added, was raised to a peak of obsolescence. Speedup brought slowdown. The decision makers, systems wizards, programmers, and planners were so busy developing a mechanized Mecca where productivity was Allah that no one ever thought to ask, "How do you program job satisfaction into the setup?"

Operation Backfire. For all the prodigious values and efficiencies brought to American business by the computer's invention, it's ironic that it also created one of industry's most serious problems, a problem that threatens to grow worse in the months ahead unless we succeed in throwing a harness over the tiger and using the machine as a tool instead of a tyrant. The key to the problem lies in the computer's very usefulness and productivity potential. However rich that potential is today, it promises to grow richer tomorrow, in part because of its regenerative capabilities, techniques spawned by techniques in an endless progression.

However, this does not minimize the problems the computer creates for this country:

- Many large bottom-line-pressured companies, most notably the conglomerates, have been on a hiring binge in recent years recruiting the brightest math-and-numbers-oriented recruits they could find from the B schools. Typically, these stars—devoid of actual business experience, oblivious to "people problems and needs," never having interacted in a work environment with fellow humans—are put into key staff jobs at corporate headquarters in an environment replete with charts, printouts and matrices. There they make decisions for the divisions that should properly be made by divisional managers who, deprived of the managerial function they were theoretically employed to fulfill, wind up feeling emasculated and dehumanized and certainly turned off on the company. A growing number of executives in name only throughout this nation are either deserting their posts or, what is probably worse, enduring the condition in a state of bitterness and frustration.

- In Japan, typically, when a problem must be solved or a decision made, people get together and talk about it, often at exasperating length which at times could result in costly delay or lost opportunities. But of one thing you can be certain: The manager responsible for making the ultimate decision will have a pretty good idea how everyone involved in the decision *feels* about it and how it will impact on their lives and their jobs. Too often, in the sophisticated, highly computerized American operation important decisions about a plant relocation, personnel placement, compensation arrangement, training and development program, processing system or some other critical issue will be based on "input" produced through a combination of operations research-based formulae and the latest computer printouts. What it boils down to is depersonalized management, the physical and intellectual separation of the decision enactors and those upon whom the decisions are enacted. Even where the decisions make sense, all human feeling and warmth are plucked out of the enterprise. And more often than not, in deciding, the all-important human factor isn't even considered.

- According to *World Business Weekly*, Japan "already has the world's highest per capita computer usage and employs more industrial robots than the rest of the world combined. The micro-electronic fever gripping Japan has made industries that produce electronic goods or use their technologies . . . the main growth areas of the current decade. Unless other countries rapidly follow suit, therefore, Japanese export penetration of world markets is likely to intensify. Japan will flood the markets of Europe and North America with goods their rivals cannot yet make—as is already the case with two types of videotape recorders—or cannot make with the same degree of sophistication."

Everybody I talked with who returned after visiting Japanese plants expressed awe at the degree of automation they saw there. Of special concern to thoughtful U.S. managers must be the realization that in close cooperation with the unions, Japanese industry has taken steps to convince employees that since automation helps produce a competitive edge, it is good for the company and hence, beneficial for them as well. In Japan the work force uses the computer as a management tool and productivity aid; in this country the work force often fights the computer. Already scores of labor leaders are gearing up to make automation and its uses a key issue in upcoming negotiations.

Noted a *Business Week* Special Report: "The new wave of factory and office automation in the U.S. will raise the productivity of American workers, improve the quality of the products they make, and increase the ability of domestic industries to compete with the imports that have eaten away at America's industrial strength. But these gains will be realized only if workers are convinced that the new machines are tools for improving their working lives rather than an extremely efficient means of controlling behavior on the job." Or a strategy for reducing the work force and depriving them of their jobs. In the end productivity and corporate growth inevitably come down to the way workers think and feel about the company that employs them and their role in the workplace.

A Matter of Focus

The old axiom about the wheel that squeaks the loudest getting the most attention applies to management as much as it does to customer complaints or shop maintenance. So far as the executive is concerned, in the U.S. the wheel that squeaks the loudest is profits; in Japan it is people. It is by and large a matter of focus. If the corporation one works for is hectically bottom-line oriented, and the boss keeps hammering away at earnings-related issues day in and day out, profit performance is going to consume the major part of a manager's time and attention. In the process he is apt, understandably, to give people issues short shrift. If the organization is people oriented so that management views the satisfaction of human needs as essential to the fulfillment of earnings objectives, a whole different climate exists. A different focus is drawn.

When recently deceased Sazo Idemitsu, head of Idemitsu Kosan, Japan's giant oil refiner and, like Matsushita, something of a legend in his country, was asked to define his management philosophy, he said: "All I can say is that I was brought up as a Japanese, educated as a Japanese and the way I manage my company is typically Japanese. Therefore, when people say there is a philosophy in my management, I believe they mean the philosophy inherent in the Japanese people."

Idemitsu Kosan is famous throughout all of Japan for its close family ties and humanitarian activities. Matsushita spells out his philosophy of management a tenet at a time. Idemitsu generalizes on the subject. But it adds up to the same thing: People. And in both corporations, if the leaders were asked, "To what do you attribute the remarkably long running success of your company?" they would answer in unison: "People."

Benefits: How Beneficial? The standard fringe benefits, the so-called "hidden" part of worker compensation, that are received by U.S. employees—health and hospital allowances, holiday and vacation pay, etc.—are also received by Japanese workers. Educated estimates cite a figure of about 40% of the average employee's annual paycheck as the amount paid in fringes by the typical large U.S. corporation.

People

But even here there is a difference in outlook or philosophy between U.S. and Japanese payouts ascribable to the human factor. Call it corporate giveaway motivation.

Generally speaking, in U.S. corporations, one can find either of two motives responsible for exceptional, or out of the ordinary, benefits. Both are directly linked to the dollar sign. Motive number one is union pressure where extra payouts are negotiated after hard and often bitter bargaining into the labor agreement. In some industries, for example, such as steel, auto and shoe, supplemental payments are granted to workers whose companies suffer from foreign competition. In fact, cases can be cited of steel workers whose total benefits due to "hardship" were in excess of their total take-home pay.

Other fringes—dental cost reimbursements, pension entitlements, cost-of-living add-ons, and the like—also are won after hard-fought battles between corporate and union attorneys.

Giveaway motive number two is a byproduct of the hot competition in some industries to lure talented recruits on the one hand, and keep key employees loyal on the other. Examples in this category include executives offered stock options of as high as a half million dollars fully redeemable in six years, home and car purchases financed by the company, and other perks too attractive to turn down.

Despite such lures, notes Deutsch, Shea & Evans, an executive search firm which studies such things, "most (U.S.) companies expect half of their new employees to leave within five years."

And William James, a partner in the consulting firm of Hewitt Associates, adds, "There is probably not enough money around to guarantee that a person won't leave. A valued executive can likely get his package matched somewhere else."

By way of contrast, fringe benefits paid by Japanese corporations, while often equally costly in terms of cash payout, are for one thing, not grudgingly given, and for another, not paid out to keep key employees from leaving, or to purchase workers' loyalty. If unusual (at least by American standards) benefits aren't pressured by unions or offered to keep executives in harness, what else motivates them? A Japanese manager to whom I posed this question considered it almost too simplistic to answer. "Management," he explained, "is responsible for the secure and comfortable lifestyle and future welfare of employees and their families. The benefits program is merely another way of helping to fulfill this responsibility."

Apart from the universal paid vacation and holiday time off, social security, health, hospital and other benefits given workers in most developed countries, Japanese employers provide a gamut of benefits which relate largely to group and family living. Typical of these are extensive clubhouse and athletic facilities, family allowances, corporation-subsidized meals and dormitories for unmarried workers, exercise work breaks, employee weddings in corporate social halls, and financing assistance for young marrieds in the establishment of permanent housing.

The U.S. employee, upon receipt of a new fringe benefit, appreciates it until his third or fourth paycheck after which he takes it for granted as a part of his income inveigled out of management and his natural due. The Japanese employee equates the extras he receives as further proof that his employer is concerned about him as a person and as part of the family, and is dedicated to bestow upon him a rich and satisfying life. For the average American worker, fringe benefits have a minimal effect on his loyalty. For the Japanese worker, they reinforce the feeling of loyalty that already runs deep.

The Power of Positive Self-Perception

In a nutshell, what the Japanese are demonstrating to the world is a truism as old as commerce itself: We must have good feelings about ourselves as jobholders before we can feel good about the jobs we hold or the organization that employs us. "Above all things, reverence yourself," the Greek philosopher Pythagoras counseled 25 centuries ago. The advice is difficult to follow if one's self-confidence and self-esteem are systematically eroded on a day-to-day basis by work that is dull and demeaning and a restrictive work environment as rule-oriented and confining as a third-grade classroom.

Francois de la Rochefoucauld wrote: "There is a kind of greatness which does not depend upon fortune; it is a certain manner that distinguishes us, and which seems to destine us for great things; it is the value we insensibly set upon ourselves; it is by this quality that we gain the reverence of other men, and it is this which commonly raises us more above them than birth, rank, or even merit itself."

In recent years especially, with job expectations rising throughout the U.S., routinization and dehumanization at all levels of employment from middle management down, due to computerized decision making, remote control management of divisions by conglomerateurs in ivory towers, and depersonalized administration in general, have been on the increase. One costly by-product of this condition has been the "burnout" effect among corporate managers. Notes Robert S. Greenberger in *The Wall Street Journal,* "A growing number of corporate managers are experiencing the feelings of frustration, cynicism and helplessness known as executive burnout, experts say. And most of these managers aren't likely to talk about their problems."

The industrial psychologists are having a field day. They have never been busier. But corporations are paying more than their fees.

Burnout is chronic and gets worse if it isn't treated, according to clinical psychologist Richard Issel. One of the best ways to treat it is the Japanese way—by applying the power of positive self-perception. Whether the "patient" is an emasculated manager not permitted to manage, or a robotized plant worker viewed by his employer as a time clock number instead of a person, the result is the same: Frustration, boredom, and a low self-image leading to bitterness.

The bitterness is evidenced by a long list of adversarial responses ranging from absenteeism, shoddy performance and worker indifference to organizational objectives, to self-indulgence and hedonism. Insurance executive James A. McIntyre describes as shocking the turndown rate when his company, Fremont General Insurance, wanted to transfer people among its branches. "We've lost the former loyalties of corporate life," he adds.

And L. Clinton Hoch, executive vice president of Fantus Co., the relocation arm of Dun & Bradstreet Corp., blames the "new generation of the 1960s for demanding instant lifestyle gratification."

Little wonder. But it leads one to speculate: Is instant gratification what employees actually seek? Or could this be a desperation grasp that masks the underlying reality? Isn't it conceivable that all they are really demanding is self-esteem on the job? And if this is so, what greater lesson than this could we learn from Japan?

Dr. Don Hellriegel of Texas A&M University's management department, states the case this way: "Since the end of World War II, the Japanese have been able to build almost anything faster, cheaper and, lately it seems, better than Americans. One reason," he suggests, "is the Japanese attention to the human aspects of life in the workplace."

6.

WE-POWER

> *The sun and moon are opposed to each other; the mountains and rivers are in opposition; and men assert a uniqueness opposed to women. But the world is not simply opposition; harmony exists over seemingly incessant oppositions to establish order in nature and in society.*
> —*Konosuke Matsushita*

According to *Washington Post* writer William Chapman, Japan has only 11,900 lawyers in a country of 116 million people. The United States has more than four times this number of law students enrolled in law schools each year. Going to court, whether for a civil case or labor dispute, isn't popular in Japan, says Tokyo lawyer Daikichi Shiratani. It is an admission of failure. The mere appearance of an attorney has an unsettling effect. The preferred method of handling disagreements is by means of reasoned discussion. If this doesn't work, a wise and mutually respected third person is often sought to fulfill the role of advisor or mediator. What it boils down to, in short, is that the typical Japanese would much rather act in harmony than in conflict with his adversary.

Herein lies the basis of the We-Approach to business and life that works so well in Japan. Where working together is a way of life, legal recourse is sought only as a last-ditch resort. When people strive to cooperate, even under difficult circumstances, lawyers are rarely brought into the picture.

Justice William O. Douglas once said: "Today it is generally recognized that all corporations possess an element of public interest. A corporation director must think not only of the stockholder but also of the laborer, the supplier, the purchaser, and the ultimate consumer. Our economy is but a chain which can be no stronger than any one of its links. We all stand together or fall together in our highly industrialized society of today."

This is a lesson which apparently comes easily and naturally to the Japanese. It is one we still have to learn. Or relearn.

Culturally, we in America are as fiercely proud of our independence and individuality as the Japanese are of the family spirit and loyalty which makes cooperation so natural. We point with pride to our famed innovators and entrepreneurs—the Henry Fords, Thomas Edisons, Thomas Watsons, and Alfred Sloanes—who helped make America great. We typify the creative process as a lonely and heroic struggle of the heart and mind against impossible odds, and have on tap a whole repertoire of quips and anecdotal jests to ridicule the committee as a decision making body, and the meeting as a communications form. What we lose sight of in the process is that without teamwork and group cooperation, the Fords, Con Eds, IBMs and GMs in this country couldn't have gotten off the ground.

"While America needs creative individual entrepreneurs," writes Lester C. Thurow, professor of economics and management at the Massachusetts Institute of Technology, "America's current economic problems spring more from the lack of teamwork and reciprocal long-run loyalties between employers and workers. The Japanese have become successful not because they have better individual entrepreneurs or because their tax laws or regulations are better than ours, but because they have been able to create an environment where workers are interested in working together in quality control circles to improve group productivity."

At a 1978 meeting called by International Paper Co.'s chief executive officer, J. Stanford Smith, to introduce the company's new president, Edwin A. Gee, to nearly 200 of IP's top executives, Smith asked all the managers who had been with the company when he himself had joined it five years before to rise. Only about a dozen executives stood. This is, unfortunately, all too typical of large U.S. corporations.

Prof. Thurow makes the point that it takes a number of years of working together and adjusting to the organization and each other before optimum efficiency can be achieved and people can function as a well coordinated team. In studies he conducted together with the University of California's Steven Sheffrin, one of the conclusions reached was that a 50% reduction in the turnover rate would raise productivity almost 30% over five years. Prof. Thurow stresses the importance of impressing upon managers that effective team play counts as a critical factor in their route to the top. And workers must be encouraged to believe that teamwork will pay off in higher wages or productivity bonuses.

"Too Many Competitors"

The author talked with Hiroshi Nomura, a Japanese executive in the office equipment industry who was in the United States on a business trip. He said that in his opinion Americans were so competitive with each other that they had trouble being competitive in the marketplace. In response to a puzzled look, he explained, "The emphasis in American business is for executives within the corporation to compete against one another when they should be working together to hack out strategies to compete against other companies at home and abroad."

Our term often applied to this syndrome is elitism; another is John Wayneism. It refers to the compulsion of the hard driving manager to stand out, win star billing for himself, prove that he's the smartest, the shrewdest, the best. More often than not, the supreme evidence of elitist success is bottom-line contribution. It triggers the tendency to become manipulative, authoritarian and deceitful. Elitism works to break down the corporate team, create splinter factions and political cliques where loyalty runs to individual leaders and their personal objectives rather than to the organization as a whole.

Questioned on the subject of group unity, the son of the founder of Idemitsu Kosan replied that "unless family members rely on each other, the family cannot exist. Our company operates with each employee relying on each other. We don't think it is so extraordinary because, traditionally, Japanese people feel just like one big family."

So ingrown and deeply rooted is this in the Japanese culture, states Nomura, that it is often an embarrassment for a Japanese worker or manager to be singled out as a star. He tells the story of an American company which opened a facility near Osaka. A supervisor came up with a brilliant idea that reduced a production process from eight steps to five for a saving of several thousand dollars a year. The plant's American public relations manager visited the supervisor in the company with a photographer in tow. He wanted to write up the young man and his idea and give him the recognition he deserved in the company newspaper.

To his surprise, the supervisor refused to cooperate and did not want his picture taken. He could scarcely conceal his embarrassment. One would think he had been called on the carpet for some wrongdoing instead of being praised for his ingenious idea. The PR manager asked a Japanese associate if he could explain the young man's response.

"But of course," he replied patiently. "Singling him out implies he is smarter than the rest of his quality circle. If you publicized this as a group accomplishment, I'm sure he would be most pleased."

We in America have become too cynical to relate genuine family feelings outside of our actual or immediate families. Part of the reason may date back to the phoney "one big happy family" sentiments promoted by some big corporations a half century or more ago when company towns were commonplace. During this era, company housing and stores symbolized worker exploitation and employees in perpetual hock to the "family." Very few of today's executives lived through this period, but students of industry know about it, and the bad taste remains.

Today an honest and genuine group—if not family—movement is being fostered by more and more large corporations. This encouraging development is due in part to the study of Japanese management by U.S. managers, and partly in response to persistent annual declines in the rate of U.S. plant productivity. The reasoning is simple. Our elitist system isn't working, the group approach is working wonders in Japan. It is worth a try here.

One key to the much publicized loyalty of the Japanese worker to his quality circle as his close familial group and his company as family in the broader sense is, of course, individual self-interest. The Japanese employee sees his company as protector, good uncle and mentor. He views his coworkers as brothers and sisters. He reasons if one is loyal to one's family, one is loyal to one's self. It follows that the worker who is sold on this premise would be a fool to act in any way contrary to his company's best interest. And the concept is so beautifully simple, its logic and good sense could escape no employee whatever his IQ or rank.

The task confronting America's high level managers and personnel professionals is something in the nature of a one-for-all-all-for-one crusade. The worker must be convinced that what is good for the company is good for the worker. By means of continuing education, benefit sharing, group-related payoffs and other *tangible* evidence, each employee must be sold on the theme that helping to make the company strong will make America strong and his own job secure. This is more than a strategy, and it's more than a program. It's the only way we can survive in the marketplace in the years ahead.

Deciding Factor

The German poet and philosopher Schiller wrote, "He who considers too much will perform little."

He didn't know the Japanese.

When the Japanese have a decision to make they are apt to consider at length. An American engineer transferred to Tokyo two years ago to become a minority member of the division's management team, recalls that his earliest and most exasperating frustration was over the rigmarole and amount of time it took for a decision to be made.

"Everyone was consulted, from the porter to the president. There were meetings and meetings and meetings. I wondered how anything ever got done."

Today this manager whistles a whole different tune. "It's the greatest system in the world. It still takes a long time for decisions to be made. But your mentality is geared to it, and you learn that patience is needed. What's so beautiful about the system is that once a decision is made, everyone is behind it. You get one hundred percent team support."

Quality Circles. "Bottom-up" decision making in Japan preceded the introduction of quality control circles to Japanese plants. Getting young and inexperienced employees involved in problems was looked upon as an important technique for helping to educate and develop them. But the inception of QC circles caused the consensus decision-making mold to settle and jell. It is now a part of the accustomed routine to get everyone involved in the decision into the act.

The initiation of quality circles in Japan dates back to the American occupation following World War II. At the time it was hammered home forcefully to corporate, government and union leaders that the identification, MADE IN JAPAN, symbolized poor and shoddy quality to the rest of the world. Although the nation already had proven to itself and other countries its capability to produce high performance products to feed its war machine, it set out, with the help of the U.S. occupation force, to rebuild the country's bombed-out industries with a strong emphasis on changing its poor quality image. Emulating America's Zero Defects (ZD) movement, workers were organized into small groups in an effort to control quality more closely and come up with new ideas to increase product reliability.

However, as a "top-down" program sponsored and supervised by management, it failed to unlock worker creativity or motivate their whole-hearted participation. The quality control circle represents a natural evolution of the ZD group. It is significant to note that it took a long time in developing. Companies that hope to duplicate the Japanese success overnight are almost inevitably doomed to disappointment.

Sperry's Michael R. Losey points out, "Quality Circles are for the most part a misnomer. They are really Improvement Circles touching on basically every aspect of the employees' environment," ranging through such interests as working conditions, tools and machinery, productivity requirements, health and safety, interpersonal relationships and, of course, quality.

Employee involvement in QC circles is high, sometimes exceeding 90% in large industrial companies, prevalent throughout all of Japan, but with a lower proportion of employees participating in most of the smaller firms. Although major quality circle activity is confined to manufacturing companies, the movement is starting to take hold in banks and other commercial organizations as well.

"In principle," says Losey, "a Quality Control Circle is a study group which concentrates on solving job-related problems—anything that could involve methods of production. They are continuous responses to inevitable problems and not created for specific problems."

They are also very informal. Meetings are brief, often lasting no more than five or 10 minutes, most frequently held before or following regular working hours, or during lunch or work breaks. Suggestions are usually simple and quickly applied. However, since no one could have the same grasp and understanding of the day-to-day job that the line employee possesses, solutions arrived at are often of a type that would be overlooked by managers, industrial engineers, and other specialists layers removed from the situation at hand.

Most Japanese companies with active QC circles have eight to 10 years of experience with them. The transition from quality concerns to a broader range of interests has been slow and gradual. Case history after case history makes clear that employee response was unenthusiastic at the outset. Only after workers became convinced that the circles would make their jobs easier, less problematical, more important, and less boring did their inspired participation take root. And only within the past three or four years did the QC circle concept begin to spark the interest of engineer and white collar personnel in addition to plant workers.

How applicable are quality control circles to U.S. industry? The following comments by Losey and others who viewed them first hand in Japan are in response to this question:

- It is important to recognize the Japanese QC circle experience as a long evolutionary process. It is not a concept that can be readily superimposed on an existing operation or system, but one of changing emphasis.

- The concept is a viable one only where the relationships between labor and management are appropriate. Thus some companies may install them effectively while, in other companies, a great deal of ground work and preparation might be necessary, the most important of which would be selling labor on the concept.

- A better understanding of the quality circles as they are applied in Japan would be required before attempting to introduce the concept to an American company. This is especially true in view of the fact that the Japanese circle is primarily regarded as an on-the-job improvement program designed largely to benefit workers—a reversal of the axiom that what is good for the company is good for the worker. In Japan the conviction is equally strong that what is good for the worker must be good for the company. Within reason, of course.

Examples. Typical of the kind of employee feedback that informs management the quality control circle concept is paying off is an incident related by labor writer Harry Bernstein that took place in a Chevrolet plant where the GM equivalent of quality circles is in force.

In a small conference room 15 workers and two supervisors were listening intently to Carl McKnight, a tall, slender machine operator. His complaint involved the quality of steel lately being received from the supplier. "The way that steel comes in," he said, "we end up with a lot of scrap for the skip loader."

Others echoed this sentiment. After 20 minutes or so of at times sharp discussion about responsibility for rejecting the unsatisfactory steel bars, Tony Kanski, the day-shift supervisor, decided it would be a good idea to get together with the vendor and see what was going on. Everybody agreed. Kanski concluded the session by saying, "Looks like we'll just have the vendor and maybe our own buyer here for our next meeting."

States Bernstein, "The proposal drew smiles of satisfaction from several members of the group."

That small group of workers, he adds, is typical of the revolutionary change taking place between workers and managers across the nation.

In another U.S. plant where quality circles are operational, a meeting was held to deal with a production backlog problem that repeatedly occurred. "Nine times out of 10 it's not even our fault," a worker was protesting. "The stuff is late coming to us from the stampers."

"That's right," another worker agreed. Still others nodded their heads.

A group leader interjected, "Why don't we check it out in the books?"

An Entry Register was kept with the time and date logged for each batch of work that was processed.

"Good idea," someone said.

It was done right then and there. Sure enough, there were frequent late batches from Stamping.

A supervisor said, "This department can't be expected to conform to the schedule if the work comes in late." His remark drew nods of approval.

Someone asked, "What can we do about it?"

Further discussion was held, a supervisor from Stamping was brought into the meeting. He conceded that batches often weren't completed on schedule, and pinpointed the problem as being triggered by absenteeism. A solution was worked out whereby fill-in workers would be borrowed from other operations when absence caused stamping machines to be idle.

Everyone was pleased with the meeting's outcome because everyone—workers as well as the company—benefitted. The pressure produced by the backlogs along with its by-product of nervousness and irritation were eliminated. Overtime was cut down. It made for a pleasanter workplace, and the operation was much more efficient.

It is situations of this type that the quality control circles, whatever they're called, are set up to deal with. Considered one at a time they may seem minor, in some cases picayune. But multiplied by the number of problems solved and suggestions adopted on a week-to-week or month-to-month basis, they can result in significant productivity improvement. Operational in an environment where workers are convinced that what benefits the company benefits them as well, the potential saving is tremendous.

A Piece of the Action. From the employee's standpoint, and this applies in different ways to different employee levels, the "piece of the action" so many workers are clamoring for these days refers to the opportunity to help decide how their jobs will be run. As a steel worker summed up the sentiment, "It's frustrating and dehumanizing when a decision is made for you when you're perfectly capable of making it yourself."

A co-worker chimed in, "Yeah, and it's doubly frustrating when you know that you understand the problem and need better than the person who made the decision."

"Giving up decision-making power is tough," General Motors Vice President A. S. Warren admits. When he was personnel director at the Fisher Body division, he recalls, he tried an experiment. He started to use assessment centers, putting managerial candidates through two days of exercises to demonstrate how they could handle the personnel director's job at Fisher Body plants. In connection with the program, Warren gave up some decision-making power, as did the general manager and plant managers.

"But we saw some real benefits," he says. "Even the people who weren't selected had a good idea why they didn't make it. It was no longer a case of thinking you missed out because the guy selected was a friend of Al Warren's."

Something similar to the assessment center system is in operation today at GM to select hourly people, Warren adds, and their peers are doing the assessing. "It is important that we develop techniques like this because we have to depend on hourly people as never before."

Given the chance, he is convinced, people will do a good job and make good decisions. They must be given the chance.

One remark this executive made is a comment expressed by several Japanese executives: "Most of the productivity problems in this country are the result of management problems—not workers' problems."

"We have been examining the decision-making process at all parts of General Motors," Warren concludes, "and we find that decisions are made two levels higher than they ought to be."

Japan is a society based on consensus, noted Takeo Sagawa, who heads up Sharp Electronics Co.'s facility in Paramus, N.J. "Confucianism and Buddhism, which influence Japanese thinking, are philosophies that stress self-control," he says, and questions whether the attempt to build wide bottom-up consensus would work in this country.

Be that as it may. Scores of situations could be cited, at the management level at least, where the failure to seek consensus when vital issues were at stake resulted in serious problems or near disaster.

A classic example took place in 1975 when Chairman Henry Ford II overruled then-President Lee Iacocca and slowed the development of Ford front-wheel drives. "That decision has cost Ford plenty," reports *Time*. "Its share of the new car market slipped from almost 24% in 1978 to about 17% in 1980. The company lost $2.1 billion on its North American operations (in 1980) and $402 million in the first six months of 1981."

Had the front-wheel drive decision been made by consensus, some Ford watchers believe, the story might have been drastically different.

Elitist decision-making is blamed too by some for many of the problems currently being undergone by trouble-ridden American Can Co. If consensus decision-making accomplishes anything at all, it gives managers a clear picture of corporate or divisional objectives, strategies designed to achieve them, and their individual roles in the drama. Complains one longtime middle manager at American Can, "Morale is very low. Some of us no longer know what we are supposed to be doing or where we will be doing it."

Another victim of misguided decisions appears to be National Semi-Conductor Corp., where executives have been dropping faster than autumn leaves on a windy day. Its stock price plunged from a high of $51.50 per share to $19 in less than a year, and according to *Business Week,* the company was "grappling with an almost schizophrenic management structure."

Surely some of this can be tracked to Chief Executive Officer Charles E. Sporck's decision-making problems. Number two man and chief technologist Pierre R. Lamond, one of the most recent key managers to resign, recalls a setup that produced confusion and conflict. Decisions made within individual profit centers went smoothly enough, he says, but winces at the thought of "interbusiness decisions" that had to go all the way to the top to be made. These were resolved by Sporck in a "red-tape-ridden process" that the CEO himself now concedes was untenable. "Frequently there were problems where a final decision couldn't be reached, and it would end up coming to me," he said. "That really doesn't make sense—those decisions should be made at the division level."

That's where they would be made in Japan, and most likely by consensus.

"We Have Met the Enemy and They Are Us"

U.S. labor and management file about 45,000 unfair labor practice complaints per year, according to recent reports, up from 17,000 just 15 years ago.

Any time a personnel change is made in the courts where labor disputes are decided, or in the National Labor Relations Board, a brouhaha is almost sure to result, with labor ascribing anti-union leanings to the appointee and management ascribing anti-business feelings. Rarely if ever is an appointment made where everyone agrees that the official selected is good for society. The adversary system, it is called, and with good reason. Characteristically, when labor and management executives meet across the bargaining table, it is tantamount to battalions lining up to do battle.

Ben Fischer of Carnegie-Mellon University's School of Urban & Public Affairs, and former assistant to the president of the United Steelworkers of America, states the situation bluntly enough: "The warfare and hostility that have typified most of the nation's bargaining history are luxuries our society can no longer afford. What we need are strong unions, self-assured, secure and capable of serving as cooperative partners in the labor-management relationship. What we need is management genuinely willing to accept unions and their role as full partners in the labor-management relationship."

We obviously cannot duplicate Japan's labor-management structure in the U.S. Unions there are not set up on an industry basis. The nation has approximately 70,000 companies and approximately 70,000 unions.

But we can duplicate—and with urgent determination must make every positive and well intentioned effort to duplicate—the Nipponese philosophy and temperament in arriving at labor agreements mutually tenable for workers, management and the economy.

"Japanese workers, generally," observes Towers, Perrin, Forster & Perrin's Myron Emanuel, "are as well-paid as U.S. workers. Labor negotiations are serious and intense, and strikes do take place. But the overall union-management atmosphere is friendly, cooperative and supportive. Japanese unions seem genuinely interested in furthering company goals and profit targets."

The theory is that a successful company makes a better employer than one riddled with labor difficulties. "Underlying this attitude," says Emanuel, "is a strong faith and belief among the workers that Japanese management will do the right thing for them and that they will share fully in the company's success."

A worker-sponsored banner prominently displayed in a Toshiba plant proclaims, "Let's all get together to work more efficiently and build better profits."

It is this attitude that we must do our best to engender in the U.S.

It CAN Happen Here. It can happen here, it must happen here, and the evidence is already strong that it will happen here.

Few industries have been as hard-plagued by labor-management problems over the years as the automobile industry. Few industries have been as hard-hit by foreign competition as the automobile industry. Few industries have more soberly and seriously assessed the situation as the automobile industry.

Its conclusions and resolutions bode well for the economy in years to come, but it will be a rough and stormy trip before U.S. labor-management relations can achieve the degree of harmony long since reached in Japan. Hopefully, the automobile industry, aided and abetted by the communications and steel industries, will set the work restructuring pattern for the rest of the country. In this connection, most of the progress to date is linked to the QWL movement currently gathering momentum throughout the U.S. Especially promising, with GM as a prime mover, is the cooperation and coordination with both the United Auto Workers and the Government. Continued progress of this kind can crack the adversary system.

The ultimate objective from the worker's standpoint is to achieve self-esteem in the workplace; to make the job, if not downright enjoyable, at least a great deal more palatable than it is today. From the company's standpoint, the ultimate goal is to boost productivity to the point where it can compete successfully in domestic and world markets. From the standpoint of society, or the economy, the target all should be shooting for is to accomplish both of these goals simultaneously.

One of the chief productivity cripplers in U.S. industry in general and the automobile industry in particular is employee absence which, nationwide, adds up to more than 100 million manhours a week, an increase of approximately 15% in the past five years alone. In regard to this issue, Bill Horner, administrative assistant to UAW's vice president, admits he is more convinced than ever that the absenteeism problem is largely attitudinal. A worker who has something on his mind about his foreman, about his job, about the work environment, and yes, even about the union, he says, decides maybe he can make it without coming to work. And you can't tell us that if we make that environment a better place that we can't turn that worker around in his thinking. It's been tried by discipline and, sure you can get rid of a person or a group of people, but it sure doesn't lick the problem.

Horner adds, "To me it's just sinful to see how much sales have dropped by the wayside while companies outside of the U.S. are increasing sales. We've got a problem and it just isn't management's problem. It's our problem."

One at a time, industries are of necessity coming around to this way of thinking. Ever since the rubber industry's crippling 140-day strike in 1976, a movement has been growing within the United Rubber Workers union in opposition to the outmoded Mike Quill-tough guy kind of stance in dealings with the Big Four producers—Firestone, Goodyear, UniRoyal, and Goodrich. The new approach comes after four bad years which hit labor and management equally hard. Repeated plant shutdowns have chopped the rubber makers' production capacity drastically. Idleness has produced a severe drain on the union's and individual finances, with membership down sharply as a result.

With job security a major issue these days, enlightened union officials are urging team play in place of myopic bullheaded warfare in labor's drive to win better concessions. "Whom are we kidding?" says one union organizer. "Too many rubber plants are endangered. Forcing work-rule changes that will hurt productivity may win us a battle or two. But who needs it, if it means losing the war? We'll have to figure a way to work in better harmony with management, or we're all down the drain."

From latest reports, a "way" appears to be in the offing.

In the steel industry it's already happening. Throughout steel, reported *Business Week,* "a drive to improve productivity through better personnel relations is under way." Vice President Thomas G. Katsahnias of Inland Steel Co., which has a $1 billion expansion program in the works, states the matter bluntly enough when he concedes that "the interface between front-line management and the bargaining unit people" will be a crucial element in making the investment pay off. With this goal in mind, a major training program is under way to improve supervisory skills in such areas as effective listening and to cool the resolution of grievances.

Bethlehem Steel, which is planning three-quarters of a billion dollar modernization program, reports improved productivity at plants where it has formed labor-management participation teams whose creation was authorized in the last United Steelworkers contract. And similar progress has been achieved at National Steel Corp. which already has QWL groups operational. According to Chairman Howard M. Love, no choice exists. "We have to get everybody to believe in the need" for better cooperation between labor and management.

At Jones & Laughlin's Indiana Harbor slab mill facility built in 1966, the stated goal of 210,000 tons per month was only rarely attained. Mill superintendent Charles W. White described J&L's productivity rate as "almost shameful." Today, with workers and management in close communication and interaction, the mill produces 280,000 to 300,000 tons of slab each month. Notes company President Thomas C. Graham, "You don't overstate the case when you say that this business used to be more totalitarian than the Prussian army."

Largely responsible for the improvement, according to J&L's Louis G. Kresich, was management's move to "take the lies out of the delay sheet"—the existence of downtime documentation. Today, problems and their causes are discussed each morning Japanese style. No one is nailed to the cross, and reasoned solutions are hammered out in an honest and straightforward manner.

As Graham told the general assembly of the American Iron & Steel Institute in 1978, the industry could solve its productivity problems without massive capital spending if only management would be more creative, communicate better with its workers, and look for even small productivity gains.

It may be no panacea. But it works a damn sight better than warfare.

The Third Adversary

Cooperation and coordination for the common economic good must involve every major segment of society: labor, management, consumers and government. Japanese government interference in business is relatively small compared with U.S. government interference. At the same time, Japanese government activity geared to ways and means of achieving economic improvement is greater, if not in numbers of actions, at least in terms of profit goals and competitive objectives.

Despite Japan's minimal regulation of industry, in contrast to U.S. regulation, agreements are usually worked out amicably on issues where the societal good is involved. An outstanding example is automobile emission-control technology where Japanese automakers are at least two years ahead of Detroit. While government ministries which establish national economic priorities in Japan are powerful and capable of exerting pressure on private companies, the need to do so rarely exists. Observes Japanese businessman Hiroshi Nomura, "Where one's managerial philosophy is formed with the individual corporation viewed as a microcosm of the whole economy, pressure is rarely required. Socially detrimental actions would run counter to stated company policy."

Indicative of government's hands-off policy in Japan, so far as industry regulation is concerned, is the ratio of government employees to its overall workforce compared against other industrialized nations. Japan's roughly estimated public sector personnel of less than 10% of its total working population tells a dramatic story when viewed against the U.S.'s estimated 16.9%, West Germany's 17.9%, and France's 15%. Significantly, the United Kingdom, clearly one of the world's most trouble-ridden economies today, has a government to total workforce ratio of about 25.5%.

Japan's government involvement in business is centered largely on business-building objectives. The computer software challenge is a recent example. Although Japanese industry is one of the world's foremost computer users, it has long been dependent on software programs that were U.S.-developed and marketed. "Today," notes one IBM manager, "Americans who assume the Japanese lack the creativity to develop software for their own economic needs are in for a surprise."

To meet this problem head-on, Japan's Ministry of International Trade & Industry's (MITI) Information-Technology Promotion Agency introduced in October 1981 a $1.7 million government-funded Software Technology Center which is now busily harnessing the talents and expertise of leading engineers and technologists from industry, government and academia on a battery of long-range software development projects. At the same time, says the IBMer, "Japanese computer makers like Hitachi and Fujitsu are cranking out their own software programs in tandem."

Hitachi already has at least 17 software subsidiaries with several new facilities being planned. "It's a fairly safe bet," a Wall Street computer industry watcher concludes, "that at this rate any software lead the U.S. may presently enjoy won't be enjoyed very long. It's difficult for this country to match the effective brand of industry-government-labor coordination that is working so well in Japan."

It's true. In the U.S., the typical government official is apt to ask, "What is this or that company doing to unfairly monopolize business in its industry, or improperly control prices?" While Japan is also concerned with fair trade, the question at the forefront of official attention is, "What steps can be taken to move Japanese industry to a position of independence and world leadership?"

The GM-UAW Initiative. "Increasing attention," states Delmar L. Landen, General Motors Corp.'s director of organizational research and development, "is being focused not only on the American worker but on the larger issue of the nature of work and its specific and its broad ramifications.

"One of the ways the Federal Government has responded to these corollary issues—the need for improvements in productivity and the quality of working life—is through the creation of the National Center for Productivity and Quality of Working Life."

The center, with a Board of Directors headed up by the Vice President, spearheads the creation of conferences, publications, and information exchange designed to focus attention and resources on a broad variety of efforts to improve the working environment and employee attitudes on the one hand, and boost U.S. productivity on the other.

Closely linked to these objectives is the establishment of a National Union-Management Committee by GM in cooperation with the International UAW. Says Landen: "This committee is committed to fostering innovative approaches to the study and design of organizational arrangements that serve to enrich the working lives of employees. These mechanisms for performing work should be so conceived that they permit people to contribute more fully to the accomplishment of organizational objectives. Other systems must also be designed to assure that people receive fair and just economic and psychological rewards from their contributions."

Landen draws the following observations from the ongoing labor, industry and government cooperation relating to the quality of work life/productivity improvement endeavors:

1. Increasing concern and emphasis is being given by the Federal Government to both productivity improvement and the quality of working life. The recent establishment of a National Center is already intensifying the government's interest and involvement in efforts to bring about improvements in these two areas so critical to our economy: the health and well-being of our nation's workers and of our country's economic and social institutions. (Please note: Disappointingly, according to latest reports on the eve of this book's publication, Federal activity of this kind has tapered off in recent months.)

2. The current emphasis in the QWL movement is on a clearer definition of the concept, upon better measurement and upon the means by which the concept can become more fully operationalized.

3. The general trend of the movement is toward more active participation of workers in decisions and in other matters which directly affect the quality of their working lives.

4. Experience has shown that union and management can work cooperatively in this area, and in so doing can contribute much more to enhancing the quality of working life than either party can accomplish independently.

5. In order to avoid mandatory legislation in the future, it is essential that union and management groups work in harmony with the Federal Government in fulfilling the Center's mission as it is reflected in its full title—National Center for Productivity and Quality of Working Life.

Does this mark the inception of Japanese-style government-management-labor cooperation—the WE-Approach—in America? Hopefully.

Is WE-Power Exportable?

Indeed it is, to a large degree, many experts of Japanese management agree. One of these is Harvard University Business School's Prof. Kim B. Clark, who believes that although special care and patience are necessary, the basic managerial concept that inspires trust and loyalty and their automatic by-product of employee cooperation, is adaptable by all peoples.

Few executives appreciate the importance of fostering WE-power more than Marvin T. Runyon, president of Nissan Motor Co.'s Tennessee-based operation. A former Ford Co. manager, he has more than three decades of hard-won experience behind him with the woes that befall management under the adversary system. With this recollection sharp in his mind, Runyan has hired a consultant to help set up a "participatory management system" as close as is feasible to the Japanese model. On the drawing board are plans to initiate quality control circles, a corporate family environment, and other innovations aimed at instilling Japanese-style loyalty in American workers.

But Runyon is well aware that his objectives cannot be reached overnight, and that a continuing communications and educational program will be needed to win work support and sell the American plant force on top management's sincerity. To help ensure the program's success, 430 employees, more than one-fourth of them hourly workers, will be sent to Japan for intensive training programs lasting one to four months. The investment is admittedly large, but if the WE-power goal is achieved, it will pay for itself many times over in years and decades to come.

7.

THE WORKPLACE

> *Developing management potential in others is one of the manager's most important roles. Even seemingly unimportant work can be done with a sense of self-management.*
> —*Konosuke Matsushita*

The first essential step toward U.S. economic renewal is the creation of a work environment where productivity will be a natural by-product of the system rather than an artificially forced and inveigled phenomenon. It must be an environment that is friendly rather than hostile, where workers derive the maximum psychological and financial benefits possible from their day-to-day jobs. It must be an environment where workers and executives work together toward common objectives, not because they are coerced or cajoled into cooperating, but because they *want* to cooperate.

How can the corporate community achieve this marketplace mecca?

The Japanese experience suggests three main conditions designed to turn around employee attitudes toward their jobs and employers from negative to positive, from the ME approach to the WE approach:

1. *Freedom from job anxiety and debilitating work pressures.* Workers must enjoy much greater job security than many of them experience today. Positive managerial strategies instead of pressure tactics must be applied to boost productivity. Workers must look upon the company that employs them as a protector and safe harbor instead of a swirling whirlpool with uncertain and dangerous currents.

2. *An opportunity to function as a person instead of a robot.* Workers must be given a chance to participate in the day-to-day problem solving and decision making that relate to their jobs. They must be made to feel *part* of the operation, not equivalent to a machine's extension. They must be permitted to acquire the self-respect and self-esteem that derives from contributing one's thinking as well as mechanical actions.

3. *Drudgery reduced to the minimum extent possible.* For all its propagandized glorification, work that is mindlessly repetitive ad infinitum tends to be oppressive to a good many people. A certain amount of repetition is unavoidable, especially in low level jobs, but there are a number of techniques that have been proven effective in relieving the dull deadly boredom.

Getting Rid of That Backpack

The 19th century Nova Scotian humorist Thomas Haliburton once said, "To carry care to bed is to sleep with a pack on your back."

The Workplace

If this is true, at least 60 million Americans are burdened down by this encumbrance. U.S. corporations play host to a worrisome workforce. Low level employees in many industries are in a continuing state of apprehension ranging from mild to acute that they are liable to be laid off any time with little or no notice due to a slack period, an economy drive, a merger, or because for one reason or another they incurred a supervisor's displeasure. Longer seniority employees, while less prone to layoff, worry that their skills may become obsolete because of technological advances or system restructuring, that they may be automated out of a job or that because of advancing age they may no longer be able to keep up with the young bucks.

Supervisors and managers are often in an even more precarious situation. In large corporations especially, the infighting for attractive key jobs becomes rougher as the pay scale and perks rise. And too many executives pit combatants against one another and let the fittest—or most ornery—survive. Very often, the closer the competitive battleground to the top executive suite, the more savage the warfare becomes. Cooperation tends to become superficial. The number one concern is for No. 1.

There is the story of an insurance company vice president who, following a run-in with his boss, quit in utter frustration. At one point during the argument he muttered, "Make up your mind: Do you want me to compete against John Smith, or against the competition!"

His boss's response: "If you can't stand the heat, stay out of the kitchen."

He got out of the kitchen and now teaches insurance courses at a nearby university.

Job-induced anxiety is self-defeating for two simple reasons:

1. The anxiety-ridden employee, whatever his level, retaliates to his employer-imposed stress with feelings of bitterness and disloyalty.

2. The individual forced to function in an anxiety-ridden work environment is less effective mentally and physically than his counterpart who is not thus impaired.

The Japanese work environment, while not worry-free, is far less productive of anxiety than the typical U.S. work environment, in large companies particularly, where lifetime employment is virtually guaranteed.

The Employment Factor. Typically, the Japanese employment recruit is introduced at a young age to industry. If he is hired by a large successful corporation the odds are strong that he will hold this job for all or most of his working life. Even if he is hired by a smaller, less well-heeled company, the prospects for long-term employment are excellent. The psychological impact of this condition is significant. The American worker's reasoning: "How I make out here isn't important; I won't be on board very long anyhow." The younger and less experienced he happens to be, the less mature his rationale.

From the young Japanese recruit's point of view: "This is it! I'd better make good. There's no second chance just around the corner tomorrow or the next day." This is only one factor toward the creation of positive thinking from the Japanese standpoint. But it is a powerful one. The simple logic is inescapable.

From the day the young Japanese starts on the job his feeling of team membership and security is reinforced and starts building. He is absorbed into an intensive training program which tells him more effectively than any words could that he is important to the company, to his group, and to the organization's future well being. The company is making a major investment in him, betting its money and resources that he *will* make it and function as an important and *equal* part of the team. It makes him feel that he *belongs* and will belong for a long time to come.

Normally, lifetime employment extends until age 55, although this number is slowly and gradually inching upward. Even at this point—and it is not a characteristic of the young to worry about retirement during one's 20s and 30s—the termination of one's career in his mid or late 50s doesn't mean he will be "put out to pasture" as too often happens in America. As mentioned earlier, the older worker is in demand by the small company where the perks and wages are less attractive. An estimated 75% of employees retired from large corporations find jobs, usually with their employers' assistance, with smaller organizations. So that lifetime job security is assured for most Japanese.

It takes little imagination to speculate upon the comparative work attitudes of the anxiety-free employee and his stress-plagued counterpart.

The Magic Word. The magic word in the U.S. economy has long been *performance.* Chief Executives in some companies change hands with the frequency of square dance participants. The measure of a candidate's eligibility to the top spot is based on a career track record, or performance. Investors weigh a corporation's earnings potential more often than not on its short-term stock market performance, hence the bottom-line syndrome so detrimental to scores of U.S. companies. The corporate employee, whatever his rank, customarily receives wage increases or promotions if his job performance warrants it, a seemingly fair and sensible arrangement.

However, in the view of many Japanese watchers, the magic word has lost its luster. Especially insofar as "job advancement" is concerned, applying performance as the criterion while it unquestionably triggers extra effort and drive on the part of ambitious employees, often produces feelings of frustration, and charges of unfair treatment and favoritism. The reasons are clear. For one thing, performance evaluation frequently is left in the hands of supervisors or managers who may or may not be prejudiced in their judgment, and/or may or may not assess individual performance accurately. On top of that, employees with low self-esteem may drop out of the competitive race because they subconsciously believe they could never win out over Charley, Sue, Betty, or Jack. Finally, employees who do compete and lose out to Charley, Sue, Betty, or Jack are rarely objective in assessing the judgment which condemned them as losers. The result: anger and bitterness, which adds up to disloyalty.

Under the Japanese system, increases in pay and promotions are largely based on seniority. Almost invariably, Shogo, Jin or Shigero, having been exposed to X years of training, experience and service, will be upgraded in rank in the natural course of their careers. A Japanese executive was asked, "But what happens if a person isn't intellectually qualified for the job?"

The manager smiled. "He would probably get an able assistant."

The rationale is an essential—and beautifully sensitive—part of the Japanese culture. Notes Sperry's Michael R. Losey: "Japanese industry is based on the Oyabun-Kobun relationship. This is the parent-child relationship and contributes to the paternalistic or family profile which exists in most Japanese companies. Under such a system, there exists a great respect for senior members of the company and the most senior individual is generally given available promotions. If he is not totally qualified, it makes little difference. In such cases, a junior, more qualified individual may be made his assistant. This is viewed as an appropriate compromise by Japanese standards."

The concept is one that promotes equality among employees within specific work categories. That is, while it is not customary for, let us say, a production machine operator to advance to managerial post, he would be treated the same as all other workers of his general class. At Kobe Steel Corp., for example, approximately 95% of all employees are promoted to supervisory jobs some time during their career.

The impression is fairly widespread that Japanese wage levels are low. This was probably the case a decade or two ago. But in recent years wages have been creeping steadily upward so that today workers in large industrial corporations earn almost as much as U.S. workers, and in some cases more, when such perks as subsidized food, housing and loans, etc., are taken into consideration.

What it adds up to is another dimension of job security and peace of mind. It is humiliating and stressful to be bypassed for wage increase and promotion when others—perhaps some of whom the bypassed worker feel are no better than, or inferior to, himself—are getting ahead.

But what about the worker who, given the company's best attention and consideration, is still lazy and indifferent, an out-and-out dud? The author posed that question to Matsushita Electric's Ken K. Shimba, a manager in the company's Overseas Publicity Division in Osaka.

"That is rarely a problem," he explained. "First, every effort is made to find the particular job or niche in the company where the employee will feel most comfortable and can put his best talents to use. Ninety-nine times out of a hundred this will solve the problem."

"But what if it doesn't?" I persisted.

"In that case the worker might be given very little work, or obviously unimportant work, to perform. He would stand out in the workforce as a failure and lose the respect and esteem of his co-workers. Who in his right mind would want to get himself into that kind of a situation? As I said, it is rarely if ever a problem."

With less anxiety on the job and little if any boss-imposed competitive pressure, it seems fair to assume that the average Japanese worker is subjected to far less stress than his American counterpart. It is also common knowledge that stress, along with diet, exercise, smoking, and heredity, is one of the five major inducers of hypertension and heart disease. And it is a fact that the Japanese male enjoys the longest life expectancy (72.97 as of 1978) of any male in any major industrial country, and the Japanese female the longest in her category (78.33 as of 1978). Is the Japanese work environment a prime contributing factor? It is a question to ponder.

Organized Nonproductivity

For decades management experts from F. W. Taylor to H. B. Maynard plotted and planned to devise scientific new methods to boost worker productivity. They came up with some brilliant creations. The science couldn't be challenged. The systems were flawless on paper. Only one problem existed. The human aspects were found wanting. The system didn't work on the job.

Management consultant and work restructuring specialist Roy W. Walters has his own theory to explain the failure: "The trouble with such systems as Short Interval Scheduling, Skill Structuring, and Methods Time Measurement is that they keep the work fractionated and simplified. The trick is to make the work more interesting and enjoyable." The consultant's salt and pepper beard wags from side to side as he shakes his iron-gray head. "Frederick Taylor's disciples are still raising hell, but Taylor's been dead for almost 70 years."

Japan today has about 75,000 robots in operation compared to approximately 3,700 in the U.S. Yet no one knows better than Japanese executives that attempting to robotize human beings won't work, however ingenious and sophisticated the system. As one manager puts it, "A half ounce of trust is worth a ton of mechanization when it comes to boosting productivity."

One of the main keys to Japanese managerial success is the self-management that prevails in most Japanese plants. It works because the managerial state of mind is conducive to making it work. For one thing, the Japanese manager assumes that personnel at all levels are sufficiently well qualified to do their job right. For another, he assumes his people have the company's best interests at heart, and so doesn't go to the time and expense of hiring supervisory watch dogs to continually monitor and review performance. His reasoning is that the employee possesses the initiative, intelligence and training to do this himself.

High productivity occurs when the maximum number of high quality products are produced at the lowest possible cost. Every avoidable nickel that is spent to make the product, or make the product come out right, is an added drain on productivity. Thus if 50 workers are employed in a department, and it takes four supervisors to keep tabs on them, and three inspectors to check their work on an ongoing basis, the productivity level will be much lower here than in the department of 50 workers doing the same job with only one or two supervisors and a single inspector, or no inspector at all. This, actually, is the basic difference between many U.S. and Japanese companies today. The Japanese company typically eliminates layers of staff personnel and, with guidance and counsel in place of watch-dogging and instruction, gets more production and better cooperation from the less-supervised workers.

The typical American company, applying Douglas McGregor's Theory X approach—which postulates that the average employee must be coerced, controlled, directed and threatened with punishment if top efficiency is to be achieved—invests in the extra staff needed to deal with untrustworthy employees, and hence achieves low productivity. This boils down to organized nonproductivity. The Japanese manager goes with McGregor's Theory Y assumptions that the average worker is capable of assuming responsibility, possesses a high mental potential, and will operate responsibly and productively if properly motivated to do so.

What the Japanese competitive edge proves as much as anything else is that in the X vs. Y race, the Y strategists win by a mile.

The very establishment of self-management at the line or operational level is, of course, an executive statement in itself; it is a way of telling workers that you trust them to manage themselves, that you don't think they have to be watched while they work to make sure they are doing their jobs properly; that they don't need to have their job duties explained on a step-by-step basis. Selling U.S. executives on this concept may well be the toughest challenge confronting industry during the remaining years of this century. The author talked with the general manager of a medium size electrical supplies manufacturing company who equates "permissive self-management" with economic hari kari. Despite all the success stories in magazine articles and books, he regards the Japanese edge as a temporary fluke.

He pointed to a list of productivity improvement techniques installed in his plant in recent years, techniques that worked in terms of "bottom-line performance." The general office was rearranged so that clerical employees no longer face one another, making it impossible for them to chat conveniently. A system was initiated requiring plant workers to obtain a chit from their foreman in order to replace worn out work gloves; a similar setup was introduced in connection with office supplies. The office's two Xerox machines were relocated, put in the line of vision of the office services supervisor, so that any unauthorized use would be spotted.

The Workplace *159*

He cited additional productivity improvement innovations, assuring that for each he could quote a specific dollars and cents savings.

This conversation was discussed with consultant Roy W. Walters, mentioning a few of the items on the list. His response was predictable.

"Workers view such moves as degrading."

This is indisputable, of course. Still, the general manager feels he can relate the actions to improved productivity and profits. What he can't do, however, is put a gauge on the psychological consequences of telling people in effect that he mistrusts them.

Within the context of the Theory X operation, productivity innovations of the type described by the general manager make sense. What doesn't make sense is the Theory X concept. The typical Japanese worker doesn't have to be watched for fear he'll spend his time gabbing instead of working. He doesn't have to be closely controlled for fear he'll steal work gloves or ballpoint pens from his employer. He doesn't have to be observed by a supervisor for fear he'll misuse the company's equipment. He will function honestly, fairly and reasonably because it's in his company's best interest for him to do so *and because his employer trusts him to do so.*

How does self-management work? What are its advantages? What makes it different from the conventional form of management that prevails in most U.S. plants today? Walters stresses three main features of the system:

1. Workers at the operating level are permitted to make many of the decisions traditionally made by supervisors and managers.
2. Good feedback exists from the work itself. Members of the work team are kept constantly informed about how the work and the team are progressing.

3. Each team member is trained to perform a variety of skills. An individual or group is responsible for an operation in its entirety rather than a piece of an operation.

Self-management upgrades the worker from third grader to adult; it gives him self-respect and self-esteem; it changes his perception of the job and workplace from one that is demeaning to one that is uplifting. What follows is an example of self-management, American style.

The Story City Experiment. Notes Ezra F. Vogel in his informative Harper & Row book, *Japan As Number 1*: "When asked to describe a Japanese company, most Japanese managers list as one characteristic the practice of 'bottom up' rather than 'top down.' The lowly section, within its sphere, does not await executive orders but takes the initiative. It identifies problems, gathers information, consults with relevant parts of the company, calls issues to the attention of higher officials, and draws up documents."

Butler Manufacturing Co.'s plant in Story City, Iowa, was built on a 58-acre tract in 1975 to provide a single manufacturing source for the company's grain conditioning products. Its procedures in many respects are similar to the Japanese style of management. The product line, notes Michael R. Simmons, Vice President-Corporate Personnel, is a reasonably complex one, consisting of 5,000 different parts, and includes the Kan-Sun continuous flow grain dryer among a variety of other farm products.

"The goal in planning the new plant," he adds, "was to develop a highly profitable and productive operation, with, at the same time, an eye toward worker satisfaction. Since about 1972, management had been tracking the experience of companies experimenting with the innovative techniques. By mid-1974, Butler became convinced that some of these new philosophies could be incorporated in its new plant, and had

The Workplace

the benefit of senior management commitment to pursue implementations.''

As mentioned in a previous chapter, the Story City operation consists of several self-managed work teams made up of five to 12 workers who have collective responsibility for specified functional areas. Four unit coordinators oversee the activities of 20 to 22 shop teams on day and night shifts.

Production expectations are predetermined. Team members decide among themselves how to allocate manpower to meet goals and are accountable for the results.

> As an example, a number of assembly teams are responsible for the complete assembly of Kan-Sun dryers, including plumbing and mechanical components, electronic controls, hydraulic and hydrostatic drives. Each team member is trained and competent in each phase of the assembly procedure. With the production schedule in mind, team members meet to decide who will be responsible for specific portions of the work. The group as a whole is held responsible for fulfilling the overall production objective.

Similarly, team members are responsible for all testing and inspection of individual units and the finished product. There are no formal inspectors within the plant. Team members also handle the routine maintenance and repair of tools and equipment within their specified area.

Each day teams receive a tally of their own production and performance so that members know on an ongoing basis where they stand so far as goal fulfillment is concerned. Teams falling behind are encouraged to seek help from other teams in the plant.

Formal weekly meetings are held by each team at a time convenient to both night and day shift members. Meeting moderators are selected on a rotating basis as productivity and safety problems, needs and performance are reviewed, and ideas for setting up work areas and resolving operating, behavioral and disciplinary problems are exchanged.

> For example, if one team member feels a co-worker is not pulling his or her weight, this issue is placed on the weekly meeting's agenda and the group thrashes it out by means of discussion or counseling. Unit coordinators and/or other staff group representatives attend team meetings to provide information where necessary along with a general business perspective. Monthly plant-wide meetings are held to review the previous month's production, financial, operating and safety results. Quarterly meetings provide similar feedback and keep workers up to date regarding business conditions and their effect on the corporation. Thus safeguards are built into the system to avoid limited and parochial operating decisions due to the lack of broad scope knowledge and experience.

Ad hoc team meetings are called to handle immediate problems. Rather than "going through channels" to unit coordinators or supervisors, team members are encouraged to resolve problems within the group if possible, and to deal directly with other plant personnel where information or guidance are needed.

Customer correspondence, favorable or not, is shared with employees. Team members are also encouraged to make field trips when schedules and workload permit. Thus, team members are able to relate personally and on a first hand basis to the ultimate purpose and use of the products they help make, and get a chance to see how their own performance translates into customer satisfaction or problems.

Communications and feedback, therefore, are key ingredients of the Story City experiment. This includes daily production reports, weekly formal and ad hoc meetings, monthly and quarterly plant-wide briefings, customer contact and feedback response.

Two special purpose teams perform unique roles. The six-member Safety Team drawn from various shop and office areas, investigates accidents and develops programs to improve plant safety. Membership rotates every six months to give as many workers as possible an opportunity to participate and to heighten safety awareness. The Advisory team is similar in structure to the Safety Team. It deals with issues of plant-wide significance, such as personnel and plant policies, holiday schedules, recreational activities, etc.

Teams also participate in the employee assessment and hiring process. Job applicants meet first with an office worker who provides company background information and screens out candidates who are clearly unsuitable. Surviving applicants tour the plant in the company of a team representative. They are then interviewed by at least two members of the group. After reference checks are made, final interviews are conducted and successful applicants chosen by the team with whom the new employee will work.

In summary, then, work teams are individually and collectively responsible for the following plant operations:

- Standards and goal setting.
- Motivation.
- Safety.
- Materials handling.
- Housekeeping.
- Setting up jobs and work assignments.
- Skills training.
- Allocation of manpower.
- Methods, operation and product improvement.
- Purchasing of supplies.

- Scheduling of work within the team.
- The team's profit performance.
- Inspection and quality assurance.
- Equipment maintenance and repair.
- Tool maintenance and repair.
- Hiring.
- Behavioral problems, counseling, discipline.

It is clear from this brief description that management places a high degree of reliance and trust in its workforce. The Story City experiment has been rated successful as of this writing in terms of improved productivity (28%), upgraded morale, and an absenteeism rate well below the industry average (under 2.0%). Notes Simmons: "Butler's recipe may not fit other organizations, to be sure. The production and quality of work life results, however, may provide stimulation for others in assessing their own work design alternatives."

He also points out that a variety of factors—rural location, employee product identification (as consumers), relatively small size, younger work force, nonunion environment, and consultants' assistance—all helped contribute to the Story City success.

The Battleground

The Organizational Behavior Institute, in its Management Psychology Letter, *OBI Interaction*, categorizes boredom as an industrial "battleground". . . .unquestionably a major problem of our age, calling for decisive management action." The report goes on to quote authors Charles R. Walker and Robert H. Guest on the subject: "We suggest that the sense of becoming depersonalized, of becoming anonymous as against remaining one's self, is for those who feel it a psychologically more disturbing result of the work environment than either the boredom or the tension that arise from repetitive and mechanically paced work."

The Japanese experience tends to support this conjecture. The overwhelming majority of Japanese workers are conscientious and loyal regardless of the level of work they perform.

One long-standing managerial approach to the problem of boredom-stimulated indifference has been the propagandized sanctification of work. History suggests that this supposed productivity boosting strategy, less effective today than ever before, yields limited and meagre results. In a 1976 book the author wrote, "Maybe you can sell the fun and glory of work to the dynamic decision-making manager, or the guy who plays in a band, or the player who covers left field for the Yankees. But show me an employee who doesn't enjoy a day off more than drudging away at a day-in, day-out job, and I'll show you a looney bin prospect."

The average Japanese worker may well fit this bill, and generally speaking, his psychological problems are markedly less than those of his Western counterpart. One reason is that the drudgery in his day-to-day job is reduced to the maximum degree possible. And equally, if not more important, his self-esteem and self-respect are maintained at the highest possible level.

The Fine Art of Despecialization. As consultant Roy W. Walters urges, so-called "work simplification," a Western productivity boosting objective, often serves to routinize the job and reduce the number of decisions a worker must make in performing his or her duties. When this is compounded by work specialization—confining the employee to the task or limited number of tasks for which he has acquired the most practice and experience, on the premise that since he knows these tasks best he will do them best—the deadly repetition is multiplied. This has been attributed in large measure to the rebellion of workers in the communications and automobile industries in the 1970s, and the communications industry's publicized fed-up-with-it-all assertions that "we're not robots, we're people."

Specialization in the U.S. is by no means confined to production and clerical employees. The traditional approach in the hiring and operating activities is to slot people according to the career function emphasized on their employment application form or resume. In fact, if the specialization isn't sufficently clear, the chance of employment is diminished. Thus, production people are classified as operators of specific machines, for example, or according to certain aspects of the manufacturing process. Managers are slotted as sales oriented, accountants, quality control specialists, advertising or public relations people, etc.

The Japanese concept is drastically different. With long-term employment in mind, the production recruit is indoctrinated into one specialization after another, with intensive training provided for each function and skill. He is shifted about from section to section and in time becomes qualified to perform a wide variety of tasks. During the course of the work day and work week, he may be switched from one area to another a number of times. Thus the drudgery of repetitive tasks doesn't set in, and at the same time all aspects of production are covered by qualified workers as required by peak workloads, vacation and absence.

The executive is similarly shifted from function to function. In the process he becomes knowledgeable about the operation as a whole, understands the problems and needs of all functional groups, and acquires expertise in a variety of areas which may be applied as required.

The deroutinization and humanization of the workplace is not confined to Japanese corporations. In addition to a growing number of work restructuring programs started by U.S. corporations, the movement has been mushrooming in Europe as well, most notably in West Germany, Sweden and France. The Siemens Co. plant in Karlsruhe, West Germany, is an outstanding example. There employees are organized into "work islands" of three to seven people where jobs are rotated, a reasonable amount of socializing is permitted, and work cycling is designed with an eye toward the reduction of boredom.

Observes a Communications Workers of America representative who has studied U.S. and European progress against work dehumanization: "Important strides are being made by American and European companies, and significant productivity gains chalked up as a result. But no place that I have visited did I see the kind of commitment and dedication that exists in the typical Japanese corporation. We still have a long way to go before we can hope to trim down that sharp competitive edge."

Work Restructuring

Oddly enough, considering the dramatically positive results of the Japanese experience, the Japanese style of management is not new in the U.S. Some of the labels, such as quality control circles, may be unfamiliar to many executives, but as we shall see in a subsequent chapter, a number of outstandingly successful U.S. companies—assiduously studied by the Japanese—have been applying many of the methods discussed long before the Japanese started cashing in on them. Nor do modest and diffident Nipponese executives claim authorship of the ideas. In fact, one manager after another was quick to acknowledge to me the debt that Japan owes the U.S. so far as the educational process is concerned.

Although they never categorized it as Japanese-style management, Roy W. Walters and several other enlightened consultants have been preaching the doctrine for years, and assisting client companies in redesigning the work environment along lines described in these chapters.

The Good Uncle Approach. Walters makes the potent point that "no organization ever hired an unmotivated worker."

Nonetheless, untold billions have been invested in recent years on a variety of strategies and techniques concocted to motivate employees at all levels and keep them productively happy. As the consultant recalls from his own long experience, benefits beyond the standard extras of health care and time off have been showered on workers in phases. A decade or so ago, a strong emphasis was placed on supervisory and executive training that focused on how to treat workers to achieve the most productive results. A fortune was spent, and is still being spent on brochures, booklets and other literature telling employees how great they are and how well-loved by management.

Then psychologists publicized the disclosure that you can't understand your people until you first understand yourself. So supervisors and managers signed up for a long gamut of courses, programs and seminars on sensitivity training, T Group Training, EST, Transactional Analysis, Transcendental Meditation and the like with self-examination and revelation in mind. There's little question that all of this training helped many people in many ways, but it hasn't seemed to solve the productivity problem. Managers today are as confused as they ever were, and still ask the perennial question: "Why aren't my people performing more effectively? Why can't we get them to work up to their full productivity potential?"

One reason, says Walters, is because it is not enough to *treat* workers well, they must also be *used* well. Since the industrial revolution began, he says, continuously advancing hardware and software technology have played a major role in productivity improvement. But company after company in the U.S. still falls short of its productivity potential. The problem is that the equipment is designed and installed without proper consideration of the human element. The focus is on the optimum use of capital investment while ignoring problems that relate to the human side of getting the job done. Regardless of how sophisticated or ingenious the equipment might be, it's up to people to see that it works. If a person hates his job, and is convinced that the machine to which he is tied is responsible for his daily ordeal, he is not apt to think kindly of either the machine or the management that installed it. Nor are the most magnanimous fringe benefits one might conceive likely to alter his attitude.

A Time for Change. "What we need," Walters insists, "is a viable balance between the human element and the technology." It entails a whole new way of managerial thinking.

He concedes that the change won't come easily. For one thing, most managers are accustomed to functioning under the old traditional adversary system. For another, most workers view any attempt to improve productivity as something management wants but they do not, since the result would only be to make them work harder with nothing gained in return. Worker wariness in response to announced intentions to restructure jobs along more democratic lines is understandable in most cases. Management has long propagandized the work force along some of the lines being discussed. It preached employee responsibility and followed up with quality checks ad infinitum. It encouraged employee involvement and called in technical staff people when even minor changes and adjustments had to be made. This no longer cuts ice. The message being hammered home loud and clear by the Japanese experience and QWL experiments is that the worker wants a bigger say where his daily job is concerned.

The way to respond to this demand to the mutual benefit of manager and managed is clear-cut and apparent, Walters believes.

1. Management must begin to realize and take action to demonstrate that most workers are capable of achieving higher productivity.

2. Management must recognize that workers *want* to achieve higher productivity.

3. Management must show a willingness to experiment with new ways of designing work in a more trusting and open environment.

We know what makes work more exciting and fulfilling, the consultant adds, and stresses that he is talking about all work levels from the top executive suite to the bottom rank-and-file rungs. For this to happen, three critical psychological conditions must be met:

1. The work must be made meaningful, not as management sees it but as workers define it.

2. Employees must be made responsible for the outcome of the work, given genuine and not pseudo responsibility.

3. They must be kept informed with regard to the day-by-day results of the work they perform.

Five factors must apply—Walters calls them "core job dimensions"—for the three conditions to be met:

1. The job must be perceived as significant by the worker; he must see the impact of what he produces or creates on other people.

2. The worker must be trained to acquire skills in a variety of functions and tasks, mental as well as motor.

3. The worker must achieve task identification—that is, carry through the whole project or job from beginning to end with result visibility.

4. The worker must be given a degree of autonomy, some control and decision-making authority so far as his daily activity is concerned.

5. The worker must receive feedback, constant and current data informing him how well or how poorly he is doing.

Walters concludes by stressing that any job restructuring effort must be preceded by departmental and organization-wide diagnosis. A growing number of progressive corporations, both commercial and industrial, appear to be going this route with a variety of results reported. The consultant is the first to concede that the redesign he espouses is not always feasible. The timing must be right. The organizational climate must be right. But one fact is abundantly clear: Job restructuring along the lines discussed will be the trend of the '80s and '90s and the corporations that accomplish it effectively will be tomorrow's industry leaders and, what is more important—survivors.

8.

BEYOND THE BOTTOM LINE

> *The* sunao *spirit is the fundamental spiritual attitude that the manager must have to be successful at management. Developing and advancing the* sunao *spirit is extremely important for everyone—managers and nonmanagers alike.*
>
> Konosuke Matsushita

A purchasing executive gives a salesman an order for component parts needed for production. The sales rep thanks him for the business, and they part with a handshake. The following day a couple of cases of high grade scotch are delivered to the manager's home.

A manufacturing manager submits a progress report to top management. The production figures and inventory statistics are accurate as far as they go, but omitted from the report in order to meet production objectives, are the final week's rejects and $5,000 in deferred accounts payable for purchased tools and equipment.

A high level executive conducts a lucrative little business on the side unknown to his superiors, using company trucks and personnel as required. Subordinate managers are aware of the action, but keep their mouths shut, applying the philosophy that you have to look out for Number One. And besides, the boss treats them right.

Jim, a young office services supervisor, is bright and ambitious and would be just right for the company's new executive training program. But, reasons his superior, he would be tough to replace. So Jim is bypassed for the program.

If you're an employee in nine out of ten typical U.S. companies, one or more of the above situations will probably strike a responsive note. They are everyday occurrences and, in the eyes of many executives, aren't even necessarily dishonest or socially irresponsible. Some may view these actions as being in the gray area between ethical and unethical managerial conduct. "But what the hell," they're apt to rationalize, "everyone's doing it, and how else can you beat inflation these days?"

Well, everyone *isn't* doing it. In fact, a growing number of executives are feeling and expressing concern over corruption and declining ethical standards throughout society in general and corporate social irresponsibility in particular. Most managers are basically and inherently ethical, given the opportunity and environment in which to be ethical. And many are deeply disturbed, wondering, how did we ever arrive at this state?

This is not to imply that all Japanese executives are lily white. Far from it. But from the reports of most observers and students of Japanese management whom I either interviewed or read, the level of honesty and fair play is higher in Japan today than in most other industrialized nations of the world. Surely part of it must be due to highly ethical corporate policies published and articulated by the majority of large corporations there and the reality that almost all Japanese employees, managers included, feel a strong sense of loyalty toward the organizations that employ them.

Even thoughtful U.S. executives who are not especially perturbed as a matter of conscience are assessing the pros and cons of engaging in transactions involving kickbacks and bribes, intracorporate deceit and shenanagins, and other forms of what the Japanese refer to as *kuroi kiri,* the corruption of businesspeople (literally: "black mist"), and having second thoughts regarding the value of illgotten gains. One of the most convincing reasons of all: Corporate managements in the U.S., Japan, and throughout the world that are most honest and ethical in their dealings with insiders and outsiders alike, are also proving to be the most efficient and profitably effective.

Not only that. More and more corporate managers, prodded both by the stirrings of conscience and the pressures of an increasingly wary and disenchanted public sector, are responding to the reality that the "business of business" does indeed extend well beyond the bottom line. As longtime chief executive officer Irving Shapiro of chemical giant E.I. Dupont de Nemours, bluntly states: "Business is a means to an end. It's not an end in itself. There is not much point in being a businessman if you're not going to accomplish something that benefits society."

A whole refreshingly new concept of managing and relating to people is taking hold in this country. It is leading many executives to re-ponder the ancient axiomatic saws about supervision not being a "popularity contest," and that a manager's aim is not to be loved. To which some executives today must surely be thinking: "Why not?"

Managers like Mssrs. Matsushita and Idemitsu long have been dearly loved by employees and countrymen alike—and both became very rich.

Love and wealth! Surely the best of all possible worlds.

The "Grabbers" and the "Grabbed"

The gathering momentum of the Quality of Work Life (QWL) movement in America, and the growing interest in Japanese management, are eloquent evidence of executive concern about the adverse effects of corporate social irresponsibility on employee morale and productivity. Comments public relations executive and entrepreneur Richard R. Conarroe: "Never before have I seen so many managers in this country so disquieted with regard to deteriorating standards of product and behavioral quality."

One concerned businessman, Albert E. Markarian, president, Kalmar Ad/Marketing, Ft. Lee, New Jersey, a small ad agency, became distressed to the point where he founded The Human Enterprise, a nonprofit public service organization dedicated to the restructuring and upgrading of life in America and took a full page ad in *The Record* (Bergen County, N.J.) to appeal to President Reagan personally following his election. In the ad he frustratedly challenged the president-elect from a "grass roots" perspective to restore and strengthen the ideals that constitute the essence of our Democracy.

In his "I Challenge You!" editorial, he wrote: "There was a time, when we were young, that we looked up to our elders with respect. We believed that the police were honest, that courts and laws were inviolate, that teachers were inspired, doctors were single-mindedly dedicated, clergymen were sacred and the President of the U.S. was hallowed. But as we grew, so did the stolen privileges of self-serving men. Our red, white and blue world became latticed with inequities that were more often than not insidiously devised by the very same figures of authority we so naively respected."

He referred further to our two-party system as an adversarial contest between "The Grabbers" and "The Grabbed," producing "a withdrawn breed of tired Americans . . . the Disillusioned Burned-outs."

Has life in the U.S. come to this pass yet? I think not. But we are clearly heading in this direction unless drastic action to restructure the system under which human beings work together and relate to one another isn't taken in a hurry.

Although statistics are guesstimated at best, and vary sharply from one guesstimator to the next, the total dollar cost of white collar crime, according to the U.S. Chamber of Commerce which has no commercial ax to grind on the subject, is in excess of $44 billion a year—more than 10 times the projected cost of street crime. Estimates on the cost of computer fraud alone, the newest and most sophisticated brand of dishonesty to plague corporations, run as high as $3 billion annually. And if there is one thing on which the experts agree it is that the largest amount of the crime is committed by employees, with corporations the most critically victimized.

What has all of this to do with Japanese management, or at least the more positive aspects of Japanese management? A great deal. To understand what, specifically, the question must be posed relative to employee dishonesty: "What causes workers to steal and otherwise defraud their employer?" A number of conditions are certainly important contributing factors:

- A display of less than unqualifiedly high ethical standards on the part of top or middle management. The corporation where bribes, kickbacks; strong lobbying for antisocietal legislation and causes, products and production processes that pollute the environment, shady transactions and the like are visible to employees, presents an open invitation to dishonesty at all functional levels.

- A climate where a blind management eye is turned to dishonesty and unethical dealings makes it easy for employees to rationalize and justify their own outright crookedness or lack of integrity. Notes management consultant Leonard J. Smith, "I know one company where the purchasing agent who earns $60,000 per year, equals that amount annually in kickbacks. The CEO knows he is stealing but ignores it. 'The guy's a terrific purchasing manager,' he says. 'I could never replace him.' "

- Unfair treatment. The employee who is underpaid, undertrained, underdeveloped, and otherwise unfairly treated, is almost sure to wind up frustrated, bitter, and disloyal to his employer. Such a person has three main options open to him: 1. He can stay on the job, and make the best of the situation. 2. He can shop the market and find a new job. 3. He can stay on the job and, given the chance, make up by means of dishonesty, the balance—or far more than the balance—of what he feels is coming to him. According to Saul D. Astor, president of the New York security firm, Management Safeguards, Inc., the marketplace is flooded with these type 3 individuals, and they rank from the top executive suite on down to the production and clerical workforce.

To get back to the original question: What makes employees dishonest? The answer is clear: Most people are basically and by nature honest and ethical in their dealings. But when exposed to a climate where unfair treatment and shady transactions are tolerated, the temptation to join the parade is often too great for many employees to resist. The ideally managed Japanese company creates an environment where integrity is taken for granted and where fair treatment and positive societal contribution are stated conditions of corporate policy and philosophy. In such a working environment, for the overwhelming number of people, dishonesty would be unthinkable. In too many U.S. companies the dishonest employee is encouraged and respected by his peers as a member of "The Club." In most Japanese companies, the dishonest employee would be shunned as an outcast.

In repeated Japanese surveys, the general public, and students in particular, rank Konosuke Matsushita, who is known as the founder of one of Japan's largest and most powerful corporations, very high on the popularity list. He is revered and loved as a national hero. For an American corporate figure to score high in a popularity contest would be an unheard-of phenomenon. In fact, Harris surveys and other polls indicate that public confidence in American business today is at or close to an all-time low, probably less than 20% positive, and the majority of Americans feel that many large U.S. corporations should be dismantled.

Periodically articles appear in the business and general press bearing such titles as: "Why Business Has a Bad Name," "What Can We Do About the Declining Corporate Image?" and "Why Public Confidence in Business Is Failing."

Unfortunately, there is the substantial weight of innumerable recorded misdeeds to support the low corporate profile. A pure body does not reflect a poor image. And in an adversary management system where the corporation is pitted against labor and the government to the degree that it is in America, it's not surprising that it is—or often seems to be—pitted against the public as well. Thus far too many businessmen appear to function on a profits-at-any-cost basis.

Kuroi Kiri, American Style

If a foreigner, newly arrived in this country, were to tune into a TV news broadcast at 6:00 PM in any major city, he would probably get the impression that the U.S. is overrun with killings, rapes and other violent crime, and that it isn't safe to walk in the streets. By the same token, if the foreigner were to leaf through the pages of any metropolitan newspaper, he would probably conclude that virtually all politicians and most corporate officials were crooks. The conclusions would be all wrong, of course. Most citizens, public servants and businesspeople are honest and ethical. The news hounds sniff where the stink is most pronounced and thus, interesting and provocative. Still, enough foul odors emanate from corporate suites to distress a growing number of concerned and socially responsible businesspeople.

Nationally known security expert Saul D. Astor, whose business it is to help companies prevent employee dishonesty and, where necessary, track down employee thieves, has file cabinets filled with sordid case histories:

Case in Point: The former chief executive officer of Intercontinental Diversified Corporation diverted $3 million to his personal use.

Case in Point: David Begelman of Columbia Pictures embezzled more than $61,000, but corporate officials still wanted to keep him.

Case in Point: The purchasing agent of the investment firm of Drexel Burnham, in many cases received only 70% of the supplies the company paid for, and split the difference with the vendors.

Case in Point: L. Ben Lewis, an operations officer employed by the Wells Fargo Bank, perpetrated, according to Wells Fargo Chairman Richard Cooley, one of the biggest bank frauds in history, a $21 million electronic ripoff.

Case in Point: Stanley Mark Rifkin, a computer consultant for Los Angeles's Security Pacific Bank, got the electronic funds transfer code from the bank's wire transfer room. Later, in a $10 million swindle, he switched money to Swiss accounts and, only because he boasted about his feat, was subsequently apprehended and jailed.

Case in Point: Charles H. Kraft, a former treasurer of Atlantic Richfield Co.'s Anaconda subsidiary, made unauthorized company-backed loans for two companies unrelated to Anaconda, plunging highly ethical ARCO into an agonizing evaluation of its moral and legal obligations regarding the criminal implications of the action.

Case in Point: Charles E. Schwab, chief operating officer of Golden Cycle Corp.'s gold mining division, and a director of the parent company, admitted knowing about the existence of misleading information in the division's annual reports. Asked by *New York* magazine writer Dan Dorfman how he could ethically have permitted his name as a director and officer to be used in reports he knew to be factually incorrect, he replied that it wasn't his job to notify the stockholders, and besides, "I didn't think it was critical."

Stories of this kind, unhappily, could go on ad infinitum—and ad nauseum. A *Time* magazine report titled "Oklahoma" and subtitled "Where the Graft Comes Sweepin' Down the Plain," describes the corruption revealed by a three-year federal investigation of the state's elected officials and says that "graft is routine and nearly ubiquitous in Oklahoma county government, and has added as much as $10 million a year to the state's road-maintenance costs."

An unpleasant aside to the corporate ethics issue involves the disposal of corporate dishonesty disclosures. In the overwhelming majority of cases, apprehended employee criminals are fired, and that's it. Wherever possible, restitution is made by the caught crook, usually over a period of time. But he is almost always free to reenter the job market, find other employment, and far too often begins stealing all over again. States Denver District Attorney Dale Tooley: "Businesses feel they have no duty to report crime. It's a real problem."

Employee crooks aren't prosecuted as a rule for a number of reasons. First, charging and prosecuting take time,

time busy executives are unwilling to spend. Second, employee rights and privacy legislation is tough and complex; an employer must proceed cautiously in following a case through the courts. Most companies take the simplest and most painless way out: they merely get rid of the crook. Third, and probably most important, corporate executives wince at the idea of the public in general and stockholders in particular receiving the news that dishonesty exists within the organization on the one hand and, on the other, that management controls were sufficiently lax to permit the company to be taken.

Mounting Pressures

Employee dishonesty is of special concern here chiefly because its primary cause is due to the improper treatment of personnel, whether improper because of the work environment, long entrenched and outmoded policies, or questionable management scruples. The unfair and/or insensitive treatment of workers is perhaps the most pervasive and antiproductive form of social irresponsibility practiced by corporations in this country and throughout the world and, from all indications, to a lesser degree in Japan. Again, the growing QWL movement and, specifically, the pressures imposed by the unions, constitute proof that the nation's workforce is in a state of rebellion with regard to the upgrading of the work environment. Nor do working conditions constitute the only form of social pressures exerted against corporations today.

It is no news to anyone that we are a society torn by crises ranging from drugs, crime, and racism to substandard housing, unemployment, and pollution. Should business share in the responsibility for these conditions? It is a question that triggers a fair amount of executive soul searching these days.

Consider the facts of the case. Business is the nation's number one energy consumer, the biggest generator of product and production waste, and thus the nation's foremost polluter. Business, through its state and federal "lobbies" and deals, sets national standards of integrity that in some cases might be kindly termed "shady." Business, because of marginal employment practices in some sectors, helps to shape adversely employee work and performance attitudes and generates rancor and bitterness among minority groups. By virtue of its products, methods of production, and marketing requirements, business spawns congestion, overtaxes transportation, and in some cases creates slums.

Any thoughtful student of business society will tell you that corporate actions and policies, directly or indirectly, have an impact on the community, influencing standards and life-styles.

Of course, the business of business is earnings. But when the conduct of business hurts people, over the long pull it's unprofitable to both business and people. The businessperson who clings to the outmoded notion that the business of business is business alone, according to the Japanese managerial philosophy of the nation's Matsushita-type managers, has no business being in business.

The pressures for corporate social responsibility are mounting faster today than the shroud of haze over polluted cities. Scores of consumer groups, religious groups, labor groups, environmental groups, ethnic groups, women's groups, senior citizens' groups, and government agencies are monitoring the system with unprecedented fervor despite Administration efforts to cut government spending.

Angry and resolute, they operate under the not-unreasonable premise that since corporate enterprise contributes a massive portion of pollution, prejudice, and endangerment to society, it should participate in attempts at social improvement and restructuring—with corporate as well as social survival in mind. What the new militants want ranges from equality, opportunity and human dignity in the workplace, and a safe, clean environment to better health care, crime control, transportation, education and housing. And now, in addition, we have the fierce competition from Japan and other countries to contend with, so that not only our life style but our whole economy hangs in the balance.

Today, we are witnessing dramatically effective organization-planned pressures being applied, which run the gamut from picketing, slowdowns, and strikes to corporate profile smears, annual meeting disruption, "responsible investor" action, student and consumer boycotts and disenfranchisements, and class action suits.

And, as one manager expressed to me recently, "We sure as hell better respond to it!"

The Growing Response. More and more corporate managements are responding to the pressures and, as is always the case, the large, progressive, responsibility-sensitive companies are leading the way. One indication, as mentioned, is the expanding QWL movement. Another is the crush of literature on Japanese management and the flood of executive visitors from industry, government, the unions and academia to Japan. A third is the increasing number of corporations, and some of these will be covered in a subsequent chapter, that are formulating formalized policies with regard to the organization's social responsibility, and issuing CEO-directed statements clarifying and spelling out corporate philosophies of management.

A fourth indication of response to societal pressures is the growing number of investigations and surveys being conducted in large corporations in an effort to determine how middle and high level managers perceive the company's societal performance and responsibilities in general, and their own in particular. As early as 1977, for example, Pitney-Bowes Inc., a leader in the national drive for the upgrading of corporate ethics, sponsored a management seminar on moral development at its Stamford, Conn., headquarters following a poll in which most managers declared belief that their peers would not refuse orders to market off-standard and possibly dangerous products. The response was anonymous, and though most respondents indicated they themselves would reject such orders, they felt young managers would, like members of Nixon's reelection committee, go along with their superior out of feelings of loyalty.

Like Uniroyal Inc. in a similar poll, Pitney-Bowes managers overwhelmingly favored a code of ethics for business and the teaching of ethics in business schools. In recent years more and more corporations are following suit both in conducting probes into the ethical behavior and perceptions of right and wrong within the organization, and the publication of ethical codes applicable to the company. In addition, courses dealing with the social responsibilities of business have been appearing in the curricula catalogs of an increasing number of colleges around the country.

States educator and social reformer David F. Linowes, formerly chairman and chief executive officer of Mickleberry Corporation, in his book, *The Corporate Conscience* (Hawthorn Publishing Co.): "An awareness of corporate social responsibility is taking hold. Whether this new awareness is brought about by government pressures, rising social and educational standards of the general public, or the enlightened self-interest of business itself is not important. What is important is that another objective has been added to the profit-making objectives of business. The corporation views the world differently now and it relates to others differently; it has taken on a new form under the old name."

One reason progress toward this end has been quicker and more pervasive in Japan than the U.S. is the culture-based personalization of the Japanese workplace in contrast to the growing depersonalization—and dehumanization—of the American workplace in recent years. For too many managers the corporation serves as a buffer between one's individual stirrings of conscience and the societal responsibility.

Obligations are directed not to human beings but to the legal entity to which no conscience can be attributed. In the process it is all too easy to lose sight of the ancient truism that the corporation is composed of people, and that when held up against people the legal entity and inanimate structure possess little significance. As Mr. Linowes points out, if a corporate conscience does indeed exist, it must mirror the individual consciences of every person the organization employs.

Notes American Management Association president, James L. Hayes: "In the 19th century, Henry David Thoreau, the New England naturalist-philosopher, posed the question: 'Did you ever expect a corporation to have a conscience when it has no soul to be damned and no body to be kicked?'"

Mr. Hayes himself answers the question: "The corporate conscience is embodied in the stockholders, the board of directors, the managers, and the employees. It may be students, faculty, and administration. Or it can be voters, elected officials, and government managers. Each person in these groups has a conscience and to some degree becomes part of the organization conscience—and thus shares the responsibilities attached to it."

In accepting, initiating, and living this philosophy of management, a growing number of increasingly animate corporations are responding to societal pressures, re-personalizing the organization and its activities and, in the process, duplicating the Japanese style of management with its results-proven effectiveness.

The Dimensions of Corporate Social Responsibility

Tracking the growth and development of Matsushita Electric Co., and the management philosophies of its founder brings to light the multifaceted dimensions of corporate social responsibility. Briefly, they break down as follows:

RESPONSIBILITIES

To Employees

Provide maximum financial security possible. Train and develop employees at all levels in an effort to uncover and make the best use of their talents and capabilities. Manage each employee as a useful individual worthy of trust and respect. Employ job rotation and whatever other strategies are available to make the work as interesting and meaningful as possible. Bend over backwards to adhere to employee privacy laws. Establish a safe and comfortable working environment. Develop a fair compensation and wage benefits program. Do your best to establish and sustain harmonious labor relations. Consider individual as well as company needs in setting up a transfer policy.

To Executives

Promote and encourage honest and ethical behavior. Create and maintain a corporate work environment where profitable performance is stressed but not at the sacrifice of highmind-

IRRESPONSIBILITIES

To Employees

Ordering an avoidable layoff. Treating an employee as "indispensable" and locking him into a job he does well instead of creating opportunities for advancement and growth. Directing and monitoring the work of an employee to the point where he is no longer able to think for himself. Assigning mindlessly repetitive tasks to individuals on a day-to-day basis with no thought or concern about the psychological impact. Creating job and performance pressures so that the pressured employee feels threatened and insecure; pitting one employee against another with this objective in mind. Failing to give individuals the credit, recognition and reward they deserve.

To Executives

Turning a blind eye to kickbacks and bribes for the purpose of increasing profits. Putting executives under such pressure to "produce" that they are tempted to engage in unfair or dis-

RESPONSIBILITIES

ed ethics and integrity. Sustain an environment where advancement is based solely on merit, not on backstabbing and political influence.

To Customers

Maintain the highest possible level of quality in providing products and service. Keep the customer's problems and needs in mind at all times, and give him as much assistance as possible in helping to achieve his objectives. Resolve never to make a profit at the customer's expense.

To Suppliers

Make sure that anyone who counts you as a customer is given the opportunity to make a fair profit on the transaction, just as you expect to make a fair profit on the merchandise or service you sell. Make every reasonable and feasible effort to help the supplier serve your account as productively as possible.

IRRESPONSIBILITIES

honest practices in order to meet unrealistic quotas and goals. Playing favorites in assigning choice projects and promotions instead of selecting the best qualified individual.

To Customers

Exerting pressure on a customer to buy a product he doesn't want, or more of a product than he needs, because he is over-dependent on you as a supplier. Unloading second rate quality merchandise on a customer. Overcharging a customer because he's in a spot and needs the goods in a hurry.

To Suppliers

Exerting pressure for price cuts when you know the supplier is dependent on your business, to the point where doing business with you is no longer profitable. Misrepresenting competitive prices to a sales rep to encourage him to undercut the competition. Expecting the supplier to give kickbacks or gifts in return for your business.

RESPONSIBILITIES

To Competitors

Conduct business in an ethically competitive manner, earning customer orders and loyalty as a result of high quality and innovative ideas. Keep abreast of competitive innovations and strategies in a fair and ethical way. Cooperate with competitors in attempting to upgrade the ethical tactics and standards of your industry.

To the Public

Produce products and services that are beneficial to users. Continually seek facilities and processing improvements to minimize adverse effects of production on the ecology. Deal only with individuals and organizations that are honest and socially responsible. Conduct research on an ongoing basis to upgrade product safety. Cooperate to the maximum extent possible with community interests and needs in conducting your business; in short, be a good neighbor. Engage in fair employment practices

IRRESPONSIBILITIES

To Competitors

Poormouthing competitors and/or spreading false information. Employing unethical or illegal methods to obtain competitive intelligence. Driving competitive prices down below the fair profit line through the use of cutthroat pricing policies. Raiding competitive companies in order to induce employees so hired to divulge company secrets.

To the Public

Excessive packaging that adds to environmental pollution. Tolerating the existence of avoidable air polluting emissions. Dumping toxic or otherwise dangerous substances in such a way as to cause air or waterway pollution. Paying money to government officials, directly or indirectly, for legislative favors rendered. Manufacturing and marketing unsafe or harmful products such as flammable clothing and drugs with improperly minimized dangerous side effects. Paying bribes to government

RESPONSIBILITIES	IRRESPONSIBILITIES
in both hiring and internal procedures. Monitor activities continuously to make sure they meet published and publicized corporate social responsibility standards. Make a top management commitment to assess and change corporate policy, where appropriate, on the basis of information received. Establish an honest and ethical advertising policy. Make it clear to all personnel that prejudice against minority groups or individuals will not be tolerated. Deal honestly and ethically with representatives of government. Insist upon honest and ethical reporting of corporate performance.	officials, foreign or domestic, in an effort to boost sales. Product misrepresentation through advertising. Dealing with repressive governments. Turning a blind eye to dishonest corporate practices because of the income they produce. Corporate lobbying for legislation with adverse social consequences. Lowering product quality standards below acceptable levels by using cheaper materials or production procedures. Misrepresenting corporate financial performance and prospects to the investment community.

The Final Dimension

The corporation that prospers and grows because of public acceptance of its products or services has an added responsibility to society: contribution to the betterment of life in the nation and community by means of corporate philanthropy. Konosuke Matsushita views "productive and progressive activity" as a "law of nature and society." Indeed, beneficence toward the body of people responsible for one's success and prosperity is a very natural response. Nowhere has this response been more aptly exemplified than in the practices and pursuits of Matsushita Electric, the company, and Konosuke Matsushita, the man. The long-held corporate credo reflects the deeply felt views of the founder:

"Through our industrial activities, we strive to foster progress, to promote the general welfare of society and to devote ourselves to furthering the development of world culture."

Matsushita, the man, has gone a step beyond this credo and, in so doing, has gone a step beyond the bottom line. A fabulously wealthy man by virtue of his organization's growth and prosperity, he has long felt personally obligated to take whatever action he can to repay society for the faith and trust it has invested in him. With this and other searching thoughts in mind, he founded the PHP Institute.

The Payoff—the Payout. Mr. Matsushita strongly believes in the balancing forces of nature. Despite his limited formal education and humble beginnings, he was rewarded for his vision and enterprise with status and riches on the one hand, the reverence and esteem of his countrymen on the other. The payoff was handsome. In balance, it seemed only natural in Mr. Matsushita's view to make the payout significant.

The PHP Institute is a natural byproduct of Mr. Matsushita's thoughts and experience. Just after World War II, the cities of Japan were in ruin. Thousands of people were without adequate shelter. Food was scarce. A restructured society was critically needed, but the rebuilding effort didn't go smoothly. Violence was rampant, the black market thrived, moral decline was apparent. With industrial growth and development vital, management and labor were in a state of perpetual conflict.

Mr. Matsushita wrote of that period: "The more earnestly you worked, the greater loss you would suffer. The more products a company manufactured, the greater its loss would be. We lived in a world where honesty didn't pay." He was deeply disturbed by this state of affairs and particularly by what he refers to as "social unreasonableness" which was, in his view, contrary to the "true and natural picture of man."

A fervent advocate of *Shuchi* (acquiring "the combined knowledge of man"), Mr. Matsushita confided his thoughts and anxieties to a diversity of individuals ranging from businessmen and judges to university professors and Buddhist priests. What evolved was the PHP Institute, founded by Konosuke Matsushita on November 3, 1946.

PHP stands for Peace, Happiness and Prosperity, in the broadest sense of these words. As Mr. Matsushita defines them:

> PEACE—True peace implies something more than the absence of war. It involves the state of the mind. True peace is established only when people can understand and help each other and share their wisdom and power. When this comes to pass, nations and people all over the world will be harmoniously and mutually prosperous.
>
> HAPPINESS—For genuine happiness to exist, three conditions must be met. First, the individual must feel subjectively happy, believe that he himself is indispensable to the achievement of happiness. Second, he must realize that his own happiness is dependent on the happiness of others, that he cannot achieve genuine happiness at the expense of his fellow man. Third, his state of happiness must be acceptable and deserving in the eyes of society.
>
> PROSPERITY—Prosperity includes not only material wealth, but spiritual riches as well. Desirable prosperity implies a good balance and harmony between the material and spiritual endowments.

The PHP Institute, says Mr. Matsushita, is dedicated to the achievement of Peace, Happiness and Prosperity for all of mankind by means of the principles and guidelines promulgated and espoused in the above definitions.

The PHP Institute sponsors the organization of "friendship associations" throughout all of Japan. The purpose is to create a forum for people of all ages and backgrounds, a congenial atmosphere where members can meet and mix, attend seminars, and exchange views of the deeper and more profound meanings of life. Close to 10,000 people participate in these activities, often forming sub-groups of their own. Busloads of people who sympathize with PHP ideas, attend meetings, rallies and seminars; their objective is self-improvement and increased self-esteem.

Discussing the PHP movement, Mr. Matsushita once explained to a *Life* magazine writer: "Life is like music, but no one really knows the score for a perfect life. We strike notes at random and the music is harsh. We must learn how to play the music, how to live our lives beautifully."

PHP can't provide all the answers. But it helps.

PHP Magazine. Out of the PHP movement a Japanese magazine bearing its name was formed in 1947. With a readership of 1.5 million, it has grown to be Japan's biggest circulating monthly magazine. The English version of PHP which was started in 1970 features articles by, and interviews with, world renowned philosophers, scholars and businesspeople from a diversity of nations and cultures.

Captioned "A Forum for a Better World," PHP ("Where East Meets West") features think pieces with such titles as "A New Vision for Mankind," "The Spirit of Coexistence," "Man's Psychological Quest for Immortality," and "Putting Our Principles into Practice." Interviewees run the gamut from leading bankers and educators to Japan's Buddha-like prime minister, Zenko Suzuki. Not surprisingly Mr. Matsushita, his age notwithstanding (88), is a regular contributor.

PHP is published in Spanish as well as Japanese and English. The magazine is, perhaps, the classic example of how a selflessly devoted effort to help mankind so often reaps prosperity (in the material as well as spiritual sense) as a by-product.

The Matsushita School. In 1980 Kappei Morishita, then 23, answered an ad in a Japanese newspaper, sent a resume and his college transcripts as required, took a gruelling examination, and was selected along with 22 others from approximately one thousand applicants for enrollment at the Matsushita School. This in itself was quite unusual. Having graduated from college in 1979, Kappei Morishita already had a year's experience working for a Japanese firm. In Japan, employees are rarely terminated, and as rarely resign. So in this case a special dispensation was necessary. After extensive discussion with the president and executives of his company, the young man left to begin a new challenge. Even more surprising, from a Western perspective, is the fact that under his name on his business card (at age 24) appears the title of Assistant Vice President.

What prompted Mr. Morishita to answer that ad? He felt he would like to continue his studies after graduation from the university. But in Japan only scholars go on to graduate school as a rule. Kappei Morishita still isn't sure what direction he would like his career to take, but he doesn't plan to be a lifelong scholar. In a personal interview with Mr. Matsushita, he confided his feelings and interests, expressed a fascination with America, received his sponsor's blessing and today, as part of his advanced training is ensconced in a spacious office at the PHP Institute's U.S. headquarters in Secaucus, New Jersey, where he has a secretary and reports to Mitsumasa Aoyama, who is president of PHP Institute of America, Inc. Despite the status and importance of his job, the first characteristic one observes in speaking with this young man is his Japanese inbred humility.

This author may not be around to witness the event, but it would be a fairly safe bet to assume that in one capacity or another Kappei Morishita will be a "leader of the 21st century." It is with precisely this objective in mind that Mr. Matsushita opened and generously endowed the Matsushita School of Government and Management, in April 1980 in the seaside city of Chigasaki, 30 miles southwest of Tokyo. Unlike the U.S. which each year turns out thousands of MBAs and Ph.Ds for eventual infiltration into business and government, Japan has very few executives with advanced degrees in positions of leadership.

Mr. Matsushita who, at the age of 9, was compelled by family poverty to leave school for apprenticeship to a hibachi store, in his mid-eighties worried that with Japan coming into its own as a world industrial leader, the nation was short of high level managers as educationally advantaged as those in the U.S. and other developed Western countries. With this concern in mind, the societally sensitive billionaire drew approximately $30 million from his personal reserves to help build the school, staff it with a top rated faculty, and prepare for the influx of candidates. Each year anywhere from 15 to 30 applicants are selected for admission out of the thousand or so who apply.

In the school's inaugural address Mr. Matsushita is quoted in *Time* as saying, "I was determined to open this school even if there were but one applicant."

The lucky candidates who make the grade are given free tuition, full board, and a $600-a-month stipend. Among guest lecturers at the Matsushita School are such names as economist John Kenneth Galbraith, Tea Ceremonies Master Soshitsu Sen, and Masaru Ibuka, founder of Matsushita Electronics Co.'s prime competitor, Sony Corporation. The school's officers include some of Japan's foremost businessmen and educators, in addition to a noted union leader, critic, economist, news commentator and novelist. Mr. Matsushita serves as Director and Executive Advisor.

The tycoon, who goes in for publicized credos, has one for the school as well: "With untrapped mind, we firmly dedicate ourselves to the gathering of wisdom; to seeking out the intrinsic nature of reality through independent, self-fulfilling study; and to searching anew each day for the path which will lead us to growth and prosperity."

It is clear that in Mr. Matsushita's view one path headed in this direction is that of corporate social responsibility. It is worth repeating that the ultimate ideal in management and enterprise is the organization wherein human decency and concern for one's fellowman combine to produce profits, work fulfillment and growth. For therein, as Konosuke Matsushita's lifetime demonstrates, lies the real bottom line.

9.

PERSPECTIVE

> *Expanding business activities must include the development of the enterprise; through enterprise activities, society also should prosper.*
> —*Konosuke Matsushita*

Throughout the decades of his leadership, one of the chief concerns of Matsushita Electric Co.'s founder was to establish a philosophy and system of management that would permit his organization to continue to function smoothly and profitably without him. His son and successor, Masaharu Matsushita, observes: "By the time the second generation of leadership comes in, a company should have consolidated corporate direction that is not changeable with presidents."

Sociologists have been writing and talking for some years now about the "instant gratification" syndrome in the U.S. We want instant results, instant performance, instant success. Our impatience is responsible in part at least for the bottom line preoccupation of so many corporate managements, and is a major factor in the emerging world leadership of Japanese enterprise.

Dr. Ezra F. Vogel sums it up aptly in his book, "Japan As Number 1," when he writes: "The Japanese firm is less interested in short-term profits and more concerned with the long run. Executives may disparage their success in planning and forecasting, but they continue their best efforts and, when appropriate, boldly sacrifice profits for several years to build the groundwork for later success. They take care in cultivating good relations with institutions that might potentially be useful. They provide extensive training for personnel in skills that might be needed in the future. They invest in technology at seemingly high prices if it might later pay off. They invest heavily in plant modernization even when present plants meet immediate demands. As products become competitive, they conduct extensive preparatory work to lay a solid grounding for markets."

Innumerable sad tales could be related of once successful, and even prosperous, companies that lost ground to competitors or went under because their managements lacked the perspective to project beyond the current period's or current year's earnings statement. Company A cut back on advertising expenditures to make the immediate profit picture look better. Company B decided to live with the inefficient old equipment another year or two. Company C reduced its investment in research and technology. Company D cut corners on its employee training and development programs. Company E failed to expand its product lines, settling for the presumably safer and less costly status quo.

In an alarming number of such cases the self-defeating rationale tracks back to domineering shareholders more concerned with today's earnings than tomorrow's structural strength. Why not? If fortunes turn down, they can simply pull out. The typical Japanese manager, however politely he may mask his true sentiments, feels little sympathy for the American executive who yields to stockholder pressure and sacrifices long-term organizational soundness to short-term profits.

Notes one Japanese executive employed by his Osaka-based company's U.S. division, "Too often the American manager's decision is influenced by statistical data registered in the last computer printout, whereas the Japanese-trained manager's decision is involved with the people who work and deal with the company, and what will be best for them over the long term. And for society as well."

Perspective on Tomorrow

Thoughtful Japan watchers largely agree that American profit projections must be drastically altered if the U.S. is to compete successfully with Japanese enterprise and regain economic world leadership, or even maintain a foremost position.

The American short-term perspective is partially built into the system, partially deepset through habit and custom, partially persistent because it is the easiest way to run a business. One harsh critic of myopic bottom-line preoccupation is Massachusetts Institute of Technology Economics and Management Professor Lester C. Thurow who writes: "A mental midget can tell whether top management deserves a bonus based on current profits. It is much harder to figure out whether top management has positioned the company well for the long haul. To (invest in) researching, designing, and building the products that will be needed in 10 years from now is to take risks. Current American management is known only for its risk aversion."

He points out further that a major pitfall of tunnel vision is the rewarding of managers who chalk up good current "performance" despite the fact that they may have undermined long-term strength and growth in the process. At the same time, managers with a healthy perspective on tomorrow are apt to be penalized for their farsightedness because their actions don't reflect well on the current earnings statement.

Japanese industry suffers from no such hindering obstacle. The typical Nipponese company positions itself for at least one decade, and often two decades, into the future. Concentrating on solidly cemented-in building blocks, the top management team is not after a quick profit payoff. The Japanese by their nature, upbringing and religious convictions tend to believe with 18th century author Josiah Holland that "there is no great achievement that is not the result of patient working and waiting."

In quest of no instant killing, the Japanese manager is willing to settle for less today—for his organization and himself—in order to ensure security and growth for tomorrow. States a survey conducted by *World Business Weekly:* "Japanese acceptance of low profitability is reflected in the ratio of net after tax income to gross sales. This was 2.4% for a selected group of foreign corporations manufacturing in Japan in 1979, against an average 1.6% for all Japanese corporations. Of 3,500 foreign companies established in Japan since 1950, 400 have withdrawn because of the low rate of return."

Management consultant Leonard J. Smith believes with other experts that the altering of U.S. profit perspectives will be one of the most tricky and difficult conversions to make. "For one thing," he says, "we have the critical difference in capital financing with which to contend. Approximately 16 percent of Japan's needs are fulfilled through the sale of stock as opposed to 50 percent or more of U.S. capital needs. So we'll have to devise ways to keep managers, and not stockholders, running the company. On top of that, the Japanese government encourages the banks responsible for most of the financing to work for industrial development; the Japanese executive is convinced that this is good not only for the corporation and community, but for the bank as well. It ensures a lasting high quality of clients, with a shared self-interest beneficial to all."

The icing on the capital formation cake is that if a client runs into difficulty it can, with his banker's cooperation, turn to the Bank of Japan for assistance.

The long-term perspective is clearly conducive to the establishment and fulfillment of long-term objectives. Stanford University Professor Steven C. Wheelwright cites a classic example in a directive handed down by the executive vice president of Tokyo Sanyo Electric Co. in 1975. The goals as set forth in his statement included the standardization of parts and components in marketing and engineering, a drastic increase in the frequency of vendor deliveries, reduced setup and changeover times, reduced warehouse space needs and inventory levels.

Five years later, the results reflected management determination—and singleminded cooperation—in responding to the directive. The 1980 warehouse space requirement was 20,000 square feet against 80,000 in 1975. Raw and in-process inventory levels were cut from 10 days to 1.5 days. Lot sizes were chopped from two to three days to one day. Production quantities were boosted from 100 index units in 1975 to 300 index units in 1980.

No one would pretend that these results were easy to attain. But spared the distraction and preoccupation with current profit pressures, the full managerial focus on long-term profit improvement was assured, as was the unified action so important to the fulfillment of difficult goals.

Leadership Grooming

A critical problem triggered by U.S. transience is that, even assuming strong current corporate leadership, one can never be certain who tomorrow's leaders will be and, equally important, the degree to which today's style of leadership will be altered 10 or 12 years down the road. Typically, a handful of high level managers, usually senior vice presidents, work closely with the chief executive. Normally it is taken for granted that when the top man retires, is fired, or resigns to take a job elsewhere, one of this group will be tapped to take over the reins. As often as not, when this transition takes place, one or more disappointed key people desert the company for what they hope will be greener pastures elsewhere. What follows is a "reorganization" which may take years to effect with the organization in a weakened and vulnerable position until the new chief and new structure are solidly grounded, after which the process is apt to repeat itself.

Japanese companies are rarely subjected to competitive onslaughts on the heels of corporate reorganization and key personnel changes. Traditional lifelong employment shapes managerial attitudes and perspectives in directions conducive to long-term corporate health. Conversely, promotions are almost invariably made from within or by means of transfer from an affiliate. Thus it is in the company's best interests to invest heavily in management development programs on an ongoing basis. It usually goes without saying that today's middle manager will be tomorrow's senior executive. Unlike the U.S. experience where managers are often groomed for the competition, the Japanese company has maximum assurance that its training and development investment will pay off in the future.

American corporate history is replete with woeful tales of corporate giants subjected to troubled times as a result of inadequate succession planning. It happened in the early days of Ford Motor Co. when Henry the First turned over the presidency to son Edsel in 1919. From then until Edsel's death in 1943, Ford senior held no official corporate title. But no one doubted who was running the company—and running it down.

Similarly, in the well-publicized fiasco at Genesco, aging W. Maxey Jarman, presumably retired, continued riding herd over his designated successor, son Franklin M., while profits rode steadily downward.

Such was also the case of Rockwell Manufacturing, where 83-year-old Colonel Willard F. Rockwell—though inactive in the company for more than 10 years—forced the president to resign.

For more of the same, corporate history buffs might dig into the files of Norton Simon, Texaco, United Air Lines, Consolidated Foods, and scores of other major corporations. In government it happened when Franklin Delano Roosevelt decided to run for a fourth term. More recently, in a letter to constituents, Wisconsin Democratic incumbent Lee Aspin described House Speaker Tip O'Neill as "a good friend of mine. He garnered a reputation as one of the strongest Speakers in our history. But now, I regret to say, Tip is reeling on the ropes. . . he's in a fog. . . he's not part of what's happening, and has no idea where to go."

Japanese corporate leaders usually have a fixed idea where to go and, based on the mounting evidence, a darned good one at that. The importance of this edge is hard to overstate as any outspoken middle manager at RCA Corp. would be quick to attest. Notes a *Business Week* editor: "In the past six years, the diversified broadcasting and electronics giant (1980 sales: $8 billion) has stumbled from one management fiasco to the next. These included: the awkward ousting of the son of the company's founder from his job as chairman; the dumping of his successor for failing to file his income taxes; the dismissal of a company president after only six months on the job; the firing of a network chairman who publicly refused to quit." And capping all of this was the departure in July 1981 of the man who presided over much of the pandemonium, RCA Chairman Edgar Griffiths. It's little wonder corporations like RCA are losing ground steadily to the well coordinated, solidly manned, and closely integrated electronic giants from Japan.

Hopefully, observes consultant Leonard J. Smith, a growing number of U.S. managements seem to be getting the message. "Long-term survival and growth are often dependent on carefully planned built-in succession. General Mills, to cite one example, has initiated an entrepreneurial training program that focuses on succession planning and the delegation of authority. A host of other companies are following suit."

The most difficult situation of all is the operation where an executive, usually an outsider, is brought in to replace the longstanding domineering chief of a big corporation. Classic examples include Lee Iacocca's head-on collision and subsequent ouster of Ford, Lyman C. Hamilton Jr.'s run-in with Harold S. Geneen at ITT, and Arthur Taylor's clash with William S. Paley at CBS Inc.

Where built-in succession succeeds it can make a world of difference from a competitive standpoint. Edward W. Carter, for example, who patiently nurtured Broadway Hale Stores into America's seventh largest department store chain, spent years grooming Philip M. Hawley as his successor and changed the corporate title to include his name when Hawley finally took over the helm. Continuity was the key, so that when the successor stepped in no confusion or trauma resulted despite differences in the two men's personalities. "The important thing," says Smith, "is that no one ever doubted who was in charge or questioned where the organization was headed."

Under the new chief executive officer's leadership, Carter Hawley Hale (CHH) has moved from seventh place to fourth nationwide in the department store industry.

It is unfortunate that in America this is the exceptional case. In Japan, it appears to be standard operating procedure.

The Key

"Technology," declares Westinghouse Corp., "is the key to the world marketplace. If we want to maintain America's competitive edge (assuming that it still exists), we must make better use of present technologies, and encourage new ones."

In an extensive institutional ad the company deplores the nation's dwindling world market share over the past 20 years.

("Not only have they—foreign manufacturers—captured part of what had been our share of the world market, but they are now successfully penetrating our own domestic markets.")

What happened? The ad goes on to answer this question: "A look at a few statistics helps reveal some of the reasons for our reversals. Take patents. The number of domestic patent applications by Americans has been flat for several years. In contrast, the number of those filed here by foreign countries has been rising every year. In 1978, almost 37 percent of the patents granted went to foreign applicants. Or take the percentage of our Gross National Product going into industrial R&D. Over the past two decades, it has dropped precipitously."

This is no surprise to students of business familiar with what is sometimes aptly referred to as the "Wall Street mentality" and the pressures it exerts on harassed CEOs. Short-term planning and projections imply the setting of short-term growth and profit objectives. This inhibits the launching of such new technology as Computer-Aided Engineering and Manufacturing (CAE and CAM) which often takes two or more years to pay off. The Japanese industrials, assisted and encouraged by Japan's Ministry of International Trade and Industry (MITI), are going full speed forward with advanced technological innovations and so can look ahead in the future to continuously upgraded product improvement and engineering productivity. If the American industrial maintains the status quo while the competing Japanese industrial thrusts steadily and deliberately ahead, it requires no crystal ball to determine what the ultimate outcome will be.

"Critically needed in this country," says Leonard J. Smith, "are top management teams sufficiently strong willed and resolute to resist the pressures that inhibit advanced technologies with long payoff dates. The U.S. is still technologically superior to any nation in the world, and the capability of applying the technology advantageously exists. But the

Japanese are masters of duplication and adaptation. As a host of rapidly growing industrials in Japan have made clear, one does not have to be an originator to attain market domination.

An increasing body of evidence indicates that the most successful and best managed U.S. companies—the survivors and thrivers— are the ones piloted by determined and courageous chief executives who make it known to employees and the public in general and stockholders in particular that corporate sights are set squarely on long-term objectives and growth. Quick kill advocates are advised to invest their money elsewhere.

Crying All the Way to the Bank. A primary MITI objective is to scout the world and bring back to Japan exploitable engineering, manufacturing and marketing innovations whenever and wherever they can be garnered. Japanese intelligence gatherers have achieved remarkable success at this endeavor and have cashed in on it handsomely. In the process the Japanese have been pegged "copiers" rather than innovators or originators, charged with a lack of creativity.

Two comments regarding this indictment: One need only drive a Japanese car to enjoy a host of innovations not available in most American cars, or review dozens of breakthrough products and product features in the lines of such companies as Toshiba, Seiko or Matsushita Electric Co. to question the validity of this charge. Comment number two is, if it is true, so what?

I discussed this subject recently with a Japanese manager who prefers to remain anonymous. He sadly and smilingly conceded, "Oh yes, we Japanese are not nearly as creative as you Americans." He didn't say it in so many words, but the implication was clear that he and his countrymen were "crying all the way to the bank."

Gilt edged crocodile tears? It would appear so. The conclusion is obvious. U.S. managers who feel secure in the conviction that ultimately "good old American ingenuity" and traditional creative superiority will prevail may be deluding themselves. All it takes is simple arithmetic to prove this point. U.S. Company A, having spent a million dollars to research and develop a new product, must reflect that investment in its selling price to come up with a fair and reasonable profit. Japanese Company B, having spent $50,000 to investigate and implement the innovation U.S. Company A invested a million dollars to develop, can sell the product for much less and still make a fair profit.

This may be an oversimplification but, for one thing, each day new evidence surfaces to indicate that the socalled technology gap between the U.S. and Japan is narrowing. And however wide the remaining gap may be, it doesn't seem to be all that important from the standpoint of market penetration and corporate growth. Of far greater significance is the overall perspective of government and industry leaders with regard to the future.

During the past two decades or so the Japanese simply adapted those technological advances they found useful and disregarded the balance. The question is, can they continue going this route? Notes the *World Business Weekly* Japan survey in response: "Now that the gap has been closed, a surprising number of Japanese businessmen and bureaucrats are asking how the country's engineers and scientists will stack up if they have to make research advances themselves. It is assumed that the technological challenge being mounted in the U.S. could lead to radical changes in computer architecture, and this could leave the Japanese industry with 'assets' that have suddenly become 'old'."

Will this be a problem for Japanese industry? Perhaps. But again the key focus must be on perspective. Taking the long range approach it is safe to bet that if the leaders of MITI and industry in Japan view the need for creative technology as one that warrants a major investment of money, manpower and time, the investment will be made. And it will be made regardless of the adverse effect it may have on the latest quarterly earnings statement.

Examples of Japanese resolve along these lines are already well past the drawing stage. One MITI objective, the Japan survey points out, is the development of a Super Computer for scientific and technical work 1,000 times faster than computers in use today. Involved in this project are the nation's leading computer makers. MITI's Sozaburo Okamatsu predicts that the Super Computer when operational will achieve much higher resolution in satellite photography, leading to more accurate weather forecasting. It will also be helpful in the design of nuclear reactors, and will enable new aircraft and space vehicle development without the use of wind tunnels.

Also in the works is the design of a "fifth-generation computer" with a projected 10 year lead time for the perfection of the system's integrated circuits. Unlike existing circuits that are silicon-based, the new technology is expected to result in speeds 50 times faster than existing high speed computers. Already involved in this MITI-sponsored endeavor are researchers from the U.S. and other foreign companies with the ultimate goal of a total system including both hardware and software in mind. "The government," states the Japan survey, "will pay for R&D, possibly up to 100% of costs, but regards this expense as more of a loan than a subsidy. Firms that profitably market products based on the research will be expected to repay the government."

As recently as a decade ago, the likelihood of a technological project of this magnitude, and in the computer field no less, being initiated by a Japanese and not an American sponsor, would have seemed rather remote to most industry watchers. At the rate things are going, says one, a decade or so from today the technological gap will still exist. But it may be up to the Americans to make the narrowing effort.

Dropouts. A growing number of American companies appear to be getting the message that an over-preoccupation with current earnings almost invariably backfires. Two years ago a perceptive product manager employed by a nationally known electronics manufacturer prepared a 12-page report for his boss, the company's senior manufacturing vice president, predicting the vast potential of the personal computer market for big company executives and professionals. He supported his proposal with persuasive facts and figures that cited the number of potential customers and applications involved. These failed to impress his nearsighted superior who had been brainwashed into a myopic hard focus on near-term profits. When he saw the size and scope of the investment required to compete in this field, a natural offshoot of existing home and small business products, his verdict was that the idea wasn't even worth exploring further.

The frustrated manager took his report to a competitor and was immediately hired, his proposed plan initiated. Today both the manager and his plan are thriving. His former employer recently entered the fray, investing in a personal computer development and marketing program similar to the one outlined two years earlier. The result: a case of too little too late. To catch up with current competitive technology, the corporation would have to shell out a sum at least three times as large as the one originally suggested. Even then the profit potential appears to be minimal when compared against the projected earnings of the handful of companies that got into the race around the time the product manager's report was submitted.

Warner-Lambert Co., the big drug maker, got itself into a similar bind. Impatient with the company's slow growth, management gobbled up a hodge podge of acquisitions in fields ranging from chewing gum to baked goods. In the process it shorted research and development causing Warner-Lambert to lose momentum in a particular segment of its drug and vision care business, while a failure to upgrade antiquated plants further crippled productivity. Today chief executive officer Ward S. Hagan characterizes this period as one of "helter-skelter, head-over-heels growth" and is taking steps to reverse the company's direction. With this goal in mind, the company is boosting R&D investment 20 percent this year. Still, with the industry's four leading competitors—Abbott Laboratories, Becton Dickinson, Johnson & Johnson, and Du Pont subsidiary New England Nuclear—far ahead in medical diagnostics research, it is going to be hard for Warner-Lambert to catch up, according to industry analyst David H. Talbot of Drexel Burnham Lambert Inc. Hard, and very expensive.

Also shooting for a turnaround—again—is Memorex Corp., the information systems company whose long-term prospects are bleak on the heels of its short-sighted profits approach. Memorex was in trouble before, however, as the result of an ill-fated move into the mainframe computer business that plunged it $90 million into the red in 1973. At that time Robert C. Wilson, a deft corporate axman, skilled at trimming fat, was recruited and by 1978, with the price of its stock topping $60 a share, the company was flying high once again. Today the stock is down to about a quarter of that price and in recent months a growing number of key executives have been abandoning ship. The familiar culprit is slashed R&D. "In 1979," states *Business Week,* "the company spent only 5% of its revenues on R&D, compared with 7% at Storage Technology Corp. (STC), one of its leading competitors."

Clarence W. Spangle, a former president of Honeywell Information Systems, stepped into the chief executive slot in March 1980, and has since increased R&D spending almost 30 percent. Whether this will prove to be enough and in time remains to be seen.

Dozens of such cases could be reported out of U.S. industrial files where R&D cutbacks are fairly typical. One significant difference between the American and Japanese business scene is that in Japan, with the long-term approach prevalent and patience a characteristic Japanese virtue, sacrificing long range growth for near-term profits would be the rare and unusual exception contrary to hard-learned precepts and behavior.

Slim and Frugal. The Japanese take the Boy Scout motto, Be Prepared, to heart. Slim and frugal is the mode for the work environment as well as the operation itself. The typical Japanese plant is so designed as to make it adaptable for quick and efficient expansion or redesign as the occasion requires. Status is secondary. Readiness comes first. Profit results and quality performance speak for themselves. The Japanese executive is less concerned than his American counterpart with impressing visitors, customers, employees and the public by parading the showy symbols of "success"—plush carpeting and posh appointments, spacious and luxurious executive offices, gigantic showrooms with a fraction of available space utilized. Managerial sights are set on the future as a matter of personal and corporate responsibility to all those whose well-being and security depend on the company's fortunes. Waste, whether in the form of time, money or space, works counter to long range corporate objectives.

From the foreign expert's point of view, the American manager's misguided emphasis on short-term profits blinds him to the importance of research and development, employee development, and other programs that ensure long-time grounding and strength. In a business report titled "The Money Chase," a *Time* editor writes: "And why has quality been declining? Partly because U.S. professional managers have cared less about what they produce than about selling it—and less about selling than about bookkeeping and tax-law legerdemain and building conglomerates that sometimes fall in ruins."

The report goes on to quote Sony Corp. Chairman Akio Morita, who says, "For much of the trouble of the American economy, American management has to take the responsibility."

Starting in the early seventies, observes 1979 Mitchell Prize Winner Dillard Tinsley, "there has been a slowdown of business investment for production facilities in the United States. This aging of the American industrial plant plays a significant role in the slowing growth of American productivity. . . . In part, erosion of the dollar's value is due to competition from modernized manufacturing plants in many foreign countries. . . . Movement toward a sustainable society will occur if productivity is improved by replacing these outmoded transformation processes with energy-efficient processes. One study estimates that as much as 25% of the American industrial energy demand projected for 1985 could be saved by installation of energy-efficient processing equipment . . . ."

However slim and frugal Japanese industry may be when it comes to the elimination of waste, it spares no necessary expense in girding for future strength and growth. A major challenge for U.S. industrials is to take action today with tomorrow's renewal in mind. If we fail to respond to this challenge we will almost inevitably slide further and further into the abyss of second class status in the fiercely competitive world marketplace.

The Lesson of Humility

The 17th century English dramatist and poet Phillip Massinger counseled: "Be wise; soar not too high to fall, but stoop to rise."

If we were to take only one page from the Japanese book—or the Matsushita credo—we might do well to select the page that teaches humility. Success, unmonitored, can become a direct route to disaster, and American industry has for long years tasted relatively unchallenged success.

When victory goes to the head of the management team, it becomes so comfortable and complacent sitting on top of the world that it forgets it revolves. Corporations too often trip over this pitfall because high level executives and directors are lulled by the delusion that success of itself breeds success. One service the Japanese have been performing for the world marketplace in recent years was to shock assorted corporate giants into the realization that smugness can be a prelude to failure. A hopeful phenomenon on the U.S. industrial scene is that a growing number of thoughtful chief executives appear to be taking Phillip Massinger's counsel to heart.

Xerox Chairman C. Peter McColough serves as a prime case in point. As of this writing his company is in the throes of a major reorganization deliberately and avowedly aimed at measuring up and girding itself for the Japanese competitive juggernaut. "This isn't a crash program . . . ," declares Mr. McColough. "It's an attempt to restructure the entire business."

With good reason. Xerox was severely burned by Japanese copier competition and is resolved not to let it happen again. Notes *Business Week,* "When a host of Japanese producers introduced low-price copiers in the U.S. in the mid-1970s, the invasion not only sparked an explosion in sales but also nearly shut Xerox out of a market segment that it had previously ignored. Largely because of this new wave of Japanese competition, Xerox's share of U.S. copier revenues plummeted from 96% in 1970 to just 46% last year —and it is still falling."

The article goes on to stress that tooling up to meet the Japanese challenge will take something more than a management shuffle and trimming down of corporate waste; it will require a radical change in Xerox's traditional organizational culture. "Accustomed to spectacular growth in the 1960s and early 1970s because of its near monopoly in plain paper copiers, the company never learned to respond to serious competition. And its attempts to diversify outside the copier market were marred by a series of missteps." So much so that one industry expert dubbed Xerox a "fat, dumb, monopolist."

Well, those days are over, according to the corporation's top brass. Under the new program every facet of the company's business will be subjected to microscopic scrutiny with plans and performance evaluated against the competition in general and Japanese competition in particular. On top of that, Xerox teams are being flown across the Pacific to study Japanese engineering and manufacturing methods in an effort to boost operating efficiency and productivity. It has already introduced such management techniques as quality circles in its plants throughout the world and, taking a tip from the master emulators, has adopted a variety of Japanese engineering and procurement practices as well.

It is a healthy perspective on tomorrow and its budding realities and a healthy resolve that speak well of the company's leadership. Nor is Xerox driving on this highway alone.

"Culture transformation" appears to be an increasingly popular game among some of the nation's most venerable companies. Another good example is International Paper Co., a textbook case study of how a complacent management can lose its momentum and marketplace niche. At IP the competitive inroads were made, not by Japanese companies, but by leaner and harder domestic competitors. Though the bolt of cloth may be different, the pattern is a familiar one: managerial smugness and laurel resting, a failure to keep up with innovation and modernization in the industry, a seeming concentration on near-term profits in years past instead of long-term structural soundness despite policy declarations to the contrary.

One short term trick of the forest trade now *verboten* at IP is to harvest an excess of trees—an inflating commodity carried on the books at modest original costs—to reflect immediate gains. What results is attractive current earnings at the expense of future growth, both forest and structural. Today the IP powers that be are firm in their resolve to avoid tricky maneuvers of this kind designed to boost short-term performance. Notes one: "Our biggest challenge is to get the investment community to accept that it is better to have a substantial fix and direction that takes longer than just a couple of blips in quarterly earnings."

It is the kind of policy declaration most Japanese businessmen take for granted. The challenge referred to is being confronted these days by more and more U.S. chief executives. Not surprisingly, America's most successful corporations are usually the ones that have long worked and planned for future strength as a matter of publicized policy. Regarded as one of this country's best-managed companies, Johnson & Johnson, the pharmaceutical-medical products giant based in New Brunswick, New Jersey, certainly fits into this category.

A management policy statement published under the headline of "Our Credo" makes it clear that "we must experiment with new ideas. Research must be carried on, innovative programs developed and mistakes paid for. New equipment must be purchased, new facilities provided and new products launched. Reserves must be created to provide for adverse times. When we operate according to these principles, the stockholders should realize a fair return."

Johnson & Johnson isn't reluctant to blow its own horn. According to its chairman, James E. Burke, "Our spending in pharmaceutical research would probably place us as one of the top five in the United States." He goes on to say: "I know of no other corporation in the world with six consumer companies each of which is number one in its basic markets." There's a strong likelihood that were it not for the reality of statement number one, statement number two could not have been made.

Staying Power. You don't have to be a behemoth or even a giant to ensure corporate survival and growth as a result of long range planning. One way to make certain your company will still be around and flourishing a decade from now is to hire managers you expect to remain on the payroll for a long period of time. It's clearly in the typical Japanese executive's best interest to provide well for the future since it's his own future he's providing for. Such a manager is apt to consider a business decision in its proper perspective if it augers well for years ahead even if a short-term loss is incurred as a result of it.

Certainly one executive who thinks long-term because it's his own skin he's protecting is Harry Cooper, president of Paterson, New Jersey's tiny Rigid Paper Tube Corporation. "Big, medium, or small," says Cooper, "the only kind of business planning that makes sense to me is the kind that projects at least five years at a minimum into the future. Every successful small businessperson I know thinks and plans this way unless he is expecting to sell the business shortly. The trouble with managers in large companies is that their personal objectives are often in conflict with their organization's objectives. The executive who regards his job as a resting place prior to moving on to another employer in the foreseeable future isn't too likely to display concern about his company's well being five and ten years down the pike."

Cooper likes the shape and size of his business the way it is. Most of all he likes the unique specialized service he is able to give his customers, and the customer loyalty he receives in response. It provides a sense of security and a feeling of intense satisfaction. One of the most important steps he takes to ensure sustaining the quality of customer he serves and the level of service he provides is through the very careful selection of accounts that his firm accepts. He seeks only customers who are uniquely positioned from the standpoint of location, size, and the nature of business they conduct to cash in most advantageously from his company's products and service, and politely rejects those who fail to meet his criteria. As a result Rigid Paper Tube has, over the years, weathered all kinds of economic climate with the help of customers who stood by the company even under the most adverse conditions.

Apex Electronics Corp.'s CEO, Michael Dorota, vehemently supports Cooper's philosophy. Born in the Ukraine, he exhibits the kind of patience, deliberation, and perseverance lacking in many U.S.-bred executives. "Today's bottom line," he says, "is secondary to the future's positioning. What good is a quick killing if it is going to return to haunt you in the future? There are times you have no choice but to bite the bullet temporarily for the good of a longer range gain. A manager owes it to himself and his people to operate in this way."

The customer loyalty Apex enjoys matches that attained by Rigid Paper Tube. His reputation in the field is second to none because he will go to any extent possible and more to rush to the aid of a customer in a bind, or to help him solve a complex problem. In large measure this is part of his nature. As one customer puts it, "Mike couldn't operate any differently if he tried." But it is also this chief executive's way of sowing seeds for the future.

A fiercely independent Wall Street favorite is Mark Controls Corp., a small producer of water tanks which makes it plain to the Street that quick kill investors would be better advised to steer clear of its stock. The company's chairman, Gary E. MacDougal, makes no secret of his conviction that responding to analyst or stockholder pressures for short-term results ranks as a cardinal management sin. He numbers one among the current new breed of manager who, resisting such pressure himself, has won the respect of the more thoughtful analyst.

It's no surprise to management consultant Leonard J. Smith that MacDougal's organization is thriving as is Cooper's and Dorota's, and he predicts such companies will continue to thrive. "We are going to see more and more of this kind of resistance in the months ahead," the consultant predicts further. "It is becoming a means of self-preservation. Increasingly, we will see outfits like Rigid Paper

Tube, Johnson & Johnson, and Mark Controls—companies large, medium and tiny—publishing avowals of their long-term perspective as a matter of corporate policy."

It's one of the most promising signs on the current business horizon.

10.

THE JAPANESE PRODUCTIVITY EDGE

> *Today's improvements are the results of yesterday's efforts, and tomorrow's improvements must follow from the efforts of today.*
> —Konosuke Matsushita

Discussing the "Culture of Narcissism" in his Mitchell Prize Award paper prepared for the 1979 Woodlands Conference, Professor James O'Toole of the University of Southern California's Center for Futures Research, cites a glowing example of self-indulgence by the "Me Generation" as reported by the Associated Press:

> Boulder, Colorado, July 18, 1979—Employers in this college town have horror tales to tell about today's young workers, a survey by the *Denver Post* found.
>
> Home builder Bob White says he is quitting the construction business because of his frustration with the work habits of area residents. Restaurant

owner Peter Brophy says he loses $700 a month in dishes and silverware because of careless employees.

Absenteeism is another general complaint of Boulder employers, the *Post* reported. . . . Boulder's average employee is between 20 and 35, well-educated and too often not welltrained to work, office managers said. Several employers said 10% of those hired for jobs fail to show up for the first day of work. White said the construction pace in Boulder is about half that in the East, where he grew up in the building trades in New York City.

"There were crews of Lithuanians, Latvians, Russians . . . all kinds of people who took pride in their work," White said of New York. But he said that Old World work ethic is missing in Boulder. These young guys are saying 'Look at me. I'm a carpenter. I have a pickup truck,' but they don't really want to know how to do the work. I can't deal with it. I can't accept it any more," White said. Brophy said he uses a crew of 70 in his restaurant. Last year he hired 192 employees. Like other employers, he blamed problems with the workforce on reluctance to settle down, the ease of group living in a university town, unemployment-pay and food stamps. "They're single. It isn't like being 25 and married with a baby and a house payment and a car payment. They just don't have any responsibilities," he said.

In Japan, employer response to such grievances would have a sharper focus on management, on where supervisors were going wrong in their failure to motivate their people.

In New York City recently a fire was reported in an uptown tenement building. Engines were rushed to the scene only to find that the fire hydrant nearby the burning building was broken. Extensive damage resulted as the fire burned on. Forty-five days later a second fire was reported in the same tenement building. Again engines were rushed to the scene to find that the fire hydrant was still in disrepair.

CBS investigative reporters, attempting to learn why this outrageous condition exists, were told by officials that far too many of the city's hydrants were broken due to abusive practices of residents in the area and the repair department was too shorthanded to cope with them all. CBS decided to get insights into the situation on its own and dispatched an undercover surveillance team to monitor repair crew activities. What they found was typical of past disclosures when monitoring garbage collection crews under similar circumstances: workers starting on the job as late as an hour and a half and two hours after their official starting time, taking lunch breaks that were twice as long as the period to which they were entitled, stopping work an hour and a half or two hours prior to their prescribed quitting time, and blandly receiving full pay, sick leave, holiday and vacation wages for a job less than half done. Officials, confronted with the evidence, admitted that it was confirmed by checkups of their own. Remarked one executive in response, "We'll have to give supervisors more training in how to improve productivity."

CBS anchorman Jim Jensen commented, "How will increased training help the situation? All the supervisor has to do is watch his people and see that the job is done properly."

Unhappily, worker negligence and apathy of this kind is more the rule than exception in many corporate and governmental work environments. The problem is that employees simply do not give a damn. They don't give a damn because they're not self-motivated or employer-motivated to give a damn. A story making the headlines as these words are being written concerns a 32-year-old sanitation department employee who has been on sick leave at full pay for the past four years as the result of an injury. During this period, he was employed by a New Jersey car dealer, collecting two paychecks each week. A week before he was finally tracked down by undercover investigators he had applied for a lifetime pension which would have retired him at full pay for as long as he lived. When he was caught he was fired, $80,000 or more ahead of the game.

What's the key to improved efficiency in low productivity situations such as those described above? Mayor John Vliet Lindsay thought he had it back in the late 1960s when he took over the administrative reins of New York City. At the time he hired top-rated management consultants who came up with a brilliant report outlining a host of techniques and strategies designed to boost the productivity of the city's sanitation, police and fire services. On paper the ideas appeared easy to implement and enforce. In the workplace they flopped one after the other. They failed to work because the workers didn't want them to work, and this has been the experience not only in government but in a host of commercial and industrial organizations throughout the U.S. over the past two or three decades.

The Japanese Productivity Edge can be summed up in a nutshell: Japanese workers want their organizations to succeed; they work hard and conscientiously as individuals and in cooperation with team members to do everything in their power to produce the most of the best at the lowest possible cost. American workers, as the evidence too often shows, simply don't give a damn because the conditions under which they work don't inspire them to give a damn; not *all* American workers, of course, as we shall see in the following chapter, but enough to make a significant difference.

When American industry gets a clear fix on why most Japanese employees *care* about their companies and take pride in their work and why most U.S. employee attitudes range from indifference to bitterness—*and takes positive ac-*

tion to correct this disparity—the Japanese Productivity Edge will disappear, and the U.S. will become a primary world competitor once again.

Ergonomics

About two decades ago the industrial catch phrase, "blue collar blues," began to see wide repetition in the business press. It referred to a seemingly new awareness by management of a growing disenchantment of plant workers with their employers and jobs. But the frustration, although articulated with greater eloquence and vehemence than ever before on the heels of organized protest encouraged by increasingly cohesive and vocal unionism, the growth of consumerism, and the budding women's movement, was neither sudden nor new. What *was* new was the most deepset and serious productivity slump in this nation's history as a result of the worker frustration.

In subsequent years the "blues" echoed from employed wearers of white collars as well and collars that come in mod shades of russet and pink. Quite clearly the managed were transmitting a message to managers, a message that was heard and most often misinterpreted. The conclusion, in response to declining productivity, made it obvious that something had to be done. But what? Scores of management consultants and computer-bred B school graduates came up with a prodigious assortment of solutions in the form of sophisticated productivity building techniques. No society on this planet can surpass the level of U.S. ingenuity when it comes to concocting schemes designed to improve productivity. But, sadly, not even the most talented and creative of the schemers can escape the hard reality that it takes people to make them work and, more to the point, as John Lindsay learned the hard way, *people who want them to work.*

Thus, inevitably, in time ergonomics came into the act. Ergonomics is a biotechnical approach to a restructured work environment designed to minimize mental strain and worker frustration, and in the process increase productivity. The objective is to create a workplace where people can identify positively with their job, organization and group, and so heighten the satisfaction and self-esteem that encourage a desire for improvement, progress and growth. "For this to occur," observes New York management consultant Howard C. Carroll, "management must develop a supervisor-employee relationship in which people have sufficient faith and trust to express their true feelings about the work and their individual roles, and where supervisors and managers are motivated and trained to respond in a constructive and positive way."

To reduce worker frustration, Carroll stresses, we must take whatever action is needed to understand its root causes. He cites a couple of cases in point:

- In a nationally known consumer products company, customer complaints long had been handled by three separate sections within the same large department. One group of employees processed the complaints, chiefly in the form of telephone calls. The information was then passed on to a second group which evaluated the complaints and decided what action to take. A third group was reponsible for scheduling and implementing the action. Productivity in all three groups, the first in particular, had been declining in recent years (between 1976 and 1978). Investigation determined that all workers in the network were frustrated as a result of their job segmentation. The complaint processors were unhappy because they weren't authorized to inform customers what corrective action would be taken and when. The evaluators complained about the depersonalized nature of their work and the lack of contact with customers. The schedulers felt they were "being treated like robots." When the operation was consolidated, with functions rotated and training undertaken to qualify workers in all aspects of the complaint handling procedure, productivity rocketed.

- Rumors were rife in an eastern insurance company that a semiautomated claims processing operation was about to be fully automated. Characteristically, some employees were worried about losing their jobs: others expected the work they did to become boring and deadly. As the weeks passed by, information carried along the gossip-fed grapevine hardened employee convictions that the rumors were true. Departmental productivity, unsatisfactory to begin with, sunk even lower. Lateness and absenteeism soared, errors and reruns became more the rule than the exception. Belatedly, management faced up to the rumors, which happened to be true, and confronted the situation wisely and openly. The department head called all employees together, leveled with them regarding the new system that was planned and its need, and encouraged them to take part in the program's development. This served to reassure people regarding their jobs and their roles and, most important, led them to feel the new setup was *theirs* and not management's alone. As a result, the productivity decline soon began to reverse.

Tailored Workplace. In Germany, Sweden, France, and other European nations, as in Japan, work environment studies are in process—often with government sponsorship—in an effort to determine how best to restructure the workplace with increased productivity in mind. But no society in the world comes close to the Japanese emphasis on matching the job to the worker's individual desires and needs.

Howard C. Carroll agrees with consultant Roy W. Walters, for example, on the importance of humanizing much of the workload by making it *more* complex instead of reducing it to the kind of simplified routines a third grader could master as well as an adult. The New York consultant points out that worker frustration tends to increase in assembly type tasks if the cycle time—the period from start to finish— is less than 1½ minutes. It is thus beneficial in some applications to make the job more complicated, and interesting, by adding steps and/or combining operations, to lengthen the work cycle time. But while this will improve the job condition for many employees, it won't improve it for all employees. Some prefer the simpler task, find it less challenging, and find they can keep pace more readily.

Old hat though the concept may be, the Japanese go to extremes of job rotation and individualized training to match the job to the man instead of the man to the job. What results is optimized job satisfaction and in the end improved productivity. Again, the procedure stems from the philosophy which centers on the human being with all aspects of business and plant operation radiating not from the profit result but from people.

Ripples. Quality and pride are not exclusively Japanese properties. Nor is the sometimes-heard claim that Japanese productivity cannot be duplicated in the U.S. because of Japan's homogenous citizenry compared with this country's heterogenous population. Notes Apex Electronics Inc.'s Michael Dorota: "People are the same the world over. If they are properly motivated, they will perform and produce."

The problem lies in finding the proper motivators, an endeavor at which it would appear the Japanese are yet to be matched or surpassed. Certainly one prime motivator, judging from the Japanese experience, is a focus on quality. Quality performance instills pride. The worker whose contribution is outstanding and who receives the recognition that is his due—whether the excellence stems from individual or group action—is proud to be part of his unit and feels a strong sense of belonging. Loyalty comes as an automatic byproduct and is a natural response to the fulfillment, support, and security he experiences.

What's more, in the U.S. today more and more workers have come to realize that quality and job security go hand in hand, another offshoot of the influx of well made Japanese products. Observes business writer Ben A. Franklin: "Based on Volkswagen's theory that it must stress quality to compete successfully in the American automobile market, precision is such a concern that it is also preached by the auto union." He quotes Rich Ferchak, shop chairman of Local 2055 of the United Automobile Workers, who says, "Our people are concerned about quality sales. They know that quality is what sells the Rabbit . . . They want to keep their jobs." Franklin also quotes Roy H. Langenbach, manager of the only foreign-owned car assembly plant in the United States in New Stanton, Pa., where the Rabbits are put together. "Our people have great pride in what they do, and they know it's a quality product." He makes it clear that the two go hand in hand. In New Stanton banners overhanging conveyor lines proclaim: "Let's Go All Out For Quality."

Langenbach, a former Chevrolet executive, says, "Those of us who have come out of the American auto industry have had to really adjust our thinking to VW quality standards. We realized we would have to do this to compete in the American market. The workforce here has made that possible."

In Germany as in Japan the government is getting very much into the work restructuring act and is helping to devise new systems to replace conventional plant environments in order to humanize jobs and improve employee productivity. During 1981, Germany's Ministry of Research & Technology shelled out an estimated $42 million on "work humanization" programs, about $14 million of which was spent to aid industrial reorganization along ergonomistic lines. Corporations that participate in such projects are reimbursed by the

Ministry for up to half the cost of restructuring investment which includes the retraining of workers.

Incorporating Self-Interest. One page the Germans are tearing from the Japanese book involves the value of quality circles. They're not called by that name, but the concept of employee teams where jobs are rotated and projects are followed through from beginning to end, is gaining increased acceptance in a growing number of German plants. Group-incentive plans are also featured with a stress on high quality and improved productivity. In group assembly situations workers become skilled at a variety of tasks, petty jealousies and resentments are largely eliminated, adaptation to product and procedural changes is rapid, and employees are happier because socializing, instead of being prohibited, is encouraged. To a limited degree, workers become involved in work planning sessions as well.

Although loyal and well motivated workers often appear to be selfless, self-interest pure and simple inevitably induces productivity improvement. In Japan the worker incentive is taken for granted as an inherent part of the system, but is a prime activator nonetheless. One of the most powerful incentives of all is the guarantee of lifetime employment in a large segment of industry. On top of that, in the majority of cases, the more profitably the company functions, the bigger employee bonuses will be, so that in boosting productivity the worker works for himself as well as the company. If automation or a labor-saving procedure is introduced, the employee stands to share in the gains from the increased productivity. What is regarded as a threat in the American plant is looked upon as a boon by Japanese workers.

Comments management consultant Leonard J. Smith: "In the U.S., middle managers and well paid technical people engage in a concentrated effort to initiate productivity improvements while rank-and-filers, often opposed to such innovation, are either passive or resistant. In Japan, productivity improvement is everyone's responsibility. Employee-based innovation is rewarded with recognition and cash. Since individuals outside the work circle, even if they are trained engineers, lack the insight and experience of the men and women on the scene, motivating the rank-and-file person to participate in the improvement effort cannot help but produce profit gains. The trick is to build self-interest into the individual job."

The Japanese do this superbly. Self-interest is incorporated into the system. In a very real sense the Japanese employee is in business for himself as well as the company. "America will never close the productivity growth gap with Japan or West Germany," states Prof. Lester C. Thurow, "unless there are major changes in the incentive structures facing labor and management." What we need is "a direct correspondence between those things that are good for society—higher productivity—and those things that are good for the individual—higher income. America does not have to adopt the Japanese incentive system, but it does have to work out the American equivalent."

Linkage. Japanese productivity is high because employees of Japanese companies are convinced that their own welfare and well being is linked to their organization's profitability. If U.S. executives could harness their widely reputed creative talents to come up with provocative new ways to produce similar linkage in this country, productivity would surely surge as a result. Robert E. Kolson, a lecturer in business economics at the University of Chicago's Graduate School of Business, cites one such proposal that might apply to a government agency.

" . . . the Transportation Department," he writes, "has about 70,000 employees and a projected (annual) budget of $20 billion. Suppose this amount were the officially established reference budget. Then, for each dollar of the $20 billion not spent at the end of the fiscal year, a small portion—say five cents— would be placed in a special agency fund. Perhaps three cents of this amount should be divided equally among all employees, four-hundredths of a penny could go to the department head and the remainder become part of a discretionary fund distributed by the department head to those employees he feels were particularly instrumental in improving the department's efficiency."

If this idea were implemented, for each $1 billion saved, each employee would earn $430, the department head would get $4,000, and approximately $20 million would be placed in the discretionary fund. The idea would be as useful to corporations as to government agencies. Any manager familiar with the acrobatics division and department heads in scores of companies sometimes go through at the end of the year to ensure that budgeted allocations are fully spent, might be able to guess at the savings and waste elimination potential. In my own personal experience I can recall at least three occasions in recent years when corporate clients for whom I write speeches, and prepare magazine articles or brochures, called in the month of December requesting that I advance bill them for work not yet performed in order to help use up the year's budget. The alternative—perish the thought—would be to wind up the year with a surplus on hand and so jeopardize the amount of budget allocations to come.

It is a fact of industrial life that employee loyalty and self-interest are closely linked just as worker initiative and self-interest are linked. This condition is as natural as scurrying out of a swimming pool when a lightning storm strikes. Whereas many U.S. corporations attempt to win employee cooperation with productivity efforts by means of a variety of techniques ranging from cost-cutting drives to inspirational pep talks, the Japanese corporation cashes in on this natural linkage by involving employees in the business on a long-term basis and tying their personal fortunes and growth to the fortunes and growth of the company.

An example of such linkage can be found in Japan's remarkably successful auto industry where productivity improvement has been little short of phenomenal. Nonetheless, however praiseworthy the results, they are still marred somewhat by a large number of small, inefficient subcontractors which, clinging to the past, operate more in the style of America's long outmoded sweatshops than the modern and highly humanized corporate giants. Although the sweatshops feature minimum wages paid for maximum hours and subhuman conditions, the failure of such firms to measure up to the productivity of the more humanely managed companies is gradually forcing them out of the marketplace. Proof sufficient that employees are willing to work hard and think hard if they can be made to believe that it is to their personal advantage to do so.

Invention's Mother

Walter Linn, an observer of the modern business scene, once remarked: "Truth as old as the hills is bound up in the Latin proverb, 'Necessity is the mother of invention.' It is surprising what a man can do when he has to, and how little most men will do when they don't have to."

When your back's against the wall, and you are attacked, you come out fighting or you perish. One reason Japan prospers today is that a couple of decades ago the nation was hard pressed, economically speaking. The leaning of Japanese industry was more than an ambitious thrust for prosperity, it was a matter of survival.

States Michael R. Losey, Vice President for Personnel of Sperry Corp.'s New Holland division: "Because of Japan's lack of natural resources, it is disadvantaged in terms of the cost of raw material when compared to Europe and America. To overcome this handicap, Japanese industries have found it necessary to produce better-quality goods having higher added value and at even lower production costs than those of other countries."

What the nation desperately needed was a system whereby higher than ordinary productivity could be ensured, plus a workforce that would conscientiously cooperate to make the system function successfully.

Hopefully, the reasons for the loyalty and cooperation of employees all down the line are being made apparent throughout the pages of this book. With the proper environment created, the evolution of the "Kanban System" developed as a natural byproduct.

Losey points up two distinctive features of the Kanban System. One is the "just-in-time-production" concept. Under this arrangement, only products that are needed are produced when they are needed and in the amount that is needed. In this way stock on hand is kept to a minimum. Feature number two is the full utilization of employee capabilities through active participation in running and improving their workshops. Blend these two elements together and the inevitable result is optimized productivity.

In activating the system, the main reliance focus is placed upon people rather than the computer as is so often the case in the U.S. Another critical element is cost reduction through the removal of waste. The assumption is that anything other than the minimum amount of equipment, material, parts and manpower—those factors absolutely essential to the manufacturing process—is simply surplus which serves only to increase the cost.

The production control function normally seeks to meet schedules by establishing an adequate, but never excessive, work-in-process inventory. Controlled inventories help protect the operation against a myriad of production problems and unexpected changes in demand. With close tabs kept on asset management, wasteful excesses of equipment, manpower and materials are avoided, keeping productivity high.

In a nutshell, the Kanban System avoids asset imbalance by shortening the lead time from the entry of materials to the finished goods stage. U.S. production, in contrast, is usually concerned with the establishment of reserve stock in response to longer range order projections and the processing of economic lot sizes. Under the Japanese system, the manufacturing effort is keyed to the projected final assembly line requirement. The intermediate stockpiling of merchandise with its attendant space, storage, insurance, and materials handling costs is largely eliminated. The standard operating procedure is to move completed units from the final assembly line to the customer's receiving facility.

To achieve these objectives, optimum cooperation and efficiency are essential. Without a smoothly functioning team, chaos and confusion would result and customer complaints would be commonplace. At Toyota, as a case in point, setup time for a hood and fender operation that formerly took one hour has been reduced to ten minutes. The typical time span in other countries ranges from four to six hours. In the achievement of such results more than systems or technical efficiency and ingenuity are involved. The employee *will to achieve* must be present. In the end this is always what productivity gains seem to boil down to.

The Japanese Diet

The Diet in Japan is something more than a legislative assembly. Applying the Western definition of the word, it is also the hardset and established modus operandi of most Japanese companies. The effectiveness of Japanese corporate dieting is so marked as to make the Pritikin, Atkins and Scarsdale advocates sit up and take notice.

Years of struggling against adversity and to overcome such natural handicaps as an extreme paucity of energy and other resources, a severe lack of space and, until recent years, a shortage of managerial and technological expertise, forced the kind of conservation of assets and economies on Japanese industrials that many American companies shoot for but rarely achieve. Today Japan's lean and hard look bespeaks a prime factor in its top positioning in the productivity improvement race.

Take the automobile industry. As was pointed out earlier, whereas in U.S. car companies eleven or twelve management layers exist between plant supervision and the top executive tier, in Japan only five to seven layers exist. If this accomplishes nothing else, it chops payroll costs and makes for smoother and more efficient communication.

In an earlier book, *Sure Fail—the Art of Mismanagement,* I write: "How does bureaucracy breed incompetence? The answer is simple enough—the system feeds on itself. Typically the new organization starts off lean, tight, and purposeful. But as it grows in size the work spreads out. Key men hire aides, and the aides hire aides. The layers multiply and flourish . . . Too many managers take Andrew Carnegie's famous counsel to heart, 'The great manager is the man who knows how to surround himself with men much abler than himself.' They interpret this to mean, 'Hire subordinates who are smart enough to relieve you of the responsibility of thinking, planning, and managing'."

The Japanese system of management militates against layerism at all levels. For one thing, with lifetime employment there is no incentive to angle for protectionism by surrounding oneself with a body of yes-men and supporters. For another, with corporate objectives clearly defined and individual goals linked to company goals, time wasted on politicking is self defeating. For a third, with unprofitable endeavors sluiced out by consensus, few if any make-work projects exist to occupy the time of nonproductive personnel.

Deadwood Preservation. The costs of layerism can be crippling and destructive of productivity improvement efforts. Sears, Roebuck & Co. was for years the envy of the retailing industry. Innovative and mammoth in both size and purchasing clout, it was able to support a half dozen or more buyers for a merchandise line where competitors made do with one or two. In time its payroll swelled to over 400,000 employees. Eventually, inevitably, the tail caught up with the dog.

Today Sears is more often sympathized with than envied. Less layered competitors like J.C. Penney and K Mart can operate profitably with a 35 percent markup on goods. Sears sometimes requires a 50 percent markup to stay ahead of the game and in today's inflationary times consumers are getting the message. Not surprisingly, the giant merchandiser's profit margin has been slipping steadily in recent years and is expected to drop further.

At long last the company's management is attacking the problem. A large scale early retirement program aimed at managers older than 55 is in the works. Merchandising groups have been consolidated, national retailing staffers reduced. All in all, a whopping personnel reduction has been put into effect which is expected to chop costs in one year by more than $125 million in executive staff cuts alone. But along with the saving must come disruption and trauma, plus an adverse effect on morale that will take a long time to counter. How much better to combat layerism by avoiding it in the first place.

Another example of weighted down layerism is American Can Co., for years as closely competitive with Continental Group Inc. as the Yankees are with the Orioles. But today it is as if the two companies are playing in two different leagues. While Continental is flourishing ($396 million in profits on $5.7 billion in revenues in 1980), American Can is, if not floundering, heading rapidly downhill with 1980 profits of $85.7 million on $4.7 billion in sales, a drop of 33 percent.

Not all American Can's trouble can be related to overstaffing; the company made some unfortunate moves into paper products, chemicals, and other disappointing performers, and took a drubbing on the record piracy scandal of its Sam Goody subsidiary. But, according to more than one industry watcher, American Can's personnel buildup is responsible for a fair share of its earnings decline. Lionel N. Sterling, the company's top financial officer until he left in 1980 to join Standard Brands Inc., serves as a prime case in point. Given top executive carte blanche to develop an internal "think tank" operation from scratch, within two years he had 900 people reporting to him. As so often happens, it took a souring of business for the empire to crumble.

The management archives are filled with such stories. Traditionally, in American enterprise, whether business or government, executive power is measured at least in part by the size of the operation and the number of people employed there. William J. Harahan, who manages technical planning for Ford Motor Co., estimates that a typical Japanese auto company makes do with approximately half as many employees as a U.S. company producing the same number of cars. The conclusion is clear. It takes a lot of selling price dollars to make up the difference.

Belt Tightening. Increasing numbers of lackluster corporate giants are taking a tip from the Japanese these days and trimming their waistline in an effort to restore some of the old glamour and shine. One newly aggressive dieter is Owens-Illinois Inc., a company that had grown uneconomically unwieldy in recent years with a host of unprofitable products being run off on ancient equipment in outmoded plants.

Responding to the challenge from home and abroad, turnaround tactics were initiated toward the end of the 1970s with O-I's glass container capacity reduced 24 percent and its workforce cut 30 percent. The result: a seven percent productivity improvement in 1979 and a nine percent jump in 1980, with a new concentration on the high-volume business that brings in the most profit dollars, and a shutdown of home-canning products, laser-glass, German box production, metal can plants and other marginal operations to sustain hard won growth.

Another corporation getting the productivity message is Jos. Schlitz Brewing Co. What most certainly must have helped the reception was an earnings plunge to a $50.6 million loss in 1979 in contrast to a $50 million profit five years earlier and a drop from third to fourth place in the industry.

Largely responsible for Schlitz's failing performance, according to beer industry watching experts, was a reformulation of the product that caused a mass exodus of longtime loyal customers. Frank J. Sellinger's first move when he stepped into the CEO slot in 1977 at age 66 was to reformulate Schlitz beer into what he not surprisingly refers to as "one helluva good brew." But as insiders are quick to admit, getting a customer to switch back once he's changed brands can be "an horrendous challenge."

Coupled with this problem was the task of boosting productivity with an earnings reversal in mind. With unavoidable belt tightening his objective, Mr. Sellinger slashed the corporate payroll of about 7,000 an estimated 12 or 13 percent.

"I believe in paying fair wages," he said, " but I can't afford two workers for one job. We eliminated a lot of people. We sacrificed a few for the good of the many."

We had grown fat and lax, he concedes. "I mean, how many WATS lines do you really need? How many copies do you have to make? There are a million ways to save."

It would appear, comments Francis J. Harrison, a New York City machinery maker's plant manager, after returning from a tour of plants in and around Tokyo and Osaka, that the Japanese have found them all. Or more likely, not permitting layerism and other waste to build up in the first place, they managed to remain lean and hard despite rapid growth.

Xerox Corp.'s new chief executive officer, David T. Kearns, is one manager whose purpose in life is not to be outdone in the department of lean and hard meanness. "If you really want to see how good you have to be to compete," he told a *Business Week* reporter, "the Japanese are the ones to look at. We want to be remembered as the company that took on the Japanese and were successful."

Mr. Kearns sees the toughest problem confronting him as a trimdown of the company's bloated workforce. Typically, during its years of breakneck growth, new staff was put to work as quickly as they could be hired and trained. States one middle manager who escaped the ax by opting for early retirement, "For at least a decade or more, the last thing on anyone's mind was productivity. Today it is all that you hear."

There were simply too many layers of management, and Mr. Kearns wasn't the only one to reach this conclusion. The result is a shakeup of unprecedented proportions. Will the restructuring survive the shivers and shudders jolting personnel from the clerical level up to inhabitants of some of the company's most spacious and thickly carpeted offices? This remains to be seen. But it certainly will if Mr. Kearns has his way.

The Key Is Not Numbers Alone. "Any manager who believes the automatic solution to poor productivity is an indiscriminate slashing of staff," cautions consultant Leonard J. Smith, "could be in for a stunning surprise."

As innumerable case studies bear out, whether the impulsive and insensitive treatment of people takes the form of mindless head chopping or callous change that produces psychological shock, employee response is predictable: the kind of bitterness, resentment, and defiance that cripples productivity and defeats profit objectives.

Payroll paring that weeds out supernumeraries along with make-work and waste is another matter entirely, especially when it is performed of necessity with survival and restored corporate health in mind. In such situations the perceptive employee is quick to understand that, as Mr. Sellinger of Schlitz states the case, sacrificing the few for the good of the many is essential surgery for the body's future health. It is not so much how many people are employed as what those people are doing.

Globally known management consultant Peter F. Drucker would be the first to agree. In his book, *Managing in Turbulent Times,* he writes: "The employee in most companies, and even more in most public service institutions, is basically 'underemployed.' His responsibility does not match his capacity. He is given money instead of the status that only genuine responsibility can confer."

Perhaps the single most notable attribute of the Japanese managerial system is the effort expended by supervisors and executives in the best run Nipponese companies to slot every employee into the place where his maximum potential will be uncovered, developed and refined, and most advantageously utilized.

"The Japanese firms may well have more people," concedes Columbia University Professor William H. Newman, "but they are in profit-related jobs. The Japanese will train their smartest engineers to identify problems, then put them on the shop floor. In the U.S. they'd be sitting at a desk reviewing things."

Not in all companies. A couple of years ago President Dee W. Hock of Visa International returned from a four-month leave of absence to find an empty in-basket, a silent telephone, and subordinates who were too busy to talk to him. Out of such staffing the company has rocketed to first place in the credit card industry, outpacing its closest competitors. Reports *Business Week:* An hierarchical reporting structure is singularly lacking in Visa. Mr. Hock and his second-in-command Charles T. Russell "operate jointly in a free-form office of the president, requiring no formal reports from any staffers but keeping informal tabs on all. 'Hock makes it his business to know each individual within the organization and is fully aware of the performance of each of his people,' notes Robert H. Potts, Chairman of Bank One, of Columbus, Ohio, and a Visa director."

This echoes sentiments heard about the best managed companies in America and, coincidentally, the ones whose management philosophies most closely resemble those of the outstanding Japanese corporations. The implication is not always clear, but it is there nonetheless. Japanese management, featuring closely integrated groups, constitutes a way of coping with bigness without letting it run out of control. Comments business writer James Flanagan about a handful of the nation's best managed giants: "It may be an accident of history . . . , but there is no monument anywhere called The IBM Building. As at Texas Instruments, Hewlett Packard and Intel (all nationally recognized top flyers), the Armonk, N.Y., headquarters of IBM is a group of unpretentious, low-slung buildings. To some analysts, it is a sign that IBM with its $23 billion in annual sales, still knows how to think small," and knows how to avoid becoming a superbureaucracy with its traditional overabundance of "programs" and underutilization of people.

11.

THE LOOK ALIKES

> *I think that however much education and knowledge you may have, or however great your ability, the wisdom and ideas of many people are still very important. Without them, you cannot achieve true success.*
> —*Konosuke Matsushita*

Two important questions exist for the thoughtful student of Japanese management:

1. Can the American executive learn lessons from the Japanese that will help him manage more effectively and successfully?

2. Given the cultural and religious differences that exist between the U.S. and Japan, the difference in upbringing and background, the reality that Japan is an homogenous society and this country heterogenous, do we in America have the capability of achieving the degree of corporate success being achieved in Japan?

The answer to both questions is an unqualified yes. Increasingly, teams of U.S. executives, academicians, labor leaders and government officials are visiting Japanese companies, studying Japanese management methods, and successfully applying them in American profit and nonprofit organizations.

As this chapter will disclose, not only are Japanese philosophies and management strategies being applied successfully in the U.S., but in a handful of U.S. corporations, although differently labeled, Japanese style management is being practiced today—and indeed, was practiced in this country *long before the Japanese experience*—with outstanding success. The startling conclusion that can be drawn from this study is that almost invariably the U.S. corporations whose management philosophies and practices are in the more important aspects most similar to the successful Japanese companies are the profit leaders and most revered in their industries. Conversely, from the Japanese viewpoint it might be stated that those corporations in Japan which most effectively emulated this handful of U.S. companies are the ones which have become most successful.

In 1980, the internationally known management consulting firm of McKinsey & Co. released a study of 10 of this nation's best managed companies. From the standpoint of the businesses they are in, the companies have little in common. From the way they are run and the success they achieve in their fields, they have a great deal in common—with each other, and with the Japanese models of excellence as well. The 10 companies are: IBM, Hewlett-Packard, Procter & Gamble, McDonald's, Dana Corporation, Texas Instruments, 3M, Johnson & Johnson, Digital Equipment Corporation and Emerson Electric. There are other superbly managed companies, of course; but these are the ones selected for the McKinsey study.

It's particularly significant that in each of these companies a major managerial emphasis, first and foremost beyond corporate objectives profit-based and otherwise, is on the needs and problems of people. In each of these companies the most important reasons for success can be traced to people, the way they are handled and treated, and the way they respond.

"In the past," states *The Economist*'s survey of Japanese industry, "the Japanese liked to say how different they were and how inscrutable their lifestyle was and so forth. Now that westerners are saying that they cannot compete with the Japanese because Japan is just so different, the Japanese are naturally keen to reply that Sheffield could work like Kawasaki if the British tinkered a bit with their management."

The U.S. companies described in the pages of this chapter need do little if any tinkering. And American executives too proud, independent or sensitive to select foreign companies as models to emulate could do no better than to examine the U.S. corporations herein discussed in order to pinpoint the factors that work together to accomplish progress and growth.

Delta Airlines

Since 1929 Delta has advanced from a tiny one-route operation with a handful of employees to the world's fifth largest airline employing more than 36,000 people. Described as "the world's most profitable airline," its cumulative earnings over the past 10 years exceed $857 million. No other airline comes close.

President and Chief Executive Officer David C. Garrett remarks on the unusual similarities that exist between Delta and such companies as Nissan Motors and Matsushita Electric. "Interestingly," he says, "all three companies developed in much the same way. Nor did any of Delta's founders and, indeed, the company's senior managers who followed in later years, before and after the war, have the remotest idea what was happening in Tokyo or Osaka."

James L. Ewing, III, the airline's director of public relations and a 20-year veteran with the company, echoes this sentiment. "Mine was the privilege," he says, "of personally knowing nearly all of Delta's founders, and in that long span of time I cannot recall any of the company's senior people traveling to Japan to study Japanese industrial techniques. Nor, to my knowledge, did any Japanese executives come to Monroe or Atlanta to study Delta."

Ewing has come into contact with several Japanese executives in recent years, all of whom agree that the key to corporate growth, productivity improvement, and profitability lies with top management's philosophy regarding the people the company employs, deals with, and serves. "We have agreed," he adds, "that human nature is a remarkable force and that beyond vast cultural differences, even those of a disastrous conflict, success is based almost wholly on the quality of the people involved in the enterprise, and on service to others and superior quality products whether they are airline seats and cubic feet of aircraft cargo space, or electronic units and automobiles."

Two axioms, he adds, dominate Delta's lifestyle and workstyle: "Only people make the difference," and "Maximum utilization of all personnel and equipment." These developed as a natural byproduct of the airline's operation, not as a managerial dictate.

The public relations executive and journalist has, for many years, been a Matsushita fan. He states that several years ago he read, "amazed," Konosuke Matsushita's guiding philosophy that thrust his corporation into the posture of an industrial giant. "His is not a complicated philosophy," says Ewing. "Mr. Matsushita expressed a genuine concern and enthusiasm for people, so much like the feelings expressed by Delta's founder and the senior officers who followed him. Very frankly," he concludes, "I know of very few organizations where 36,000 people actually look forward to coming to work every day!"

He is understandably biased and, as a PR man, has an image ax to grind. But whether he grinds it or not, the Delta reputation of quality and excellence is already firmly established, and I for one am convinced that Ewing's enthusiasm and excitement are genuine.

Accidently on Purpose. It's no accident that both Delta and Matsushita Electric are top rated in their industries from the standpoint of managerial excellence and profitability. The two companies have been walking the same garden path for decades.

Delta's family consciousness matches Matsushita's. Like the top Japanese companies, the airline promotes from within; no executive exodus occurs here as a result of disgruntlement or "reorganization." CEO David C. Garrett, Jr. himself joined the company as a reservations sales agent in 1946 and has been steadily developing and climbing ever since. The company, like Matsushita, takes care of its "family." One would be hard pressed to find the equal of its employee benefit plan. It virtually guarantees lifelong security. In the event of death, widow and children are provided for. Should disability strike before or after retirement, provision is made for that contingency as well. And Delta listens in earnest because the company earnestly cares. It is no sin here for a foreman to bring his problem directly before a VP without going through "channels." And a top management program calls for a meeting of all employees in groups of 25 or 30 at least once every 18 months with a member of Delta's nine-person top executive team. Here achievements and plans are reviewed, problems aired, ideas exchanged.

Delta, like its Japanese counterparts, keeps its managerial eye on the long-term picture, sticks doggedly to its 15 year planning perspective with regard to flight equipment and support facilities through all kinds of adverse economic weather—air controller strikes, fuel emergencies, reduced air travel periods. With the middle and late 90s in mind, the company is engaged in a $5 billion expansion program from which it refuses to deviate. Result: its productivity is the highest in the industry.

Lifetime employment? Well, practically, within the American context. There have been no layoffs because of economic conditions in over 25 years. During slack periods, surplus pilots and flight personnel are put to work on a variety of tasks ranging from cargo loading and ticket selling to manning reservations desks; it may temporarily cost the company in earnings but its seniority and benefits programs remain intact. When the air controllers struck, severely curtailing flights, thousands of airline employees were furloughed. Not at Delta. In 1973, when air traffic was crippled by the oil embargo, Chairman W. T. Beebe proclaimed, "Now the time has come for the stockholders to pay a little penalty for keeping the team together." In times of disruption, family members must come to each other's aid.

Nor is the Delta employee tied down by union strictures to a single job. In fact, the International Association of Machinists has long since given up trying to organize the airline. There's not a union contract around that could match Delta's compensation and benefit programs. Working under a job rotation system, employees are trained and qualified to pitch in where and when they are needed.

As in Japan, consensus management is practiced extensively. Task force teamwork is commonplace from the top down and back again. In fact, the nine members of the top executive team, operating as a kind of president's office, are in touch with each other constantly in connection with internal and external problems and the hammering out of crucial decisions.

How successful has Delta's "Japanese managerial style" which is so purely American been? One indication might be the reaction of Japan Air Lines which regularly sends teams of managers to Atlanta to study Delta's techniques.

IBM

Proclaimed on signs and plaques nationwide, IBM's single syllable byword is THINK. Its management quite apparently thought.

One-time Ford Motor Co. president and retired Stanford Business School Dean Arjay Miller, calls International Business Machines Corp. the country's best-managed company. When Courtney C. Brown was dean of Columbia University's Graduate School of Business, he noted: "It is now a commonly accepted truism that the corporation is more than a legal entity engaged in the production and sale of goods and services for profit. It is also the embodiment of the principals and beliefs of the men and women who give it substance. More particularly, the corporation is the expression of those who have given it leadership in its development and in the conduct of its affairs. Perhaps no corporation is more illustrative of these characteristics than the International Business Machines Corporation."

Like Konosuke Matsushita, Thomas Watson Jr., son of the company's founder, believes in the establishment, publication and dissemination of a corporate managerial and operating philosophy as a set of guidelines for the organization's diverse endeavors and activities. Typical excerpts from Watson's IBM credo include:

"I believe the real difference between success and failure in a corporation can very often be traced to the question of how well the organization brings out the great energies and talents of its people."

"I firmly believe that any organization, in order to survive and achieve success, must have a sound set of beliefs on which it premises all its policies and actions."

The belief that is most important in IBM's philosophy is *"our respect for the individual.* This is a simple concept, but in IBM it occupies a major portion of management time."

"We believe that an organization should pursue all tasks with the idea that they can be accomplished in a superior fashion."

"More and more there seems to be entering into relationships between government, industry, and labor a fourth force—the force of the public. Anyone particularly interested in some segment of the economy must increasingly realize the force of public or national interest. Ultimately we are held accountable to it. We exist at its tolerance."

Shades of Konosuke Matsushita? Perhaps. In 1930 Thomas Watson Sr. visited the Matsushita plant in Japan, was impressed by what he saw and by the founder's philosophy, and was apparently influenced by his thinking.

An interesting indication of IBM's concern with and respect for the individual can be gleaned from a deal recently made between the company and Jerome H. Lemelson, a 58-year-old inventor, with regard to the nonexclusive licensing of some 20 patents related to data processing and word processing technical innovations. Said Mr. Lemelson: "I first wrote to Thomas Watson Jr. . . . in 1963. Would you believe it? He answered me within a few days. It was a big thrill."

IBM's roots trace back to 1911 when it was known as C-T-R, for Computing-Tabulating-Recording, a small equipment manufacturer. Today the company's gross income exceeds $26.2 billion. In over 40 years, no person employed on a regular basis by IBM has lost as much as a single hour of working time because of a layoff. The company's reputation as a long range planner is almost legendary. Advancement is from within wherever possible and strictly on the basis of merit. Its employee training and development program is second to none.

IBM's Open Door Policy, states *About Your Company*, a manual distributed to all employees, "is deeply ingrained in IBM's history. . . . Should you have a problem which you believe the company can help solve, discuss it with your immediate manager, your manager's manager, or your location's personnel manager. . . . Or, if the matter is of such a nature you prefer not to discuss it with (any of these people), you should go to your local general manager, regional manager, president or general manager of your division or subsidiary, whichever is appropriate." If none of this produces a satisfactory resolution, the employee is invited to contact the company's chief executive officer by mail or in person.

IBM compensation is well above the industry average, and its benefits program is one of the finest in existence.

Product and service excellence is a fetish at IBM, a goal extended to employees and the public as well as customers. As any of the best-managed companies' executive teams could attest whether in Japan or America, it is a goal that pays off in profits, reputation and growth.

Hewlett-Packard

HP's 1980 net sales of $3.10 billion marked a 31 percent increase from the previous year. Net earnings increased 32 percent to $269 million. The figures are representative of corporate success by any and all measures over the years, up from net sales of $378 million and net earnings of $24 million in 1971.

President and Chief Executive Officer John Young wholeheartedly agrees that the management practices and philosophies of the most successful Japanese companies are already in force in some of the best managed U.S. corporations. And Young feels it is flattering for the company to be cited for excellence in so many books and articles in the current wave of business literature comparing top rated Japanese and American companies. But he is quick to point out that while the Japanese practices alluded to are essentially of post World War II vintage, HP's management philosophy and style date back to 1939.

So be it! What, precisely, is what is so often referred to by the company and outsiders as "the HP way"? Corporate literature stresses its "Management by Objectives" concept and philosophy—seven objectives specifically. Here they are presented in summary:

1. PROFIT

Objective: To achieve sufficient profit to finance our company growth and to provide the resources we need to achieve our other corporate objectives.

2. CUSTOMERS

Objective: To provide products and services of the greatest possible value to our customers, thereby gaining their respect and loyalty.

3. FIELDS OF INTEREST

Objective: To enter new fields only when the ideas we have, together with our technical, manufacturing and marketing skills, assure that we can make a needed and profitable contribution to the field.

4. GROWTH

Objective: To let our growth be limited only by our profits and our ability to develop and produce technical products that satisfy real customer needs.

5. OUR PEOPLE

Objective: To help HP people share in the company's success, which they make possible; to provide job security based on their performance; to recognize their individual achievements; and to help them gain a sense of satisfaction and accomplishment from their work.

6. MANAGEMENT

Objective: To foster initiative and creativity by allowing the individual great freedom of action in attaining well-defined objectives.

7. CITIZENSHIP

Objective: To honor our obligations to society by being an economic, intellectual and social asset to each nation and each community in which we operate.

"The dignity and worth of the individual," notes William R. Hewlett, chairman of HP's executive committee, "is a very important part of the HP way. Relationships within the company depend upon a spirit of cooperation among individuals and groups, and *an attitude of trust and understanding* on the part of managers toward their people." He goes on to say "that men and women want to do a good job, a creative job, and that if they are provided the proper environment they will do so."

Observes HP psychologist and training specialist "Rick" Gilbert, commenting on Hewlett's remarks: "The assumption here is that people will strive to do the best they possibly can by meeting their own inner goals. . . . People gain their 'motivational horsepower' from an inner desire to do the best they are capable of doing."

Dr. Gilbert further capsulizes the sum and substance of the HP philosophy when he says, "If you believe people can't be trusted, are motivated primarily by external rewards, and need to be told what to do by an all knowing authority figure, you will create a company along the lines of the military.

". . . if you believe people are trustworthy, capable of making good decisions, motivated by inner satisfaction to do better, more creative work in a non-authoritarian atmosphere, then you are more likely to pattern your management style along the lines of HP."

Like the leading Japanese companies, Hewlett-Packard believes solidly in the group or teamwork approach. Chairman David Packard: "In basketball and football I gained the idea that you have to work together to achieve a team goal—back up the other fellow, and not act like a bunch of individuals working independently."

In an effort to keep a big company small-minded and informal, management makes individual executives responsible for enterprise segments ranging from $40 million to $250 million in sales.

Within practical limitations, employees are permitted leeway and flexibility so far as personal needs and individual preferences are concerned. They are not required to start work at a specified time, for example. They can report at any time within a two-hour "window." This makes it possible for many working parents to take their children to school before reporting to work. Where an employee feels the need exists, he is encouraged to "go over his boss's head" to seek satisfaction or justice if a problem concerns him.

The importance of open and honest communication receives special emphasis at HP. "Open Line," by the company's own definition, "is a communication process involving many people and all levels of the company. Initially it took the form of an attitude survey in September 1979, during which 7,966 employees of the U.S. organizations were asked to give their views and answer questions on more than

The Look Alikes

100 topics. Their responses were reviewed by an independent survey organization (International Survey Research of Chicago) and placed in 17 categories. The results then were compared with the results of similar surveys of 200 leading companies."

Using the results as a launching point, analysis teams of from 7 to 12 people began a long, searching process of formulating specific concerns. They generated about 3,500 problem statements falling into 22 categories. Most of these concerns could be addressed at the local level, with corporate actions and resolutions made in response.

Another HP communication program is labeled MBWA which stands for Management By Wandering Around. It refers to the way executives visit operating departments and work groups, seemingly at random, but on a regular basis. The objective is to encourage Open Door communication and mutual trust. Or as John Young puts it: "What can we do in a pro-active way that tends to anticipate rather than react to the tensions that inevitably arise in the work place?"

Under MBWA, in a relaxed and informal atmosphere, managers listen to employee problems, complaints and concerns, exchange ideas, impart information. The payoff speaks for itself. When executives show a willingness to listen and respond, it is proof that they care.

Texas Instruments Inc.

TI normally stands for Texas Instruments, the world's largest producer of semiconductors. It also stands for Total Involvement.

At TI, *Fortune* writer Max Ways writes, "Employees at all levels participate actively in the planning and control, as well as the performance of the job. Seventy-three percent of TI's manufacturing employees and 49 percent of other employees form teams of four to ten members each" with methods improvement in mind. Ronald J. Ritchie, a TI vice president with responsibilities in Europe, Asia and elswhere, is convinced that the company's participative culture—in existence since 1930, a spokesman is quick to point out—can be transplanted anywhere. Says he: "I've never seen a job level where the guy wants nothing but pay." Ritchie believes the key to transplantation is a manager's willingness to involve himself with his people where the action takes place, and absorb their ideas of how the work should be done.

The company's commitment to this policy extends well beyond the lip service so often encountered elsewhere. Under TI's "people effectiveness programs" employees plan and control their own jobs. Worker teams aren't called quality circles, but they meet voluntarily, and that's what they are, causing an observer to wonder if, in initiating quality circles, Japanese industry didn't take a page out of Texas Instruments' book. The concept, incidentally, was transplanted in four TI plants in Japan about 12 years ago, where it is working quite well.

The team approach to problem solving is a longstanding management strategy. After natural work teams are formed, they meet to come up with solutions, suggest (and implement) improvements, and find ways to increase productivity. An example from the company's Freising, Germany plant involves an error rate reduction effort in the order entry department. With team members setting their own goals, they worked on "manageable parts of the problem" with a specific time commitment for solution. Measuring their own progress toward established goals, in this case as so often happens, the goal was surpassed: an error rate reduction of 1.2 percent points as against the stated 1.1 target.

As is the case in leading Japanese companies, a major reason teamwork succeeds is that each participant is given a personal stake in the program. Under TI's Success Sharing and People Involvement strategies, notes Executive Vice President A. Ray McCord, "employees must receive rewards for improving productivity, and more important, they must realize that they do. Most managers understand that improved productivity rewards employees by making jobs more secure and opening new job opportunities. But this is a remote and vague motivation for most employees. TI's Profit Sharing Plan makes a direct connection between productivity efforts and economic benefits to the individual, and we communicate this direct connection frequently and clearly."

Under the Plan, a People Effectiveness Asset Index is combined with an Asset Effectiveness Index to arrive at the Profit Sharing percentage, which makes Profit Sharing a unique overall measure of productivity growth. In one recent year, the profit share yield amounted to 15 percent of an eligible employee's income deposited as stock in his individual Profit Sharing account.

He thus enjoys an accumulation of cash along with an increasingly substantial piece of the company.

One of the company's major objectives as defined by TI Group Vice President L.M. Rice, Jr. is to make "every employee of TI, wherever located in the world, a part owner of the company, proud of his involvement, sharing in its profit, and striving for individual and corporate excellence."

TI is clearly committed to the long-term approach. In 1979 a goal of $10 billion in net sales was set for the late '80s; in 1980 this goal was revised upward to $15 billion. In support of this managerial philosophy the much emulated OST planning system was initiated over two decades ago. The letters stand for "Objectives," "Strategies," and "Tactics," each identified O, S, or T in the actual operation representing a corporate goal to be pursued by some organization or group.

"Taken together," comments E.W. Helms, manager of TI's Corporate Engineering Center, "the sum of the Objectives, Strategies and Tactics adds up to our total strategic business thrust. So OST is a goal structure, imbedded in our organization, that pinpoints responsibilities in that organization for strategic performance."

You can be sure the structure isn't likely to be altered as a result of stockholder pressure for a quick bottom line boost.

Nor are stockholders about to complain. If any segment of our economy apart from the automobile makers has been injured by the infiltration of Japanese products, certainly the electronics industry must rank high on the list. But TI, which produces a host of products from electronic watches and calculators to minicomputers and air traffic control systems, couldn't care less. In a nation by nation bar graph comparison of productivity growth since the year 1950, the United Kingdom and U.S. are at the low end with Japan well in front as the leader—and Texas Instruments, well ahead of Japan. The company has exceeded Japan's productivity growth rate, high as it is, for several years. Over a period of more than three decades, both billings and income have grown at almost 24 percent per year. An exception was 1981, a year during which TI was hit hard by competition from Japanese companies and such American stalwarts as Hewlett-Packard, Apple, and Tandy. The marketing blitz the Dallasites were subjected to would have sent less visionary corporations reeling. But despite its stock plunge toward the end of the year, most insiders are predicting the company will, over the longer pull, recover its punch and thrust once again.

Widely known as the orginator of zero base budgeting and a host of sophisticated financial, planning, marketing and manufacturing techniques, TI's major emphasis has been largely on people, people within the company, and people in general. In the McGraw-Hill book, "America's Competitive Edge," written by Richard Bolling and John Bowles, the authors write: "Texas Instruments' management believes that if they do not meet the genuine needs of society and their global markets, the company's profits will dwindle and the company will disappear." They go on to say that TI is "an unmysterious, hard-hitting and real-world example of how a company can integrate human, capital, and R&D resources to increase productivity, cut prices, expand business, and increase employment."

The company is run in a Spartan non-elitist environment where such signs of status as thickly carpeted offices—the higher level the manager, the thicker the carpet and the more wasted space—are conspicuously absent. The entire staff regardless of rank eat in the same open, spacious cafeteria where the strongest and most popular drink served is iced tea. There are no "dress codes" at TI, no special status-bestowed perks, and no hat-in-hand social barriers such as the requirement to address managers who have achieved a certain rank as Mr. So-and-so. Nor must employees wade through a chain of command if they have a suggestion to make or a complaint to register. And through OST, every employee, whatever his level, gets a chance to be his own boss and get his own ideas across.

TI Director of Public Relations Richard M. Perdue recalls a mammoth training program undertaken some years ago in which approximately 9,000 supervisors were introduced to the finer points of teamwork and participative management. "I personally participated in this special training," he says, "and it was merely a formalization of what I had learned to do the first year I joined the company in 1959. I had to unlearn a lot from my experience in other organizations."

He adds, "I think you'll find that the team approach exists in any operation where there is mutual respect. I was raised in my father's general store, and I find the same kind of family atmosphere at Texas Instruments. In fact, my father was probably *less* receptive to suggestions."

Dana Corporation

Dana, a Toledo, Ohio manufacturer of automotive parts, has more than doubled employee productivity over the past eight years. Based on a 10-year return to investors, the company is ranked second (behind Philip Morris) of the nation's top 200 industrial companies.

A variety of techniques, strategies and programs could be cited to explain Dana's remarkable performance and productivity growth. But when it comes to productivity, former Chairman Ren McPherson prefers a one-word explanation: *People!* His solution to America's productivity decline is simply to ask people, "What do you think?" a hundred thousand times a day.

McPherson lists five major ways to keep productivity high:

1. *Nothing more effectively involves people, sustains credibility or generates enthusiasm than face-to-face communication.*

2. *It is critical to provide and discuss all organizational performance figures with all of our people.*

3. *We have an obligation to provide training and the opportunity for development to our productive people who want to improve their skills, expand their career opportunities or simply further their general education.*

4. *It is essential to provide job security for our people.*

5. *Create incentive programs that rely on ideas and suggestions, as well as hard work, to establish a reward pool.*

Above all, the company believes in simply treating people like people, like intelligent adults who want to do a good job if they're given the chance. The work environment at Dana is friendly, unhurried and informal. McPherson says he spent five years "taking the handcuffs off people." Nobody is required to wear a suit on the job, and relationships regardless of rank are on a first-name basis.

The Look Alikes

The company has no use for time clocks. A time clock, McPherson believes, tells the employee, "You're a crook, and I got you on the clock so you won't steal from us." He contends that's ridiculous, that three people out of a hundred will steal, time clock or not, so why insult the rest? Time clocks already have been eliminated in more than half of the company's plants.

Another goal Dana is shooting for is to break the barriers that exist between hourly and salaried people in most companies. The company believes that working by the hour is demeaning and is experimenting in some of its plants with putting all employees on a salaried basis. Highly decentralized, Dana top management believes no one knows as much about his job as the individual who is doing it. Employees, including supervisors and managers, are given as much autonomy as they are willing to accept—plus the accountability that goes with it.

McPherson refers to this as "The People Principle." Managers, in the main, are permitted to operate with little headquarters control. Explains Gerry Mitchell, who in 1979 stepped in as president and chief operating officer, "Let's suppose a plant manager asks for a $4 million increase in his capital budget for the next fiscal year. He doesn't have to tell us what he wants it for, and I don't want to know what he wants it for; it's his plant." But if that money goes down the tube, the manager will be expected to justify it.

States Mitchell: "How can I tell another fellow, who spends a good deal of time operating a particular machine or plant how to best run it? He should be the one telling me how to run it and to get the most work out of it."

The participative management doctrine and promotion from within have been long in effect at Dana. Mitchell himself started his career with the company 35 years ago as a grinding machine operator. Employee involvement in functions beyond the routine is encouraged and assured by two powerful plus incentives:

1. Eighty percent of U.S.-based employees own company stock, so that the more productively and profitably Dana operates, the more valuable their holdings become.

2. Beyond that there is the uniquely effective Scanlon Plan in force in several U.S. plants. Under the system, bonus payouts for ideas that pay off can run as high as 30 percent. The average take is 16 percent as opposed to the 10 percent on first year earnings payoff in most companies with employee suggestion plans. At a Dana packaging and shipping plant in Churubusco, Indiana, bonuses are running about 25 percent of gross monthly salary. Employee morale? It's sky high.

Managers have as much of a stake in the participative approach as the rank-and-filers. At the twice-yearly accountability sessions, in order to put their best foot forward they must prepare assiduously by reviewing ideas and approaches with subordinates on the line, a process that takes place continuously. As in the best managed Japanese companies, it is in everyone's personal self-interest to cooperate with profit objectives in mind.

Layerism? It's a dirty word at Dana which has about half as many tiers as most major companies. Corporate staff is kept minimal in order to bring middle managers into close contact with top executives. Direct contact is encouraged in place of memos and reports. With less time spent on paperwork, executives have more time to listen, and managerial doors are wide open all down the line. How do you make people more productive? "In our opinion," says Ren McPherson, "you communicate with them. And what's the most important part of communicating? It comes very hard to a lot of us who are professional wind machines, and that is to listen."

It doesn't come hard for McPherson. "Scrapping the rulebook" was his first move when he took over the reins, according to business writer Thomas C. Haynes, and Mitchell is following suit. But you can be sure of one thing: A rule that will never be scrapped is Dana's adherence to the tough, lean, hard approach with a realistic perspective on what people need from the company and what the company needs from its people. In the early 1970s, Dana employed about 450 people at its headquarters office. Today with sales more than doubled, only 200 staffers are on tap.

Digital Equipment Corporation

The more the world's best managed and most successful companies are studied, the more the echo effect seems to appear. Writing about DEC, editor Bert Kirchner notes, "Everything conspires to force the manager to rely on people—not only on his own self-confidence and sense of responsibility, but also on his trust in his peers."

Trust is a word you hear emphasized in every top rated corporation I have yet come across.

And like most of the best-managed, DEC publishes its corporate management philosophy as a set of guidelines for employees to follow in varying business situations. Representative excerpts:

HONESTY—We want to be not only technically honest, but also make sure that the implication of what we say and the impressions we leave are correct. When we make a commitment to customers or to employees, we feel the obligation to see that it happens.

QUALITY—Growth is not our primary goal. Our goal is to be a quality organization and do a quality job which means that we will be proud of our product and our work for years to come. As we achieve quality, growth comes as a result. The product we are selling includes the engineering, the software, the manufacturing, and the services, which include field services software support, sales, order processing, training and manuals.

CUSTOMERS—We must be honest and straightforward with our customers and be sure that they are not only told the facts, but that they also understand the facts. To the best of our ability, we want to be sure that the products we sell solve the needs of the customer even when he is too naive to understand these needs exactly. When we sell a product to a customer, we want to be sure the Corporation fulfills the obligations we took on with the sale. We sell our Corporation, not a single individual, to our customers and we must be sure all DEC commitments are met.

COMPETITORS—We never criticize the competition publicly. We sell by presenting the positive features of our own products. We want to be respectful of all competition, and collect and analyze all public information about competitors. When we hire people from competitors, we should never press them for confidential, competitive information nor should we use confidential literature they may have taken with them.

SOCIETY—We are committed as a Corporation to taking affirmative action in providing equal opportunity for employment and promotion for all persons regardless of race, color, creed or sex. We encourage all employees to take responsibility in community, social and government activities. We are always open for proposals as to what the Corporation or an individual on Corporation time may want to do in these areas. However, activities done on Company time or with Company funds should have a formal proposal including ways of regularly measuring success towards goals.

Another echo heard from Toledo, Ohio (Dana) to Osaka, Japan (Matsushita) is the exhortation often made by Kenneth H. Olsen, DEC president since its inception (the title of chairman doesn't exist): "Listen to what people tell you *they* want to do."

Listening to people has thus far paid off handsomely. Voted one of America's five best-managed companies in 1979 by *Dun's Review,* the company started in 1957, according to *The Wall Street Journal,* "with old lawn furniture, a small, roll-top desk and three employees in 8,500 square feet in the corner of a woolen mill." Today DEC is a $2.4 billion company, number one in its field (minicomputers), employs 62,000 at 50 plants and more than 400 sales offices and, as Ken Olsen casually mentions, doubles every two years.

Like every other well managed company, Olsen attributes DEC's growth and success to its people. Here "participation" is more than a byword. Shades of Dana's Mitchell's conviction: "I believe that the worker always knows more about his job than his boss."

Olsen's office is as unpretentiously functional as the man and, most important, it is close to the source of "the action"—the development of new computer technology. As in the leading Japanese companies, everyone gets a piece of that action. The stress is on bottom-up management, and the company goes to great lengths to make sure individual engineering creativity isn't stifled. But the president bluntly states the importance of holding people accountable for their actions. "There is freedom to set your own directions," he says, "and to set tasks for yourself. . . . But there is no freedom without accountability."

Lifetime employment? It isn't unique to Japan. Digital has never had a layoff, not even when times became slack (a rare occurrence, admittedly).

More shades of Japan: Consensus decision-making. "At Digital," notes business writer Theresa Engstrom, "teamwork is everything. Marketing, development, production—all facets of a product must be approved by consensus before a project can roll. This 'diffusion of responsibility,' as Digital people call it, produces at least two side effects: endless rounds of meetings and a subtle kind of peer pressure." Engineering vice president C. Gordon Bell confirms this observation. "We tend to beat issues to death in a very open way, and one's always subject to public scrutiny." It takes a darned good management team, he concedes, to operate in this kind of a climate.

DEC's concern about its people is also evidenced by its no-commission compensation system for salespeople. On straight salary, the thinking goes, the rep is encouraged to think more about the next customer and less about "performance." Nonetheless, DEC salespeople perform at least as well as other industry reps, chalking up an average individual yearly revenue of about $850,000.

"Commissions are eschewed," *Fortune* writer Bro Uttal reports, "not just for tactical reasons, but because Olsen and his colleagues feel they are cruel. With commissions, some salesmen will never be able to make a living wage, and almost every salesman's compensation will plummet when demand is slack. 'The goals for our sales force,' notes Andrew C. Knowles III, vice president for corporate marketing, 'are loyalty, customer satisfaction, and low turnover.' "

Sales-force turnover at DEC is among the industry's lowest.

The company's sales goals are also indicative of Olsen's long-term perspective on business and growth. So is DEC's no-dividends policy, one that may be altered by the time this is published. But for now the CEO explains, "While in a fast-growth stage, we needed all the money we made, and then some, to reinvest in the company."

Regarding the long-term outlook, Bro Uttal recounts one of Ken Olsen's favorite parables. At the outset of business, return on assets was substantial partly because of

DEC's false building economies. When the plant's roofs fell apart in five years, it cost a bundle to replace them. Today's roofs have a 20-year life expectancy. "Unfortunately," says Olsen, "that kind of investment for the future doesn't show up on your annual statement for the year."

But it shows up in that two-year growth doubling rate.

The Japanese Have Plenty of Company

Needless to say, this is only a sampling. Several more successful U.S. companies could be cited which are managing their people and enterprises the Japanese way or, in some cases, the other way around, for many Japanese managers explain that exhaustive studies of top rated U.S. companies were made before their own management philosophies were solidified.

Nor must an American company, newly established, restructuring, or initiating a philosophy of management, turn to the Japanese as a model. As a growing number of successful corporations are proving, they can do as well or better emulating one or more of the top U.S. performers. A glowing example is Tandem Computers Inc., modeled largely after Hewlett-Packard, not surprising since James Treybig, Tandem co-founder and president, worked for HP along with three of his top aides.

Like its Palo Alto paragon, Tandem did away with time cards and features informal, humanistic management with a focus on open communication, and an employee participation philosophy that gives people as much sovereignty and responsibility as they are willing to assume. Peer pressure is virtually nonexistent, and class privileges awarded by rank aren't visible.

One thing Tandem strives hard to maintain is the entrepreneur's vision and perspective, a difficult quality to achieve as a corporation grows in size. The Cupertino, California company's growth is little short of phenomenal—at a rate of 100 percent annually. Few experts doubt that its projected 1983 revenue target of a half billion dollars will be exceeded. Though Tandem took its style from HP, it seems to be a bold step ahead of its model in its unorthodox management. From the standpoint of employee benefits, for example, it is more "Japanese" and family conscious than some of the leading Nipponese corporations. Every employee is eligible for its stock option plan. It grants all employees fully paid six-week sabbaticals every four years, throws Friday afternoon beer parties, and offers such recreational activities as a swimming pool and volleyball court for its workers.

Little wonder that in the face of a minicomputer average industry turnover of 23 percent, Tandem's runs only eight percent annually.

The evidence grows more overwhelming each year that success hopes are dim in companies where management and labor regard each other as The Enemy, and promising in organizations where employees trust and respect one another. Notes Mitchell Prize winner James O'Toole, some companies continue the outmoded adversary type management until it is too late to recover; others restructure their operations just in time. He describes one such last minute rescue in his award winning paper.

> In 1973, the managers of Kaiser Steel decided to permanently close their mill in Fontana, California because they were convinced that the mill could not compete with imported Japanese steel. Faced with the loss of their jobs, the workers at Fontana persuaded Kaiser to keep the plant open by agreeing to change their behavior. The hitherto adversary labor relations at the plant were quickly turned around, and workers started accepting the necessity for such things as limited lay-offs and overtime work. The managers changed their behavior too.

Previously unwilling to listen to the advice of "dumb" workers, they now started listening. For example, they followed the suggestion of the workers to improve the maintenance of machines, a simple act they had long resisted, but one which reduced the rate of rejects by 39% in the first instance it was tried. The managers had never believed the plant could be run profitably; but it is still in operation. . . . A union official identified the secret: "Nobody really knew what the workers could do if they cooperated."

A similar success story comes out of Fort Worth, Texas where Tandy Corp. bought Radio Shack for $5,000 in cash and $300,000 in working capital—all nine stores—and built it into a 6,150 store operation pushing the $2 billion sales mark. Notes *American Business:* "An investor who purchased 1,000 shares at $15 each in 1967 would find the investment worth $2.35 million today."

The chief reason? You guessed it. It starts with a capital P. The key focus is on People, and the "personalized approach" is a hallmark at Tandy. That applies to both employees and customers. Also, to what Charles Tandy, son of the founder, refers to as "institutionalized entrepreneurship." Basically, this means that in a very real sense employees, although they work for the company, are in business for themselves. Says one Radio Shack store manager, "This isn't a Radio Shack store, it's my store."

Tandy's biggest shareholder group is made up of employees who own 25 percent of the company's outstanding shares. Called "the McDonald's of electronics," according to Garland Asher, Tandy's director of financial planning, 40 percent of all American households are on Radio Shack's mailing list for advertisements.

The Giant Is Stirring. Then we have General Motors Corp.'s divisions all over the U.S. and abroad. It's no news to anyone that GM has suffered tremendous losses in the past due to strikes, cost overruns, layerism and worker frustration in general, and continues to experience some of these problems. But in response to foreign competition, the company is trying hard to delayer where possible and humanize its operations. More than trying, it is, from an auto industry standpoint in the U.S., pioneering and innovating with promising progress reported. Two cases in point are GM's Delco Remy Division in Albany, Georgia, and its Fleetwood Fisher Body Plant in Detroit.

At Delco all workers are divided into teams; you're either a team member or support person. Even the plant manager is a support person. Teams elect their own leaders from the hourly ranks. The first line supervisor has been converted into the "team advisor." At the weekly team meeting, he presents the next week's production goals and the team members decide how to meet them. The team copes with all problems, personal and otherwise, and peer pressure works its magic toward solution.

There are no "janitors" at Albany. Housekeeping is an individual and team responsibility. Maintenance people only handle the big jobs. Individual status and sensitivities are respected. The plant's products, Delcotrans, received one of GM's highest quality ratings. Productivity is up, absenteeism down. Grievances register less than 10 percent of those at comparable operations with the traditional management structure, according to Vice President A. S. Warren.

Notes Mr. Warren: "Even the design of the plant is open to continuous review by the workers. A blueprint of the plant is left in the cafeteria. People can suggest changes in the plant's facilities and operations. And nearly all of their suggestions have been implemented."

Though unionized, Delco's traditional rate structure has been altered. Workers are paid for their skills, not their time on the job. They exchange jobs to learn new skills and attain

The Look Alikes 269

higher pay. The result, says Mr. Warren, has been high quality and increased flexibility.

The approach at Fisher was somewhat different. Management held meetings with first-line supervisors to get their ideas for improvement. This was followed by meetings with union officials to bring them into the act. Now two-day workshops are being offered to hourly people on a voluntary basis, with a union and management facilitator helping to moderate the meetings. The focus for the present is on working environment, not on quality and productivity. The program is proceeding a carefully planned step at a time.

Though still in its formative stages, the effort's results are already noticeable in terms of an improvement in quality, reduced absence, upgraded communications. Some departments have started their own newsletters—run by hourly people. They discuss quality, productivity, and give employees personal recognition where warranted. Transition to automation is a whole lot smoother as well, Mr. Warren reports. "As a result of their better understanding of the operation, workers see the need for new tools."

As one manager put it, everyone benefits. "We don't have to spend all our time putting out fires. Engineers have more time to engineer. Managers have more time to plan."

GM has a long way to go, but its auspicious start is encouraging.

In the "Money." Money Magazine ran a piece a few years ago titled "Ten Terrific Companies To Work For." The Procter & Gamble Co. and 3M were two of the names on the list (which also included IBM, Eastman Kodak, Xerox, General Electric, Weyerhaeuser, Cummins Engine, Du Pont, and J.C. Penny).

Money wrote about P&G that ". . . People who work for P&G believe the products they make and market *are* better." Observed David North, a consultant: P&G is "a great school, not a great place to work." A couple of years there, he adds, are worth a second MBA.

Like all "terrific companies to work for," P&G stresses humanized management and mutual trust. States P&G Chairman Owen B. Butler, ". . . mutual trust pervades everything we do. We trust each other to be truthful. When a recommendation comes forward, when a forecast is made, when data are analyzed, when a future action is promised, we accept the promises, the conclusions, the estimates, because we know that we won't deliberately mislead each other or try to hide the truth. . . ."

Every chief executive *says* this. Whether the words ring true or are merely hollow pronouncements is tested by the company's popularity in the job marketplace. Butler also remarks that "it is declared to be the policy of the company to recognize that its interests and those of its employees are inseparable." This philosophy is held sacred by the leading Japanese corporations and by every top rated company described in this chapter. It might be added that P&G's employee profit sharing plan is probably second to none in the country.

Another featured credo of the Cincinnati giant ($11.4 billion in sales for the year ending June 30, 1981) is "Progress Through Individual Initiative." This is evidenced by "a deep respect for employees as individuals and a strong desire to provide each the opportunity to make the most of his or her individual talents." Notes executive Committee Chairman Edward G. Harness, "The character of the Company starts with its inward face—the way it is seen by its employees. Once this inward face is recognized, accepted and perpetuated by the employees, it soon becomes the Company's outward face, or the manner in which P&G is seen by shareholders, customers, suppliers, the government and the general public."

P&G apparently takes this pronouncement seriously. Management—top, middle and lower—is largely developed from within. Also indicative of the company's long-term perspective is the fact that most P&G employees spend their entire working lives with the company. As is flatly stated in the annual report, "the long-term development of the business is much more important than the results of any single year." A philosophy shared by the world's outstanding managers, wherever they function.

Also well up at the head of the class as a desirable place of employment is $5 billion-plus 3M, headquartered in St. Paul, Minnesota. If this company has one key operational word it is innovation, and the climate for it—however cold it may get in St. Paul in the winter—is red hot for ideas. If entrepreneurship is your cup of tea brew, 3M recruiters may be the people to contact. 3M employs more than 5,000 people in approximately 50 individual research laboratories. Cross-communication between the labs is an ongoing process in a continuing dialogue.

3M has an informal practice of allowing research scientists to devote 15 percent or so of their time on unassigned personal research pursuits, the ultimate demonstration of trust. States Vice Chairman and CEO Lewis W. Lehr, "Our management has also created a structure and a personnel practice whereby one individual can enjoy a series of several different careers without leaving the Company. The innovator who is so inclined can become the entrepreneur who goes on with his development to build a business. He or she may become the product champion in front of senior management or even in the marketplace.

"Such a person may also have the option of moving into technical and/or general business management. Or, the bench scientist who shuns administrative duties can remain a bench scientist while still advancing, because of a dual ladder personnel policy, to a corporate scientist rank, which is the equivalent of senior top technical management."

How successful is 3M in the marketplace? It boasts a growth rate twice as fast as the nation's GNP and can point to 20 to 25 percent of each year's sales resulting from products or services new in the previous five years. According to *Money,* "Working at 3M is fun. Recruiters describe 3M as shrewd, aggressive, well managed and good to its employees. It's been decades since 3M put an outsider into a senior job."

The Japanese in America

"Sure, the Japanese companies can win employee loyalty and willing cooperation in Japan, but the situation in the U.S. is different."

It's a commonly heard argument offered by American executives in explaining the significant difference in results between many large Nipponese and U.S. corporations. This is then followed by references to Japan's homogeneity, capital financing system, family ties that are culturally rooted, and other factors. Without denying the influence and weight of these factors, it is interesting to note that Japanese style management appears to succeed in the U.S. and abroad as well as Japan and—this bears endless repetition—wherever a company operates, its chances for outstanding performance appear to be multiplied if it demonstrates a clear regard for and sensitivity to the problems and needs of its people.

The Panasonic Company

Panasonic is a U.S. subsidiary of Japan's Matsushita Electric Industrial Co., Ltd. located in Secaucus on 46 rolling acres of New Jersey's sprawling Meadowlands complex. The company employs approximately 2,000 people nationwide, 800 of them in Secaucus. About 10 percent of Panasonic's workforce, including it managerial workforce, are Japanese. Several members of its top executive team are Americans.

Secaucus serves primarily as a sales office for more than 1,000 products made by the company, these ranging from pocket alarms and electric pencil sharpeners to TV sets and microwave ovens. Originating in 1959 as the Matsushita Electric Corporation of America, it was reorganized in 1979 into three separate divisions: Panasonic Company, Quasar Company, and the Matsushita Industrial Company under the MECA umbrella.

Panasonic ranks number one in the U.S. in the sales of tape recorders and is an industry leader in radio and other home entertainment products with an average annual growth rate over the past five years of 26.6 percent.

Ken Kurahashi, president and chief executive officer of Panasonic since early 1980 (currently president and chief executive officer of Panasonic Industrial Co.), a characteristically humble and courteous man with an incisive mind, is the first to admit that much of managerial knowledge and style stem from what he learned while studying General Electric Corp. and other leading U.S. companies. "I was surprised," he recalls, "how similar many of them are to Japanese corporations." He believes that the Matsushita style of management is applicable anywhere in the world, for human aspirations and needs aren't limited by national boundaries.

A framed sign in Panasonic's personnel office capsulizes Kurahashi's feelings about people in general and employees in particular. It reads: "Treat individuals as human beings. Respect them for what they are not what you think they should be."

Part of the human approach is the personal touch. Kurahashi makes it a point to get out into the field at least once a month, to talk with dealers, shake their hands, and meet their wives. In many U.S. corporations, when a new chief executive takes over the reins, all too often a "reorganization" takes place. This doesn't happen at Panasonic. Not a single executive was fired since Kurahashi stepped into the number one spot.

The company's training and development programs are planned with the long-term in mind. Since a major investment in manpower is made, Kurahashi stresses the importance of careful and efficient hiring and evaluating procedures. He personally interviews management applicants in an effort to employ the highest caliber people available after the candidate has been approved by personnel and other executives. "There are no big machines in a sales organization," he explains. "People are our only asset."

Equal care is taken with the assessment of personnel to avoid any possibility of error or unfairness in their development or advancement. The individual is evaluated by a succession of executives in addition to his immediate boss, then by an evaluation committee and, if one of the company's 60 top managers is involved, the evaluation is submitted to Kurahashi for his personal review and okay.

"The difference between good and not so good isn't always easy to pinpoint," he says. "We go out of our way to ensure that a good person will remain happy and stay with the company."

One way of doing this is through a system of job flexibility. Thus it is not unusual for a data processing employee to be transferred to Sales at his request, or an engineer in the products division moved to a spot on the sales engineering team. "We lack generalists," Kurahashi says, specifying generalization as a route to further growth. Even high level people are free to switch from job to job, and from one department or division to another.

Characteristically, the CEO is a strong advocate of consensus decision making. He feels it's a mistake to discuss issues with top people alone. One risk is that if this is done policies may not be carried out as desired by middle managers and rank-and-file people. At Panasonic, when problems and decisions are tackled all employees are consulted from the top

The Look Alikes

ranks and right down the line. Kurahashi also meets regularly with union leaders to keep abreast of how they perceive the company and its management. "If you talk only with top people," he adds, "you wind up with distortions which work their way to the botton."

Kurahashi was asked, "What advice would you give to a U.S. manager or student of management?"

His response was an engagingly modest smile. "I would not presume the qualifications to lecture to an American manager. But I will tell you what I tell myself, the ideals that I strive for." He cited these in addition to the standard characteristics of the good businessperson such as strong leadership, problem solving and decision making skill, etc.:

1. The manager must be a basically optimistic person, in decision making especially. If one is an optimist he can find many solutions.

2. The manager who is cynical or negative is not trusted by his boss or subordinates.

3. The leader must behave properly. He must be constantly conscious of many thousands of eyes on him. The higher one climbs, the more eyes. You sometimes find managers who are very strict with others, but not strict enough with themselves.

4. You must treat people fairly at all times. Your superiors and subordinates must come to expect fairness of you as a natural course.

"For a company to be successful," he concludes, "the people who work for you should be happy. The company's neighbors and the people who deal with the company will be happy. If you don't satisfy your own people, you cannot do the rest. This means everything."

It means everything in Japan. It means everything in America. It means everything anywhere in the world.

Quasar Electronics Co.

Improved employee morale plus quality awareness and concern can change a faltering operation into a viable enterprise. Quasar, another Matsushita plant located in Franklin Park, Illinois, and recently renamed Matsushita Industrial Co. (MIC), has been identified as a "model of efficiency" by *New York Times* writer Thomas C. Hayes. In 1974, when the company was purchased by Matsushita from Motorola Corp., it was a drowning enterprise with its head under water.

Most notable in the company's turnaround is the new evidence of employee loyalty seen only in top rated American companies and a reputation for quality that is tops in the field. Most significant is the reality that the majority of workers employed there today are the same workers who were employed in Motorola's bumbling plant.

Notes Hayes, quoting James I. Magid, an L.F. Rothschild broker who keeps tabs on the consumer electronics industry: "If you visit Motorola's present semiconductor and communications manufacturing facilities, you would see a combination of high productivity, worker satisfaction, low-cost, high quality products and a reliability record second to none in the electronics industry worldwide."

Within three years of acquisition, MIC turned the operation around. The average defect rate in the U.S. television industry, for example, is about 140 defects for every 100 sets built. MIC's average defect rate was brought down to five to seven defects for every 100 sets. A remarkable achievement—but Richard Kraft, who heads the company's manufacturing operation and worked for Motorola 23 years preceding the sale, still isn't satisfied. A sister MIC facility in Japan chalks up only one-half defect per 100 sets.

Motorola's chairman and chief executive officer discounts the reversal, according to Hayes. He claims to have purposely let the operation slide. "We couldn't earn a good return or build the market share, so I decided to get out."

Sour grapes? Perhaps. Maybe not. Whatever the case, the philosophy of the matter is worth noting. Settle for third rate quality? Deliberately allow an enterprise to go down the drain? The prospect is one that would give most Japanese business leaders—and most CEOs of the U.S. corporations described in this chapter—the willies.

According to Hayes, Motorola's resolve to let the operation slide was made in 1964, 10 years before the sale. Wow!

Workers at the Franklin Park plant shoot for individual and team targets called "quality bogeys" instead of overall plant goals, and in an adaptation of the quality circle arrangement, meet weekly with supervisors to discuss a range of issues from job problems and needs to employee working conditions.

It is ironic, perhaps, that Motorola which now enjoys a good quality and reliability reputation in the field, presently bills itself as "A World Leader in Electronics" that achieves "Quality and productivity through employee participation in management."

It is currently running an expensive two-page spread series of ads in leading publications headlined: "Meeting Japan's Challenge." In ad number four of the series, it insists that Japan isn't ahead of the U.S. in productivity, research and development, and amount of goods exported. This is true. But, while admitting that "Japan may be gaining," Motorola ignores the annual rate of gain in recent years and the reality that Japan is at the top of the productivity improvement list and we are, along with the United Kingdom, at the bottom.

The overriding theme of this book is that we'd better do something effective about it damned fast or it will be only a matter of time before the Japanese and other foreign manufacturers relegate the U.S. to second class status. Blowing our horn and proclaiming how good we are simply isn't the answer. A more effective show of patriotism would be to make the changes that are needed.

Motorola ad number two states: "Many factors contribute to productivity: producible designs, superior tools, clever processes, minimal regulations. But, heading the list is people. Most of us are aware of the impressive productivity improvements Japanese companies have realized with their people by using teams of cooperating workers called Quality Circles. Wisely, hundreds of American companies now are duplicating these efforts in their factories."

Where were these concepts and pronouncements in 1964?

How well is MIC doing in the bottom line department? It's hard to say. Although the turnaround is impressive, the company doesn't release earnings figures. Some industry watchers believe the company still is not profitable. It currently produces about 900,000 sets a year in a market that averages 11 million sets annually. In the meantime MIC's reputation for topnotch quality and reliability is steadily solidifying. Is the company satisfied to settle for slow steady growth with the long-term in mind in the classical Japanese tradition? Or does it have other objectives in mind? One cannot say for sure at this point. Clearly, the end of this story is yet to be written.

Others

A host of other Japanese companies are operating offices and plants in this country, largely staffed by American rank-and-filers and managers, and in varying degrees adapting Japanese style management to the U.S. work environment.

Sharp Electronics Corp., for example, with its sales office and headquarters in Paramus, New Jersey, runs several operations nationwide. With a topnotch reputation for quality, quality circle management is in force in Sharp's Tennessee plant. Although President Takeo Sagawa, a publicity shy man who steers clear of Japanese-American comparisons, believes the Japanese edge is due largely to deeprooted cultural factors and the desperate need for Japan's hard-pressed, energy-starved economy to come up with winning ways following World War II's devastation, surely his managerial philosophy must count in building his organization to its niche amoung consumer electronics industry leaders.

According to business writer Robert C. Wood, evidence from Toshiba, Nissan Motor, and other U.S. operations of Japanese manufacturers is proof sufficient that Japanese style management can work in America. He writes that at Toshiba's Lebanon, Tennessee, plant, "the Japanese have hired Americans to run most of their company—but quality control they supervise themselves. And their methods seem to work well . . . in a product whose assembly involves over 200,000 operations. . . . The average (reject) rate in recent months has been less than one percent."

And according to Shuichi Yoshida, a vice-president for quality assurance at Nissan Motor Manufacturing Corp.'s U.S. division, his company attributed cost reductions of $23.6 million last year to quality control circles—an average of $668 per worker.

At Sony's television manufacturing plant in San Diego, Japanese style management concepts ranging from consensus decision making and family-type integration to the interaction of line employees and top management pays off in high employee morale and its natural byproduct of high productivity. Time clock makers would go out of business if they had to depend on Sony. Managers and workers are on a first-name basis. Uniforms are provided, but not required and no dress code exists.

The low reject rate in San Diego proves that Americans are as capable of achieving high quality as the Japanese if they are properly motivated and given the standards and goals needed as targets. Promotion from within is an important part of the managerial credo, as is the company's concentration on training and development, and not a single employee has been laid off in a decade. When sales dragged in slack times, people were put to work on maintenance, cleanup and other chores.

Does the system pay off? In spades—and good attendance as well! The Sony plant's absentee rate is an impressive five percent. Efforts to unionize the company have been consistently defeated. "More significantly," states *Time,* "company officials now proudly say that the plant's productivity approaches that of its Japanese facilities."

Can the Japanese experience happen in America? There's no question about it.

Osmosis

Here near the conclusion of this chapter it is well worth including a talk by Dale Romine, Personnel Director of GM's Fisher Body-Fleetwood Division at the company's Quality of Work Life Executive Conference in 1980.

DEVELOPING SOLUTIONS: LEARNINGS FROM OTHER COMPANIES

In December 1979, Drew Danko of Organizational Research and Development and I visited 3M Corporation Headquarters and the Sony San Diego Plant to learn more about their approaches in controlling absenteeism. These two organizations were recommended because of their low absenteeism record and reputation for effective management.

Taking into account the differences in how absenteeism is measured in these two organizations, we established that

3M's absenteeism rate is about 4.8%. This 4.8% includes all lost hours contractual, controllable, and paid sick leaves and therefore compares to GM's rate of 19%. Sony's absentee rate of 5% includes both contractual and controllable but excludes paid sick leaves and therefore compares to GM's rate of 10%. Their record is accomplished with a higher proportion of females in their work force (average 50%, with some locations at 40% and others as high as 70%). In the past this has been viewed as leading to higher absenteeism rates. Both organizations were experiencing increasing trends of absenteeism and both were very concerned about it.

A significant point of interest is the lack of any "sophisticated" absence control program. Basically, theirs is a combination of management control and behavior management strategies based on a strong "people" orientation. Both use variations of progressive counselling for poor attendance and rewards for good attendance. Most significant is that both companies work at keeping the controls flexible, individually oriented and safe from abuses. Both companies believe the key factor to be the supervisor employe relationship with every absence followed up by the absentee's supervisor.

Based on our contacts with these two companies, we extracted the following learnings:

1. An organization's philosophy about people is fundamental in that it dictates what they do about controlling absenteeism and how they do it. Both organizations we visited are decidedly employe oriented and characteristics such as supportiveness, accommodating, trusting, dignity, cohesiveness, honesty, helping and a satisfying work experience are detectable in their management of this problem. Most locations of 3M do *not* require medical excuses if the person is sick.

2. Perhaps equally important as philosophy are the standards which the organization sets, communi-

cates and implements through its policies and practices. Both 3M and Sony have very clear standards about attendance and communicate that *both* management and employes are responsible for meeting these standards.

3. A third critical element is management's attitude toward ownership of the absentee problem. Our visits revealed concerned management who actively support attendance improvement efforts, who are directly involved in them and who are committed to continual improvement of attendance through experimenting, making mistakes and changing. This commitment is by line managers (plant managers or production managers, superintendents) not just personnel managers.

4. As indicated previously, the programs for dealing with absenteeism in 3M and Sony can be described as use of rewards (positive reinforcement), progressive counselling with release (negative reinforcement), and supervisory contacts. Supplementing these programmatic efforts though is training and/or selection which promotes or enhances healthy employe-supervisory relationships.

5. Communicating is an important process at 3M and Sony. At 3M, there is a great deal of work on measuring and monitoring attendance at the individual level; at Sony, there is a great deal of emphasis on two-way communications between all levels of management and the production levels even to the point of having daily meetings before the production line starts.

With specific reference to our visit to 3M and in support of the foregoing, generally we found the key ingredients to be: measurement, commitment, consistency, involvement,

The Look Alikes 283

and human relations. With respect to measurement, 3M emphasized the necessity for accurate records and used charts extensively to keep the problem in the forefront. Almost constant attention was paid to the problem of absenteeism through regular daily reviews and contacts. Any employee who was absent was talked to by his supervisor on the day of return. This discussion was related to counselling and working to solve the problem rather than discipline (correction by force). The following guidelines are provided supervisors at one 3M location:

- Try to determine the "real" reasons for the absences.

- Stress the need for correction and the problems caused by absenteeism.

- If the absences appear to be due to actual illnesses, try to determine what is being done about it, and stress the employe's obligation to correct the situation.

- Severe problems such as alcoholism, drugs, etc. require special handling. The employe must take steps to immediately seek help. If necessary, the services of 3M's Personnel Services Group should be called on through the Industrial Relations supervisor.

Although discipline was not used extensively, it did have its place in certain instances to bring the seriousness of the problem to the employe's attention. Coupled with this was the reality that failure to correct an attendance problem could lead to employe release.

Employes were made to feel involved in solving the absence problem in that discussions with the employes centered around the "real reason" why the employe was absent.

The following determinations had been made by 3M relative to absenteeism:

1. There is no discernible connection between an employe's attendance record and the amount of work he is required to do.

2. There is a very definite connection between an employe's record and his overall morale.

3. There is a very definite connection between an employe's attendance record and the way he feels about his supervisor.

4. Curbing absenteeism is a one-to-one proposition—the supervisor and the employe. Effective supervision will keep absenteeism at an acceptable level.

5. Curbing absenteeism requires a company policy and some reasonable rules supporting it. These are part of the supervisor's equipment, but he's got to use them intelligently, allowing for differences in people, differences in situations.

These findings led 3M to conclude that absenteeism can be reduced if:

- We realize that absenteeism is a human relations problem that you can control; it's never inevitable.

- We prove to every employe that he and his supervisors are concerned about absenteeism by never neglecting to question an absence.

- We keep accurate records to spot an absence pattern before it gets out of hand.

The Look Alikes

- We probe to find out the real reason people stay out, and avoid the false notion that people are all alike.

- We apply our policies consistently but are flexible enough to exercise good judgment.

- In other words, improvement of an employe's quality of work life results in improved attendance.

One example shared with us to illustrate this point was a program designed to bring together all levels of employes to work to identify, prioritize, and attack technical problems. A significant side benefit was an increase in "presenteeism" from 95% to 98% over a three year period. This change was attributed to *involvement* of machine operators in the various task forces created to solve the technical problem.

Another point emphasized by 3M was their view that *poor attendance* is just *one symptom* of a *poor work environment* and that in order to improve attendance, being at work has to be a positive experience. One application of these principles to a plan for a specific location improved presenteeism from 90% to 93.5% in just one year.

The message we learned at Sony was very similar. Sony utilizes an extensive pre-hire orientation process, organizes around work groups supported by the supervisor, believes in an honest, friendly relationship and stresses communication. Sony also shared the feeling that progressive counselling was an effective and practical way to approach the problem. Both 3M and Sony looked not just at the reason for the absence, but also the frequency. Both emphasized, however, that frequency and reason required individual examination of each case to assure that fair treatment was given. Although using some positive reinforcements such as certificates and dinners, Sony like 3M felt that this did not really work to correct an absenteeism problem but was effective in supporting and maintaining a good presenteeism level.

In conclusion, I would like to share with you the operating philosophy of one of 3M's plant managers who has a work force which is 40% female and whose absentee rate is 2% including paid sick leaves:

1. I treat people like I want to treated.

2. I treat people like respected adults.

3. I trust.

What about the vitally important hardware and software tools essential to the efficient and productive operation of a modern manufacturing plant in today's increasingly competitive marketplacc? Focusing almost exclusively on people, doesn't this approach sell them short? Not at all. In this author's and ex-manager's rather extensive experience, when you treat people like people, all the rest falls into place.

12.

MAKING IT HAPPEN

> *Looking carefully at Japan's development, we find that companies were dependent on outside assistance.*
> —*Konosuke Matsushita*

We can no longer afford to theorize and hypothesize. The time for action response has long since arrived. In the first three quarters of 1981 about 12,000 U.S. companies filed bankruptcy petitions, 42 percent more than the same period of 1980. The decline of the auto industry on which so many Americans depend is scary. Latest estimates reveal a Japanese cost advantage of $1,500 to $2,000 per car over non-Japanese models. One out of every three cars sold in America today is a foreign model, in California one out of two. Patchwork solutions no longer work. Detroit must rethink and restructure its whole business approach and philosophy.

Hopefully, the Big Three's aggressive interest in the national Quality of Work life movement augers a recognition of this imperative. In April 1980 Harvard University conducted a symposium on U.S. competitiveness in the world marketplace. Jointly sponsored by Harvard, the Senate Finance Committee's Subcommittee on International Trade, and the

New York Stock Exchange, one goal was to determine the level of domestic concern regarding U.S. economic decline in recent years.

Present at the symposium were representatives of government, industry, labor and academia. If the conference accomplished nothing else, it hammered home the message unmistakably that the public in general and business people in particular were deeply concerned over the decline and prepared to take drastic and unprecedented steps in an effort to turn the economy around.

Bluntly speaking, no other alternative exists. Happily, there is a positive side to the picture. Although the Japanese edge may appear at times too great to overcome, the truth of the matter is that American industry is in many respects in a more advantageous position. There are no doubts in this author's mind that given the triangular cooperation and support of industry, labor and government, the U.S. can not only catch up with Japan in the world marketplace, but surpass the Nipponese and regain the economic leadership that we held for so long.

The Japanese Never Had It So Good, But . . . .

The first step prior to formulating a plan and policy for corporate change is clearly one of assessment from the standpoint of both the individual organization and the total U.S. economy. What are the company's, industry's, and economy's competitive strengths and weaknesses? What steps and strategies will be required to cash in on strengths and shore up or work around weaknesses? What kind of agreement between management and labor will be needed for the company and/or industry to compete successfully with Japan and other foreign economies? What cooperation and assistance from government must be sought?

Japanese corporations are vulnerable in certain respects. U.S. corporations likewise. The trick is to compete ag-

Making It Happen 289

gressively where we have a clear competitive edge, to eliminate our own vulnerability where we can, and with the cooperation of government and labor to stress the enterprises where we are strong and steer clear of those where we are soft with no hardening tactics in sight. The Japanese have proven themselves to be masters at this art. In this respect we can take a page from their book and, of course, other pages as well.

But . . . The Japanese edge is misleading. Inroads have been so remarkable in such industries as automobiles and electronics, it tends to blind us to Japanese failure in other industries from tires and aircraft to pharmaceuticals and chemicals. The truth of the matter is that corporate performance is unexcelled and growth outstanding primarily in industries where the products are largely capital intensive, or where competition is efficient with narrow profit margins prevailing. What's more, however successful the leading Japanese growth companies may be, they have a great deal to worry about and, taking the long-term in perspective, some of Japan's business and economic problems may be harder to overcome than our own.

Few nations are as crowded or as resource-poor as Japan. While on the one hand these conditions made government-industry-labor cooperation critical to survival, on the other, all the cooperation in the world can't squeeze another pint of oil out of a barrel gone dry. The wheels of Japan's well tuned industrial machine will continue to turn into the 1980s and '90s only so long as the energy to run it is made available. With the Middle East situation as volatile as it is and some other countries less than enthusiastic about helping to sustain the swift growth of Japan's superefficient industrials, the problem is serious enough to keep some of the island's business leaders sleepless at night.

One alternative is nuclear, but this too is beset by its problems and bottlenecks. States *Time:* "In Japan, where 22 facilities now generate 12% of the country's electricity, another 15 plants are set for completion by 1985. Yet a major mishap (in March of 1981) at a reactor in Tsuruga, where a ton of radioactive water leaked into nearby coastal waters, captured national headlines and fueled opposition to atomic power across the country. Japanese officials last year (1980) proposed dumping low-level wastes into the Pacific, but an international wave of protest quickly forced them to table the plan."

If Japan's energy dependency fails to produce its fair share of insomniacs on this tight little island, surely protectionism will be able to step in and take over the job. A key issue being debated these days among economists, businesspeople, and government officials in most major industrialized countries—the ones Japanese industrials rely on to gulp down its products—involves the pros and cons of Japan's industrial growth from the debater's point of view. The faster the growth, the louder and more vehement the cries for protection are sure to become. The more badly domestic industrials are hurt by Japanese inroads, the more feeble and ineffective the free trader's arguments for open world competition will be. Japan's smart and shrewd corporate leaders started heeding worldwide climate changes with trade balance in mind a long time ago. Hence the decision to export not only products but industries as well, and the startup of so many Japanese facilities all over the globe and in the U.S. in particular.

Then we have the breakneck pace of industry itself. How long will the Japanese be able to sustain the present level of productivity improvement that is in large measure attributable to optimized worker time utilization? Employee loyalty and dedication notwithstanding, it's unrealistic to imagine that workers—with or without quality circles—can continue exceeding productivity records indefinitely. Some industrial relations experts and psychologists, in fact, question the wisdom of shooting for ever-higher targets. At a certain point, they believe, the negative stress factor tends to override the positive performance result.

During the past decade or so in Japan, the work ethic was revered with near-religious intensity. But this attitude appears to have peaked in recent months and now appears on the wane for two compelling and logical reasons. The first was revealed in a study conducted last summer (1981) by the Japan Productivity Centre which found that the hectic work pace of Japanese industry leaves one employee in ten suffering from nervous stress. The second is a very natural response to affluence we in America should understand better than anyone. Summed up by a Japan Survey published in the September 14, 1981, edition of *World Business Weekly,* a caption used tells the story: "The workaholics turn into leisureholics."

Last year, the report goes on to say, the Japanese "leisure market was estimated to be worth around $150 billion, 14% up on 1979 and an eightfold increase since 1965. The Leisure Development Center reckons it will be worth more than $500 billion by 1990 at today's prices."

As consultant Leonard J. Smith states the case, "Once the hard and lean Japanese begin to reap the material reward of their industry and frugality, they will inevitably turn some of their focus from job responsibilities to recreation to an increasing degree as time goes by. That doesn't mean they will be any less loyal to their employer; it simply means they will succumb more to affordable and attainable lures like gaming and travel."

Utopia or Bust. The peoplization of industry, the single factor more responsible than any other factor for the Japanese edge, will be increasingly put to the test as this century weaves to its uncertain close. Lifetime employment and benevolent paternalism, along with such inbred cultural attributes as respect for authority and the kind of family-type integration that encourages teamwork, have contributed mightily to Japan's productivity leadership among industrialized nations. But the nation's investment in its impressive nurturing of human resources is becoming more and more costly. The question is: How long can it continue?

This presents a problem for two reasons. One, with Japan the world's biggest user of robots, as an example, is the rapid expansion of automation and technology. As more and more corporations and divisions become highly robotized with a single machine performing the functions of several workers, what will become of the workers? Is Japan heading for a utopian three or four hour day? If so, will it be able to continue competing in the world markets as effectively as it does today? On top of that, what provisions will be made for all the free time of employees? If Japan develops into the world's foremost leisure society, how long will the current work ethic persist?

Another disquieting question relates to the ageing of the Japanese labor force, a question that raises new worries. Today's 30, 40, and 50 year old worker is loyal and docile, the work ethic imbued into his life rationale and philosophy. Much less so, the employee in his early 20s. And considerably less industrious is the youngster in school, judging from current reports. Young people in Japan are less inclined to work hard than their elders; like young people in the U.S. and Western European countries, they are restless and more preoccupied with self-gratification. Nor are their temperaments so conducive to a lifetime of loyalty with and to a single employer. It is a subject of concern to Japanese managers.

Within the next decade or two Japan will have the oldest workforce in the industrialized world. Today's "retiree," at an average age of 55, is in some measure absorbed by the large number of smaller and lower paying companies (lower paying by about 60 percent on the average). Inevitably the retirement age will push closer to 60, unless automation restructures the society in a still unpredictable way. Inevitably, increasing numbers of seniors—traditionally revered and treated as the nation's wisest and most worthy group of citizens—will be competing for a decreasing number of jobs.

Most of these people will want to continue working, will not be intellectually or physiologically prepared for pasture-ization. How will Japan's economy cope with them?

The Japanese have acquired a justified reputation as adroit strategic planners. Do they have a master plan for dealing with the country's problematical old and young workers? Or does the ultimate answer lie with some Skinnerian type of a utopian society?

The Tradeoffs

Business in a way is like contract bridge. Bidding conventions help the partnership to exchange much needed information. But there is usually a tradeoff involved. For each gain you achieve when a convention is used, you give up something in return. So it is with Japanese management. Its mighty values and strengths have been demonstrated and proven. But in competing with Japan it makes sense to keep the system's vulnerabilities in mind as well.

Inbreeding. No industrialized society has ever more assiduously sought and emulated new ideas from abroad than the Japanese. Yet, ironically, it is still a very closed society. Foreigners are regarded with mistrust and suspicion. Outsiders are not easily accepted and integrated into the mainstream of Japanese life.

Inbreeding certainly is not unique to Japanese corporations. It's a common pitfall for U.S. companies as well, especially companies which have become so accustomed to success that they take it for granted. A reluctance to revise and adjust plans, policies and procedures to new market conditions and requirements can be pinpointed as the primary cause of innumerable corporate disasters and individual managerial downfalls. Management theorist William Ouchi singles out inbreeding as "perhaps the greatest risk" of the "Theory Z" or egalitarian type of management.

As McKinsey & Co. consultants Tino Puri and Amar Bhide state the case: "Homogeneity breeds ethnocentricity" which makes any ideas that originate outside the core suspect.

Inbreeding also produces conformity, a weakness often attributed to Japanese society as a whole and to industry as well. Ralph Waldo Emerson wrote, "Who so would be a man must be a nonconformist." And the 19th century philosopher Arthur Schopenhauer said, "We forfeit three-fourths of our selves in order to be like other people."

Every individual is unique with a unique potential that is entirely his own. When one gives up his individuality he relinquishes his opportunity to be an exceptional person. Where an organization—or society—fosters conformity, it invites mediocrity.

No nation's commitment to individuality and independence can match or surpass the U.S. commitment. Atlantic Richfield's communications manager Bill Stephens, although much impressed with Japanese style management, observed after his visit to and study of leading Japanese corporations: "Japanese corporations aren't perfect. Critics say that the price the Japanese have paid for their success is over-conformity to group norms at the expense of the individual and creativity. It can be humiliating for a young person not to land with the right firm and it can be next-to-impossible to go elsewhere once you're inside."

The difficulty of switching employers is another problem that disturbs many Japanese workers. Sperry New Holland's personnel vice president Michael R. Losey describes an unplanned encounter he had in Japan while enjoying a Big Mac at one of the nation's McDonalds fast food establishments. He engaged two young Japanese men in conversation, one of whom spoke English and was particularly interested in the theme of American individuality. In this Osakan student's view, lifetime employment wasn't good for either himself or the company.

Said Mr. Losey: "He felt he could learn much more by working with different people in different organizations. He said he did not plan to work for just one company," but didn't know how he could "beat the system," since employees who leave their organizations are looked down upon in the labor market. Perhaps he would go to the United States, he added, after graduation three months hence. Which only proves that even the presumably *ideal* work situation is only ideal when it is so viewed from the worker's perspective.

Author Adam Smith sums the problem up in a nutshell: "The homogenous corporate systems of Japan cannot cope with internal cultural diversity. And options are closed off at an early age."

A Japanese manager told me after serving two years of a three year stint with his company's American division: "If I were empowered to make one change in the Japanese system, that change would be in the form of a managerial strategy designed to encourage more individuality and greater independence of thought. I would not abandon the concept of lifetime employment, but I would make taking advantage of it optional."

The American Edge

While the American edge—success factors where the U.S. enjoys an advantage over Japan—is substantial, given the situation today, the power of the Japanese edge over the American edge is still sufficient to result in an ever-widening gap in the race for productivity rate increases. Most experts agree that overall U.S. productivity is still better than Japanese productivity, but if existing conditions continue, this won't apply too much longer.

Women. The Japanese manager smiled when I brought up the subject of women in management in Japan and was reluctant to pursue this line of conversation. The fact is that the woman in management in the large Japanese corporation is a rarity. The manager explained that much of business is conducted during off hours in bars and men's clubs, where some of the language and topics of discussion would be offensive to the female ear, and where "a woman's inclusion simply would not be appropriate."

What's more, he added, the Japanese woman customarily leaves the job market after a few years to marry, raise a family, and keep house for her husband. Women in management is not a practicality in Japan. He expressed the further opinion that all of this would change some day, but the change is still a long way off.

The typical woman who charges a man with being a male chauvinist has never been to Japan. The Japanese male culturally and traditionally loves and respects women. But he is firmly convinced that "a woman's place is in the home" making and raising her children, and otherwise serving her husband.

Few would question that it is still "a man's world" in America. But it is much less a man's world than in Japan. In the U.S., innumerable middle and high level management jobs are capably held down by women, and the number is growing each year as the scales continue to balance more and more favorably toward sexual egalitarianism in business.

States San Francisco's Bruce A. Nelson who recently lectured extensively in Japan on equal employment opportunity laws in America, "Certain employment practices that are standard in most of the world—especially the relegation of women to subordinate roles—are illegal in the U.S."

Indeed, a host of suits claiming sex discrimination have been filed in recent months against employers whose managerial payrolls are overbalanced in favor of males. Interestingly, in one such case, a class action suit was initiated by secretarial employees of Sumitomo America Inc. in New York, charging that only Japanese males were being hired for management-level jobs. In 1953, a court of appeals ruling held that Japanese businesses in this country are not exempt from antidiscrimination laws.

America may still have a long way to go in granting female employees equal job opportunity, but it has made impressive strides in recent years toward this goal. Given the tough leadership and resolve of the women's movement coupled with the growing recognition by business leaders of the inestimable value of this yet to be fully tapped human resource, further progress in the decade ahead is inevitable. In this author's opinion, women's increasingly important role in business and industrial management—a virtual doubling of the human resource asset over Japan—represents the single most important advantage in the American edge. As progress along this line continues to accelerate, that advantage will grow more and more powerful.

Technology. More technical innovation and automation have been pioneered and initiated in the U.S. than in any nation in the world. America long has and continues to be the world's undisputed technological leader, and critics often charge Japan with being adept at copying, but second rate when it comes to creativity. This may have been so in the past, and may continue to be so to some degree, but it would be a mistake to sell the Japanese short so far as technology and innovation are concerned.

Japan is surely one of the world's most stubbornly persistent societies; on top of that, Japanese national pride and pride in performance are second to none. Tell a Japanese manager that he falls short in this or that attribute, and he will work 14 hour days in an effort to correct the flaw. So it seems to be with innovation.

Matsushita Electric Co.'s advertising persistently proclaims its technological prowess, touting such products as

"3-Dimension TV", a "1½-inch pocket TV that plays most anywhere in the world," "talking ovens that also see," and "eyeglasses to help the deaf hear." Hitachi's "voice response system lets a computer speak with a natural human voice," and the company bills itself as "the world's advance technology leader."

Another company, Fujitec, is challenging U.S. giants Otis and Westinghouse with "the world's fastest" elevator said to run on 30 percent less electricity than the American models. Japan now produces an estimated 80 percent of the world's production of high-speed facsimile machines, according to *Business Week,* and nearly 20 percent of all fax machines made in Japan are for export. "Because foreign competitors are not keeping pace with Japanese product development," the report continues, this trend is expected to accelerate.

Not surprisingly, Nipponese auto industry innovations are keeping pace with if not exceeding Detroit's. To cite a few, *Time* reports that Japanese manufacturers are using computers on a chip to improve fuel economy, monitor the engine and even make a new electronically controlled transmission operate smoothly. Toyota's radar-activated cruise-control senses vehicles ahead and applies the brakes when necessary; if it starts to rain, electronic windshield wipers adjust their speed to the amount of precipitation. And a Nissan-made car's "voiced word recognition system" responds to the spoken commands of a handicapped driver. Japan's Ministry of International Trade (MITI) announced recently that Japanese engineers have developed robots that not only weld, paint, stack and pack but also walk, feel, grasp and—if properly equipped—talk.

And so it goes. Surely, the U.S. is still a world leader in technology. But anyone who believes the Japanese are standing by complacently content to copy American innovations and convert them to yen, is living in a dream world which could become nightmarish if no action is taken. The question is, of course, what can we do to make the most of our technology lead?

Automation advances provide the capability of boosting, not only U.S. manufacturing productivity, but quality as well by means of improved production consistency and more precise engineering design. "Computer-aided design and analysis systems," observes Roy M. Salzman of the management consulting firm of A.D. Little, "permit better prediction of product performance and assurance that all components of the product will function properly with each other. Robots and other computer-based manufacturing systems can produce components with much greater consistency than human counterparts. Inspection devices with computer-driven 'eyes' and precise coordinate measuring machines can ensure that the product has, indeed, been manufactured to specifications."

So far as state of the art supremacy is concerned, few would question that the U.S. still holds an impressive lead in the development of computer software and computer-aided design. All we need do is cash in on our mighty advantage. This is admittedly easier said than done. Awakening U.S. business leaders to the realization that it *has to be done* isn't the problem. "Making the most of our technology edge," declares Apex Electronic Inc's CEO Michael Dorota, "is no longer a matter of choice, it is one of business survival."

This is to some degree in the hands of labor and government. Again, where a clear opportunity to make important productivity strides exists, instead of labor-industry-government teamwork taking over, the battle lines are being drawn. States more than one labor leader: "There's no question that automation will be a key issue in collective bargaining in the decade ahead." What we need, according to United Auto Workers consultant Harley Shaiken, is "a national debate on the social consequences of microelectronics."

There is little talk of a national debate on the social consequences of failing to cash in on the advantage the U.S. technology lead affords along with the opportunity it provides for narrowing the productivity growth gap between the U.S. and Japan. Quite obviously, what we need most of all is a tripartite agreement among representatives of labor, industry and government that will encourage and aid implementation without giving either labor or management an unfair advantage at the expense of the other. Japanese workers share in their employers' technological gains. There's no reason U.S. workers cannot do the same. But more on this shortly.

And More. Other advantages as well work together to make up the productivity edge potential the U.S. has over Japan. Both the U.S. and Japan are democracies, but in some aspects that apply to the workplace, the U.S. is more democratic and this constitutes a powerful plus from the standpoint of human resources optimization. We already discussed the values of cashing in on the managerial talents and capabilities of women who make up about half the available workforce, something the Japanese have thus far failed to do. In addition, it can be argued that U.S. industry takes greater advantage of the creative talents and developmental capabilities of its male working population as well. An ideal example is the case of Dana Corporation's chief operating officer and president Gerry Mitchell who started his Dana career as a grinding machine operator. It is *theoretically* possible for a Japanese worker to advance from the ranks to a high level executive job. But bridging that gap in a large corporation would be a near-impossibility due to a classification system that relegates office and factory workers to clerical and production chores, generally keeps supervisors at a level within their specified hierarchical framework and, despite the laudable degree of egalitarianism practiced, elevates executive personnel as a kind of elite. In the U.S. a bright young worker, male or female, given the proper imaginative and leadership attributes, has a much better chance of climbing to the heights with his or her full range of talents exploited.

On top of that, the U.S. is as blessedly resource-rich as Japan is resource-poor. As a *Business Week* team of writers points out, the U.S. "has more oil, more natural gas, and more coal than any other country in the Organization for Economic Cooperation and Development" and, equally important, the technological skill needed to exploit these resources to their full potential. "Transforming this potential into reality," the team goes on to say, depends heavily on our willingness "to pay the full price of energy."

From a business standpoint, the U.S. has a bigger and better educated workforce and developing workforce population than Japan, with an abundance of top rated universities geared to equip young people as generalists or specialists for careers in commerce and industry. The trick, of course, is to gear educational curricula to the more specific needs of the marketplace, an area where better cooperation and communication between educators and business people could serve to sharpen the U.S. educational edge into an increasingly productive asset.

Finally, while Japanese consensus decision-making has such clear advantages as consensus agreement and the avoidance of friction, it gives the competition an important advantage as well. Getting a quick decision out of a Japanese corporation can be as difficult as filling a cavity of a shark with a toothache. Added to this is the reality that American businesspeople are more bold and adventuresome than the Japanese when it comes to experimentation and risk-taking. As Tino Puri and Amar Bhide point out, "The ingrained habit of having to conserve inhibits (the Japanese from) committing assets to high risk ventures."

They go on to describe global, technological, and developmental opportunities which, while potentially profitable, entail a degree of risk the Japanese businessman is in most cases unwilling to assume. "In time," the McKinsey observers conclude in a *Wall Street Journal* essay, "Japanese society and industrial organizations may transform themselves in order to fulfill these new tasks. Until then, non-Japanese competitors have real opportunities to hold their own by exploiting Japanese institutional rigidity."

The American Challenge

Today's Japanese economic invasion, with significant inroads being made in one U.S. industry after the other, calls to mind Marshal Ferdinand Foch's famous wartime message issued on the eve of the second Battle of the Marne during the first world war:

> "My center is giving way; my right is pushed back; situation excellent. I am attacking."

The French commander succeeded at the time in halting the heavy German advance, which helped turn the tide of the war.

The United States has been similarly put to the test more than once. When the Nazi war machine, rolling over Europe, was at its most powerful peak, U.S. strength was puny by contrast. Yet we garnered our forces of manpower, technology, and resolve in a remarkable show of cooperation and teamwork, confronted the challenge and met it. Toward the end of the following decade we faced a challenge of another nature when America became the first nation to land a manned space ship on the moon. This project too was beset with mind-boggling technological problems which at times seem insurmountable, and required the willing and efficient cooperation of labor, industry and government. Again, in an inspiring display of national integration and teamwork, we tackled the job that had to be done and wound up victorious.

Sometimes it would appear that for the U.S. to perform in a unified, outstanding and courageous manner, a great deal must be at stake and the odds against us impossibly high. Well, today American economic well-being is at stake. How we respond could determine America's economic status among the world's industrialized nations for decades to come, the employment situation, and ultimately the living standard of every American worker. And given the current adversarial relationship among industry, labor and government, plus the overwhelming U.S. handicap of a bitter and dispirited workforce, the odds are certainly stacked high against our overcoming the Japanese productivity edge in the foreseeable future.

So be it. If this is the condition we need to excel—as any automobile industry executive would agree—the condition is well upon us. I might only add that judging from the action pledges and resolve being expressed by a growing number of U.S. corporate managers, government and labor organization officials, the time for restructuring and renewal may be closer than the doomsayers suspect.

U.S. Mandate No. 1: RESTORE HUMAN TRUST AND ALLEGIANCE. If we succeed in fulfilling this mandate, I have an abiding faith that all of the following mandates will fall into place as required.

"Do you know what astounds me most about the world?" Napoleon asked towards the end of his career. "It is the impotence of force to establish anything. . . . In the end, the sword is always conquered by the mind."

We can't force workers to cooperate with management. We can't demand loyalty. Nor can we pressure people into performing more productively. But we can win them over by honest efforts to convince them it is to their benefit as well as management's to work together in a unified effort to outcompete the competition. And we can prove that we mean what we say by indicating what the rewards of teamwork will be and producing those rewards when the revenue-creating results of effective teamwork become evident.

Restoring America's "good old team spirit" to the American workforce is clearly a two-sided task, and it is up to management to make the first move. This does not imply more giveaway programs or fancier fringe benefits. They don't work. For team efforts to succeed, workers must be convinced they, the workers, are important to the operation, and managers, sharing this conviction, must treat them as if they're important.

According to Professor James O'Toole: "The only way to change a company's or a nation's productivity/labor cost ratio is to alter the entire congeries of fringe benefits/incentive schemes/working conditions. These conditions have to be such that workers can clearly see that it is in their *self-interest* to improve the productivity/labor cost ratio. Jaw boning won't do it."

Professor O'Toole cites a partial list of strategies which, in his opinion, deserve high marks in making employee attitudes more positive:

- The Scanlon Plan (Attractive profit sharing used by Dana Corporation and others)

- Cooperative stock ownership

- Productivity sharing

- Incentives for teaching other workers

- Peer-set salaries and raises

- Access to phone for all workers (including blue collar)

- Portable pensions

- Well-pay, safety-pay

- Pay for task completed, not hours worked (e.g., finish job, go home)

Making It Happen

- Flexitime (instead of rigidly set working hours)
- Autonomous work teams
- Peer-established work/plant rules
- Self-managed quality control
- Worker-designed jobs
- Job posting and job sharing
- Permanent part-time employment

Professor O'Toole adds: "Not that these conditions are appropriate in all workplaces at all times. Nor is the list rigorously all-inclusive; it is merely suggestive of the kinds of conditions that have the characteristics of diversity, choice, flexibility, mobility, participation, rights tied to responsibilities, and security."

U.S. Mandate No. 2: CASH IN ON THE JAPANESE EXPERIENCE. Don't try to superimpose successful Japanese management tactics on a U.S. environment. But do delegate selected bright and people-sensitive managers the task of making an exhaustive study of leading Japanese companies—and leading U.S. corporations as well—with the objective of pinpointing techniques and strategies applicable to your own industry and organization. Then investigate as many American companies as possible that already went through this mill to find out how they did it, the problems they encountered, and how they are solving them.

This may be a painful reversal of roles following the long period of economic history during which Japanese and other foreign executives swarmed to the U.S. in an effort to understand and emulate our methodology. But we can learn a great deal from this process and, as a number of Japanese managers made clear to me, the Japanese stake in our successful turnaround is high since, without American prosperity, Japan's most important foreign market would be jeopardized. For this reason, and because many Japanese managers I've discussed this with genuinely appreciate America's role in Japan's redevelopment and renewal—most notably in the area of quality control—their gracious cooperation and support of many of the country's largest and most successful corporations can be counted upon.

The authors of both best-selling books—"Theory Z" and "The Art of Japanese Management"—strongly suggest that American managers turn to Japan for role models. This author vehemently agrees. And most experts on the subject of Japanese management appear to agree that while it would be a grave error to attempt to carbon copy Japanese style management in the American workplace, important aspects are most certainly adaptable.

You don't necessarily have to visit Japan to get insights into Japanese management ways. Increasingly, trans-Pacific technology transfer is being effected through cooperative deals and information exchanges between Japanese and American companies. In addition, technology transfer represents a business opportunity being seized by enterprising Nipponese firms. Career Development International, for example, a wholly owned Sony subsidiary, has introduced a three-day "intensive management simulation" service. Other Japanese companies are participating with U.S. firms in quality circle seminars and information dissemination to American companies by means of study trips. And of course the literature on the subject continues to multiply.

Commercial interests aside, Hitachi President Katsushige Mita sums it up in a nutshell: We have taken and taken for years. Now it is our time to give.

U.S. Mandate No. 3: REFUSE TO SETTLE FOR SECOND BEST. A. D. Little's Roy M. Salzman states the situation bluntly enough: "It is well recognized that cost alone is no longer the reason that U.S. industry is losing ground to international competitors." Higher quality products from Japan and Europe, he adds, are forcing U.S. companies to seek new and more efficient ways to ensure a consistently high level of quality production.

Salzman cites automation which upgrades manufacturing consistency and design precision as one important solution to the problem. A critical American plus along these lines is the continuing sophistication of computing capabilities coupled with the declining price of computer hardware and software. On top of this is U.S. leadership in the mushrooming growth of microelectronics and the vast potential of microprocessor chips which enable the development and manufacture of consistently excellent high quality products machined to close tolerances.

Equally if not more important is the generation of heightened and sustained employee quality awareness and concern. Japanese companies and, increasingly, their American counterparts, implement thousands of quality control suggestions each year communicated by means of quality circles and suggestion plans. This ties in directly, of course, with U.S. Mandate No. 1 involving the restoration of employee trust and allegiance. According to Joseph Juran, a U.S. quality control engineer who has served as a consultant to auto companies worldwide, 80 percent of the defects in the U.S. auto industry are "management-controllable." He calls for long-term quality control training in the Japanese style, beginning at the top and filtering down through the ranks, which steers us directly into Mandate No. 4.

U.S. Mandate No. 4: FOCUS ON LONG-TERM PROFITABILITY AND GROWTH. Several businesspeople interviewed pinpointed switching to a long range corporate perspective as industry's most critical and difficult challenge in the decade ahead. It is the only way, they stress, to develop a solid managerial and organizational structure and the corporate resolution and strength needed to compete successfully with foreign economic infiltration in the years ahead. "Relying on trade protectionism," Apex Electronics' Michael Dorota insists, "is a poor substitute for sound and patient corporate foundation building, will eventually weaken U.S. enterprise, and could lead to global conflicts as well."

Admittedly, bucking shareholder profits-now pressure will prove tough for top managements accustomed to quick-results operation, but it is the only way to ensure sustained corporate health and its byproduct of executive job security. Studying U.S. companies and their activities and managerial philosophies (or lack of philosophy), it is interesting to note that by and large the nation's strongest and most successful corporations are the ones where top and middle management personnel survive the longest and look upon their jobs as lifetime careers. It is mainly in the statistics oriented "performance" companies where the chief abiding interest is the daily stock fluctuation that periodic "reorganizations" take place and managers feel most insecure.

A fact of corporate life any B School student could confirm is that business growth requires investment on an ongoing basis—in product development, product and marketing research, plant modernization, employee training and development, plant expansion, and the rest. It is a parallel fact of life that such expenditures are costly and impact adversely on current earnings reports. But without exception every top rated industrial company in the U.S. or Japan pays this price, and reaps the inevitable benefits.

In some corporations imaginative new means of financing enterprise must be sought to decrease company dependence on public capital markets. Japanese executives are freer than U.S. managers to pursue long term objectives because of the major role played by banks in fulfilling capital needs. In Germany, bankers interested in long term relationships are often board members of the important companies they lend money to, and help in monitoring programs and activities to ensure continuing investment with an eye to the future. The

Making It Happen 309

challenge to enterprising U.S. bankers virtually poses itself. American imaginative capabilities are second to none in the world. If Japan and Germany can do it, with U.S. government cooperation and assistance, why not us?

In any event, for the near term at least, more courage is needed on the part of corporate leaders in response to shareholder profits-now pressures. One solution, notes consultant Leonard J. Smith, may be in some cases to revert to private ownership. He also feels that more corporations might do well to make their philosophies public, let investors know in advance that the company is interested in long term growth and not quick-kill advocacy. "Corporate policy," he stresses, "must be spelled out by top management, not dictated by Wall Street."

Management must also take the action necessary, adds Smith, to protect itself against raids. "The stronger a small or medium size company becomes," he points out, "the more greedy the hungry bigs become to gobble it up. A good executive is too often forced to the realization that if the job he does is too good, it may force him out of a job. This presents another challenge to management. It must find ways to build defenses against unwanted aquisition."

The consultant calls to mind one company that included a clause in its employment contract whereby key executives would, in the event of takeover, receive three times their regular compensation, a provision almost guaranteed to discourage would-be raiders from dive-bombing.

U.S. Mandate No. 5: SWIFTLY DEVELOP A MITI EQUIVALENT. If anything has the Japanese businessman joyfully smiling all the way to the bank, it is Japan's Ministry of International Trade and Industry (MITI). Although industrially strong West Germany gets harmonious government, industry and labor relations through a system of consultations and by having representatives of labor sit on corporate boards, it has no MITI-type operation in force. Great Britain and Italy are no longer major factors to contend with when it comes to world commerce. France's National Planning Commission and Ministry of Research and Technology, formerly useful, have been severely crimped by the business community's lack of faith and trust in Mitterand's Socialism and have bankbound Japanese smiling more broadly than ever.

This gives the U.S. its most pounceable opportunity in decades. Japan's MITI-generated edge in world industry is as important as any other factor in the nation's success with the possible exception of its humanistic and egalitarian form of management. If a challenge of challenges exists in the U.S., it is the triangular challenge of quickly structuring and drawing national commitment to a tripartite planning and cooperative alliance consisting of Labor, Industry and Government (LIG).

Given America's imagination, ingenuity and rallying power in crisis, there is no reason LIG united cannot accomplish what MITI has accomplished and more. Above all, the crisis imperative must be spelled out as simply and forcefully as possible, and national commitment mandated. With the issues clear cut and hammered home to top officials of labor, industry and government, who would not respond positively? With the realization apparent that acting counter to LIG's dedicated objective of recharging and regenerating the U.S. economy would be self-defeating and, yes, unpatriotic, what responsible leader would opt for heat in place of reason?

Obviously, each leg of LIG would have its particular function to fulfill:

- Labor must understand and acknowledge that the complete and wholehearted cooperation of workers at all levels nationwide is absolutely essential to our economy's success.

- Industry must establish policies and objectives which include profits, of course, but extend well beyond profits—and certainly well beyond "profits now"—and aspire both practically and philosophically to long range security and wellbeing for the organization in general and all of its people in particular.

- Government—our elected officials—must be committed to the establishment and sustained sound health of the nation's economic foundation; this implies consensus decision-making on issues of national and international industrial significance with *friendly and cooperative* inputs from all three branches of LIG.

It is particularly critical that legislators in cooperation with business and labor officials develop a tax structure and monetary plan that will encourage the laying aside by industry of reserves of capital for investment in product research, the application of new and developing technology, human resources development, and plant refurbishing on a long-term basis with corporate growth and continued soundness in mind.

The U.S. National Productivity Council established in 1978 appeared to be an auspicious start towards a MITI-like structure in America. But it seems to have fizzled, with few meetings held since January of 1980. Hopefully, the Council's work in cooperation with labor and management groups in the automobile industry may help respark efforts towards a unified national body that will help all segments of the economy as the Ministry of International Trade and Industry helps Japan.

Specifically, what has MITI achieved? It draws up comprehensive data of immense value to Japanese planners, spelling out which industries possess maximum growth potential and are eligible for government financial assistance. This information is produced on the heels of innumerable meetings in which representatives of government, labor and industry thrash out scores of consensus decisions. The key operational word—or co-operational word—is compromise, with the interests of labor, industry and society as equitably balanced as possible.

MITI's funding function—of most favored industries, developing technologies, and Japan's continuing internationalization—has proved to be of vital importance to the growth and expansion of the nation's economy. Contrast this, the *Business Week Team* point out in their book ("The Reindustrialization of America"), with the U.S. approach which tries to keep workers employed in declining industries, and with the European system where government attempts to prop up steel mills and other ailing industries with subsidies.

Clearly, none of these five mandates will become operative overnight. But just as clearly a sixth mandate must if we are to pull out of the bog and start moving forward on solid ground once again. *We must get the momentum under way,* convince ourselves and the world that Operation Turnaround has begun. Once it begins no one will want to, or be able to, stop it.

The toughest part of beginning, so far as corporate managerial style is concerned, states restructuring expert Roy W. Walters, lies in getting managers to understand and agree to the changes that have to be made. Education and enlightenment about what excites people in the workplace and the critical role trust must play in the manager-worker relationship will have to start from the top and filter down through the ranks. "The best way to begin," Mr. Walters says, "is simply by allowing it to happen."

Finally, we can all take a tip from the hard new Xerox approach to competition in general and Japanese competition in particular. Chairman C. Peter McColough presents the company's position and resolve clearly enough when, facing up squarely to the Japanese onslaught on his company's markets, he has set forth a plan to repel Japan's attack on the one hand and, on the other, a Xerox counterattack of its own.

Without question, the time is at hand to strike back with economic survival and refueling in mind. A big plus in our favor is that our leading economic opponent—Japan—can be counted upon to be highly supportive of our efforts, and will be rooting for us all the way, for its own economic well-being is also at stake.

TOMORROWLAND

The Dilemma of Too Much Success

We are witnessing, or are about to witness, the most exciting, unsettling, and worrisome worldwide transformation of economic coexistence and accommodation since the industrial revolution—with Japan at the fulcrum.

Japan today is a society in rapid transition. Between now and the year 2000 we will see this tight little island trembling from the shock waves of Westernization lashing hard against its implacable shores of age-old tradition and culture. At the same time, we will see a global wingspread of Japanese industry reminiscent of America's early burgeoning days of world economic leadership.

More than a decade ago, Alvin Toffler wrote in his book, "Future Shock," that he "came to be appalled by how little is actually known about adaptivity, either by those who call for and create vast changes in our society, or by those who supposedly prepare us to cope with these changes."

This is what will make the transformation worrisome and fraught with uncertainty. On top of that, the super-acceleration Toffler refers to may seem like slow motion compared to what will take place between now and the end of this century.

Already Japan is being pressed into action by a combination of pressures and circumstances, and most of all by a steamroller economy that can't afford to slow down. The repercussions from this response will have a significant bearing on the lifestyle and economic security of every man, woman and child on this planet for decades to come.

The Japanese economy today is confronted by the gargantuan task of, on the one hand continuing to flourish, and on the other, surviving. However, unlike the U.S. economy which might be compared to a disassembled car with its parts all over the place, Japan's unified and single-minded economy is by contrast like a well lubricated vehicle speeding along toward a well defined destination.

Japan knows where it is going and what it must do. In the decade ahead it must deal with and adjust to:

- Growing world concern over, and fear of, its steamroller economy and the impact it might have on corporate profits and jobs in an increasing number of industries.

- Critical Japanese labor shortages in a number of specialized industries, coupled with threats of rapidly growing unemployment due to mushrooming automation in a society which counts "guaranteed lifetime employment" as a "sacred treasure."

- Japan's internal economy slowing to a crawl in the face of mounting annual trade surpluses due to the nation's exports explosion.

- The inevitable impacts of culture shock on a number of fronts such as the opening of new tradition-smashing roles for women in the workplace, the challenge of providing for Japan's aging population in a society that pays deference to the old, and a growing Western-type restlessness on the part of the young who are more and more challenging the Japanese work ethic and demanding instant gratification and increased leisure time.

- The need to overcome traditionally xenophobic perspectives and throw open hitherto closed Japanese markets to foreign enterprise in order to promote international goodwill and help discourage protectionist leanings abroad.

- The stirrings of social upheaval in response to inadequate housing and, in some industries long working hours and mandated worker relocations, along with the inequitable treatment of women.

Operation Outreach

Japan's economic juggernaut must keep rolling to stave off widespread unemployment due to automation, if for no other reason. Since the domestic Japanese market is small compared with U.S. and European markets, and is no longer growing, there is only one way for the Japanese economy to keep thriving: that is to internationalize its operations.

If Japanese government and industry leadership possesses one attribute, it is determination. When an objective is set, every avenue of enterprise is investigated, every opportunity seized, in bringing it to fulfillment. Japan's plans for Operation Outreach, if accomplished, would not only make its global ambitions palatable to the major industrial countries of the world, but secure its positions of world economic leadership as well.

The nation's master plan may take years to become operational, but important aspects are already well under way. A major part of the strategy is, through the good offices of government and industry, to make companies abroad offers that are "too good to turn down": offers of shared technology, for example, joint ventures of various types, partnership enterprises, and offers to open manufacturing, research, and marketing facilities abroad that will provide business opportunities and jobs where they are critically needed.

The overall philosophy of Japan's Operation Outreach is as basic as Konosuke Matsushita's managerial credo: To add value to the fortunes of any individual, organization, or country that does business with Japanese industry. It achieves this goal by introducing products that are priced lower than the same products manufactured domestically, and are usually superior in quality as well.

Emerson wrote: "If a man has good corn, or wood, or boards, or pigs to sell, or can make better chairs or knives, crucibles, or church organs, than anybody else, you will find a broad hard-beaten road to his house, though it be in the woods."

Japanese industry and government are embarked on an all-out crusade to prove this premise.

Stone Turning. If the Japanese are anything at all, they are thorough. Any stones within sight that have even the remote possibility of concealed treasure beneath will be turned over, and the sightings are precise. Japanese companies, for example, assisted by MITI studies, probes and encouragement already are moving in to establish ground floor tenancy in supplying Third World communications and electronics requirements for the future. So far as specific product needs are concerned, MITI chips in heavily for the product design and developmental research. Manufacturers by and large need only worry about application and production.

Digging in to compete hard with U.S. and European electronics and communications giants, Japan has already won a billion dollar contract to install a telecommunications system in Malaysia and has beachheads established in Argentina and the Arab world as well.

Under the guidance of MITI's master plan reached through government-industry consensus, each Japanese giant is a well targeted juggernaut in its own right, concentrating on specific product and market segments: Hitachi already is turning out more 64K RAM chips (integrated circuits) than the three or four leading U.S. producers combined. Sharp and Casio together are cornering the world calculator market. Canon claims to be number one in the U.S. copier market and three out of four low price computer printers and about as many high-speed facsimile units are also Japanese.

The familiar proven strategy in markets abroad is to come in with quality products that are too cheap to resist, and gradually trade up as the Nipponese foothold becomes secure.

The Buddy System. Are other governments and foreign corporate giants standing by affably while the Japanese land and take over? Not by a long shot, and foreign resistance has been carefully calculated and accounted for in the master plan. One of the surest ways to avoid trade friction, the reasoning goes, is to cut in the export target for a generous piece of the profit pie by means of partnership agreements. It's happening in Europe and America. The strategy generates domestic employment, stimulates business, and keeps everyone happy, including government watchdogs.

The system is already working with a string of U.S. giants ranging from the auto industry's Big Three to such companies as IBM and 3M already marketing Japanese products in the American marketplace. In some cases, U.S. distributorship is set up because opening a network of Japanese sales offices would be too costly a venture, undermining the neon lighted low price advantage. In the case of large scale computer systems, for example, the ultimate goal of Nippon Electric Co. (NEC) is to establish its own distributor network in the U.S. The question is whether NEC and other companies can achieve this objective without whipping competitive resolution to new heights on the one hand and jeopardizing the Japanese price advantage on the other.

Stargazing. There's nothing like heady success to keep the stars shooting high, and that's what the Japanese have been enjoying of late. The declared long range goals of the Ministry of International Trade & Industry (MITI) are clear and concise: 30 percent of the world computer market by the end of this decade, in large measure by means of Third World penetration; worldwide electronics domination and ultimate independence in both hard- and software technology; telecommunications superiority over such behemoths as AT&T, especially in the developing world; and a redirectioning of Japanese enterprise away from energy-intensive industry (such as conventional chemicals) and toward knowledge-intensive industry (such as biotechnology).

Most significant is the Japanese resolution to convert what long has been assessed as one of the nation's primary weaknesses—a shortage of creative and innovative capability—into one of its most potentially profitable strengths. Along with the low-price-high-quality lure for international prospects and customers, one sees unique and attractive new features—on cars, copiers, calculators, TV sets and other home electronic products—thrown in for good measure. We will see more and more of this in years to come. Already, in several areas of scientific and engineering research, technologists are turning to Japanese papers for the latest developments in the state of the art.

Nor is any of this being accomplished on a catch-as-catch-can basis. MITI stresses the importance of its objective to compensate for such natural economic handicaps as the nation's meagre access to affordable oil by optimizing its creative brainpower to the maximum extent possible. Ambitious programs are already under way to make this goal a reality. Where tne Japanese have a leg up over U.S. corporations in striving toward this end is in the nation's pooling of company and government resources with consensus agreement and cooperation achieved when it is mutually beneficial—beneficial for the companies and for society as a whole. Herein lies the key to making the system work.

Two-way Street. One of the toughest challenges facing the Japanese in the years ahead will be to make its program of internationalization a two-way street. As the rationale runs: "If we expect a warm and welcome reception from host countries abroad so far as our products are concerned we must, at the very least, extend the same kind of welcome to foreign corporations wishing to do business in Japan."

Wiping out the perception in the U.S. and Europe of Japan as a country unfriendly to foreign business overtures will be a difficult task for the traditionally xenophobic Nipponese to accomplish. The telecommunications industry offers a unique opportunity to help dispel this notion. From the time the Nippon Telegraph & Telephone Public Corp. was established in 1952, NTT linkage with Japanese suppliers has been so involved and complex, foreign competitors were virtually ruled out of the market.

Today, the word is that NTT is "opening up," that it will be amenable to U.S. bids in particular. This remains to be seen. One question being raised by wary Japan watchers: "Will Japanese corporations chop profit margins to the bone and beyond in an attempt to keep NTT from buying American?" This too remains to be seen. The objective view is that the strategy would be inadvisable and would not receive government backing. For one thing, reasonable profit margins must be maintained to finance internationalization; for another, foreign goodwill will be critical for free trade to survive. If there is one thing Japan looks out for, it is its own best national interests.

Yen Flow

The yen will be flowing in some new directions as the 1980s push on toward the '90s. MITI will continue to fund research and product development in narrowly defined segments of the economy and it will continue to sponsor ambitious studies and probes into information and infiltration opportunities all over the world. In addition, government laboratories and researchers will work along parallel lines. Finally, MITI and other government agencies will pour massive funds into the financing of Japan's millions of small manufacturers which primarily service the giants as contractors.

This is all made possible by billions of yen reserves generated by a system where the government's Postal Savings department offers tax-free interest at rates comparable to commercial banks' for Japanese savers, who are the most thrifty on earth. Until recently, this diversion of funds from the banks was no significant problem since the banks were doing a heavy loan business with the big corporations. But the picture is currently changing, with loan activity in many institutions reduced to a trickle because so many of the large corporations are now yen-rich and financing their programs internally.

The government, which finances industry through the Japan Development Bank (JDB), which in turn borrows most of its funds from the Postal Savings system, will be even more selective than in the past in dispersing its yen. Stressed today are energy-related research and advanced fields of technology. Loans made for these projects are interest-free; on other loans the going rate is charged.

In recent months a growing number of corporations have decided they might be better off selling stock to the public. It's a blossoming trend that makes some prudent managers edgy. They're concerned about undue shareholder influence. "When Japanese executives start focusing on today's bottom line instead of long-term growth and development," says one, "they will start wooing disaster."

Leaving the Leader Behind

In past decades Japan has been playing Follow the Leader insofar as product development in general and technology in particular is concerned. MITI-minded managers in the years ahead, intent on pacing the field, have plans to leave the leaders behind. With this resolve in mind, the yen-rich corporate giants are investing massive sums of their own, separate and apart from government financing, in advanced technical research.

Sony, for example, is plowing back hefty chunks of its sales revenue into semiconductor research. Matsushita is doing the same, along with Hitachi, Toshiba and others. Much of the research is esoteric and far out, geared to market opportunities projected 10 and 12 years down the pike. The same story holds true for robot technology where companies like Sanyo, Yasakawa Electric, and Kawasaki Heavy Industries Ltd., have, with MITI's aid and encouragement, poured huge sums into research in recent years and expect before the end of the century to launch a major worldwide sales offensive with the U.S. market potential alone estimated at eight to nine billion dollars.

Total independence is a hardset Nipponese goal. As one MITI official states the resolve: "When a foreigner mentions the technology or creativity gap to me a few years from today, I would like to be able to answer: 'What gap?' "

The vastly ambitious Fifth-Generation Computer program painstakingly hammered out by MITI and friends with what will truly be "the thinking machines" of the 1990s in mind, is a shining example of the unified vision of Japan's business and government leadership. While Japan wants to lead, it has no desire to go it alone. MITI has scoured the world for participants and has received expressions of interest from cautious but respectful representatives of leading U.S. and European computer makers. It is MITI's hope that technology transfer and information pooling will take place in a constructive atmosphere mutually advantageous to all parties. If this hope is fulfilled, it would go a long way toward winning international acceptance of the Japanese role. After all, it is easier to do business with a "partner" who has a stake in the project than with a hardnosed competitor who is intent on beating you down.

The Barrier Busters

Point out to a Japanese where an obstacle exists in achieving a goal that's been set, and he'll work like a beaver inspired to mow down the roadblock. Innovation is the classic example. As recently as two or three years ago, high level executives at such companies as Matsushita, Sony, Hitachi, Fujitsu and Sharp, informed that while Japanese businessmen are brilliant in many respects, they lack the creative capabilities of Westerners, would have smiled agreeably as if deploring the situation, then proceeded to reverse the condition. Today it would take a tome as thick as a Manhattan telephone directory to print a full list of Japanese innovations in a growing rundown of products and industries.

It stands to reason that, given the Japanese worker's attitudinal response to corporate needs and objectives, the directory is destined to grow thicker in years to come. One of the most valuable byproducts of the quality circles is the quantity of suggestions generated by the working groups, substantially greater than those produced by the suggestion plans of U.S. corporations where material reward incentives are higher. Since productivity experts are in general agreement that the individuals best equipped to come up with improvement ideas are the men and women on the line, it's logical to assume that the upward flow of suggestions in Japanese plants will multiply as the fervor continues to spread.

It wasn't so long ago, for example, that Japan was described as "years behind" in microprocessor design. Yet only recently Nippon Telegraph & Telephone (NTT) announced its first 32-bit microprocessor, almost on the heels of U.S. announcements.

Germaine to the barrier busting effort, of course, is the consensus plan developed by Japan's powerful tripartite alli-

Making It Happen 323

ance. MITI resolutions call for software development, as one illustration, that will be compatible with advanced computer systems still in the offing. With this goal in mind the Ministry is into heavy funding for advanced software package research, and offers attractive tax advantages to companies that come up with successful programs with an opportunity to recoup their investment over a period of years. As a result, companies like Hitachi and Fujitsu are growing software subsidiaries faster than a baby octopus grows tentacles, and hundreds of small firms are springing up on their own.

Nor do the Japanese tie their hopes to Japanese efforts alone. Industry and government emissaries are going all out to induce U.S. software producers to develop packages tailored to Nipponese computers already in production and/or on the drawing boards. One hard to resist lure involves the financing of research projects. Another proposes sales minimum guarantees.

Manpower in the software field is admittedly hard to come by these days and will grow scarcer in years to come. Well then, tradition be zapped where it interferes with national goals. The latest trend, just barely blossoming, is toward *womanpower*. In an upgrading of females that is inevitably destined to expand, increasing numbers of women are being niched into engineering and programming jobs. What will happen when, in their late 20s or early 30s, these technologists quit work to keep house? One widely made guess: They'll work part time at home, which could spawn a whole new cheap skilled labor market.

With regard to technology in general, the question is more and more getting to be: "What technology gap?" Japanese universities today are turning out engineers faster than American B schools produced accountants in the 1940s and '50s, and certainly in greater abundance than U.S. universities. In addition, several large industrials have company sponsored and controlled colleges of their own where advanced education, largely technical and tailored to specific needs, is conducted on a continuing basis. We are thus witnessing a vast educational effort which combines on-the-job with lab and classroom training.

As one Japan watcher states the case: "The American student usually stops college when he gets his degree and a job; at that point the Japanese student often starts it in earnest."

Old Vs. the New

Much of the progress made by Japanese industry in recent years has been attributed to ideals and characteristics inherent to Japan's ancient and time-honored customs and culture. But today, some worried sociologists believe, the beginnings of social contamination are already in evidence in a variety of forms from designer jeans and rock 'n' roll to openly expressed gripes about hard working hours in fields where job skills are in short supply, and a budding youth culture that glorifies instant success and self-gratification.

In a nutshell, the anxiety nagging at a growing number of predominantly conservative businessmen is: What fissures will be produced in the traditional culture as a result of the jolting shock waves of accelerating change beating up against it today?

There are no easy answers. Surely one endangered tradition is the "sacred treasure" of lifetime employment. In plant after plant where robotics and other forms of automation are being installed, one finds production capabilities expanding and workforce requirements shrinking. This may be good news for productivity-minded corporate executives, but it's an Excedrin-sized headache as well. Japan's unemployment rate, still a low two percent, is growing at an alarming rate and this is only the start. What's more, hundreds of thousands of workers are swelling the workforce who could be let go tomorrow but are being retained to keep the "sacred treasure" intact.

Until now, the job displacement problem has been solved by attrition. Workers aren't being fired, but neither are new workers being employed. This is fine for today, but what about tomorrow? What about the new throngs of college and secondary school graduates entering the workforce? Will the growth of export trade continue at a pace sufficiently large to absorb the continuing influx? It is questions like this that are confounding the economists and sociologists.

The arithmetic is simple enough. As the sophistication of robots and computers increase and they get cheaper to make and to buy, they will push the cost of manufacturing down. Simultaneously, labor costs will continue to climb. Thus far most workers have been sold on the premise that what benefits the company benefits them as well and all of society. And thus far, to support this conviction, workers saw tangible proof in the benefits and security they enjoyed, and in the way they were treated. But their faith could come unglued faster than a postage stamp on a letter immersed in a glass of water if they are confronted with too many job uncertainties and expectations of sacrifice.

Already complaints are being voiced, for example, in connection with a new trend toward three-shift plant operation which makes economic good sense in wringing maximum mileage out of expensive automated equipment. And where displaced by a machine, even if not fired, many workers are unhappy at the prospect of being transferred to remote locations. What's more, with the spectre of increasing unemployment looming in some sectors, combined with the added employment of female part timers, men are caught in the friction-fraught bind of competing for jobs with lower priced women. In fact, a significant part of the workforce is already ensconced in such jobs. All of which makes the newly blossoming attempts of some tradition-scoffing militants to form independent *non-company* unions anything but surprising.

What will probably have the most rattling effect on Japan's ancient culture is the emergence of women's lib Japanese style in defiance of deeprooted tradition where the female, dominated by the male, is functionally put on this earth to serve her man and rear his children. Notes one woman graduate newly employed by a small software firm in an engineering capacity, "I already tried housekeeping and don't like it at all. And I'm not sure child raising is for me."

As Tevya described the situation in *Fiddler on the Roof*, such heresy is "Unheard of!" "Absurd!"—but it's happening. So drastic a transition as a mass exodus of women from the home to the job market will undoubtedly take years to develop. But even the most conservative Japanese businessman concedes that its development is inevitable in time.

What does it all add up to so far as the American worker, business-person, and government official are concerned? On the one hand, a worrisome outlook; on the other, an unprecedented opportunity. Japan today, it would appear, is at or close to the peak of its economic well being with an inspired workforce and very low unemployment. Sustaining that peak and controlling the tides which threaten to jeopardize the current near optimum condition will become increasingly problematical in the years ahead. Frictions are sure to develop and build, trade barriers are sure to grow, work ethical traditions are sure to be challenged by more and more workers, and by the young in particular.

At the same time, assuming that the movement toward humanized management in America continues to grow, and that increasing numbers of executives adopt managerial philosophies roughly fashioned after those of Konosuke Matsushita, U.S. worker and plant productivity could start an upward sweep that would gather momentum as the new spirit takes hold. Herein lies our hope and our dream.

What does it mainly depend on? On overcoming the mountain-high advantage the Japanese currently enjoy over the U.S. and the rest of the world, the advantage of Japan's powerful labor-management-government tripartite alliance. Therein lies the hope of that nation.

What it boils down to is that the Japanese have their act together and we do not. That is the challenge confronting us. And on that our economic survival depends.

References

CHAPTER 1

Konosuke Matsushita sections on his philosophy: From "The Philosophy of Management" series, published in various issues of *PHP Magazine*.

CHAPTER 2

Yasukawa quote: *PHP Magazine*, Apr. 1981, p. 83.

Report statistics: "Joint Economic Report," 1980.

Home-appliance material: "U.S.-Made Appliances Bomb," by Leroy Pope, *American Business*, Aug. 1981, p. 2.

Robot material: Japanese Industry survey, *The Economist*, July 18, 1981, p. 13.

Sporting arms material: "Japan Gaining in Sporting Arms," *The Record*, Aug. 14, 1981, p. C-7.

Computer printer material: "Japan's Swift Success in Printers," *Business Week*, Aug. 31, 1981, p. 73.

Motorcycle information: "The Technology War: Behind Japanese Lines," *Playboy Magazine*.

Report to management: Michael M. Losey, Sperry New Holland Co., Dec. 1980.

HBR quote: "Why Japanese Factories Work," by Robert H. Hayes, *Harvard Business Review*, July-Aug. 1981, p. 57.

Emanuel information: "Productivity Improvement—Japanese Style," Report by Myron Emanuel, *Communications & Management*, Jan.-Feb. 1981.

Stephens comment: "Visions: The Rising Sun of Productivity," by Bill Stephens, *Mgr.*, 1981/Two.

Emanuel comments: "Productivity Improvement—Japanese Style," Report by Myron Emanuel, *Communications & Management*, Jan.-Feb. 1981.

Sagawa quote: "A View on U.S.-Japanese Business," by Glenn Ritt, *The Record*, June 29, 1981, p. A-7.

Business Week quote: "Japan's Edge in Auto Costs," *Business Week*, Sept. 14, 1981, p. 97.

Hayes quote: "Why Japanese Factories Work," by Robert H. Hayes, *Harvard Business Review*, July-Aug. 1981, p. 59.

CHAPTER 3

Time quote: "How Japan Does It," *Time*, Mar. 30, 1981, p. 57.

Morita quote: "Sony: A Diversification Plan Tuned to the People Factor," *Business Week*, Feb. 9, 1981, p. 88.

Idemitsu material: "Managers Employ Unusual Techniques at Idemitsu of Japan," by Mike Tharp, *The New York Times,* June 8, 1981, p. D4.

CHAPTER 4

Fischer quote: "Taking Combat Out of Labor Relations," by Ben Fischer, *Business Week,* Sept. 21, 1981, p. 17.

Bernstein quote: "Democracy Moves Into Workplace," by Harry Bernstein, *Los Angeles Times,* Oct. 23, 1980.

McDonald and Warren quotes: Speech by A.S. Warren, at the American Institute of Industrial Engineers, Detroit, May 7, 1981, p. 4.

Simmons quote: Story City project report, used at American Productivity Center seminar, by Michael R. Simmons, Sept. 13, 1979.

Walton quote: "Work Innovations in the United States," by Richard E. Walton, *Harvard Business Review,* July-Aug. 1979, p. 98.

Story City material: See Simmons quote above.

GM EPG information: "QWL Update" (GM publication), Mar. 1981.

Bluestein comment: "Labor-Management Cooperation in Productivity," talk by Delmar L. Landen before the American Productivity Center, Apr. 21, 1980.

Butler material: See Simmons quote above.

Kofka quote: "The New Industrial Relations," *Business Week* Special Report, May 11, 1981, p. 98.

CHAPTER 5

Interpace material: "How a Winning Formula Can Fail," *Business Week,* May 25, 1981, p. 119.

Coors story: "Coors Eats the Dust As the Giants Battle," *Business Week,* July 20, 1981, p. 54.

O'Toole material: "Work in an Era of Slow Economic Growth," by James O'Toole, Mitchell Prize Award paper for Third Biennial Woodlands Conference on Growth Policy, Houston, Texas, Oct. 28-31, 1979, p. 9.

Emanuel quote: "Productivity Improvement—Japanese Style," by Myron Emanuel, *Communications & Management,* Jan.-Feb. 1981.

McLuhan material: "Sure Fail—The Art of Mismanagement," by Raymond Dreyfack, (distributed by Farnsworth Publishing Co., Inc.) p. 59.

World Business quote: "SURVEY: Japan," *World Business Weekly,* Sept. 14, 1981, p. 28.

Idemitsu quote: "Managers Employ Unusual Techniques at Idemitsu of Japan," by Mike Tharp, *The New York Times,* June 8, 1981, p. D4.

James quote: "Gold Handcuffs," *Business Week,* July 27, 1981, p. 58.

Greenberger quote: "How 'Burnout' Affects Corporate Managers and Their Performance," by Robert S. Greenberger, *The Wall Street Journal.*

References 331

McIntyre/Hoch comments: "America's New Immobile Society," *Business Week,* July 27, 1981, p. 60 & 62.

Hellriegel quote: "Successful Supervisor," Dartnell Corp. bulletin.

CHAPTER 6

Lawyer material: "... and Why Japan Has Few Lawyers," by William Chapman, *The Washington Post,* picked up by the *Bergen Record,* Sept. 20, 1981, p. E1.

Thurow material: "Where's America's Old Team Spirit," *The New York Times,* by Lester C. Thurow, July 26, 1981, p. F3.

International Paper item: "International Paper Tries Managing for the Long Run," *Business Week,* July 28, 1980, p. 94.

Idemitsu quote: "Managers Employ Unusual Techniques at Idemitsu Japan," by Mike Tharp, *The New York Times,* June 8, 1981, p. D4.

GM example: "Democracy Moves Into the Workplace," by Harry Bernstein, *Los Angeles Times,* Oct. 23, 1980.

Warren comments: A.S. Warren speech at the American Institute of Industrial Engineers, Detroit, May 18, 1981, pp. 8 & 9.

Ford material: "Where Are All the New Fall Cars?" *Time,* Oct. 5, 1981, p. 66.

American Can item: "Where Different Styles Have Led Two Canmakers," *Business Week,* July 27, 1981, p. 80.

National Semiconductor item: "Behind the Exodus at National Semiconductor," *Business Week,* Sept. 21, 1981, p. 95.

Fischer comment: "Taking Combat Out of Labor Relations," by Ben Fischer, *Business Week,* Sept. 21, 1981, p. 17.

Emanuel comments: "Productivity Improvement—Japanese Style," by Myron Emanuel, *Communications & Management,* Jan.-Feb. 1981.

Horner comments: "UAW Involvement," by Bill Horner, 1980 QWL Executive Conference, Apr. 11, 1980, p. 79.

Steel industry material: "Steel Jacks Up Its Productivity," *Business Week,* Oct. 12, 1981, p. 84.

GM-UAW information: QWL chart and other materials supplied by GM.

CHAPTER 7

Story City material: Presentation by Michael R. Simmons before the American Productivity Center, Sept. 13, 1979.

Organizational Behavior Institute material: *OBI Interaction,* Feb. 1, 1978, Vol. 8, No. 3.

Author quote: "Sure Fail—The Art of Mismanagement," by Raymond Dreyfack (distributed by Farnsworth Publishing Co., Inc.), p. 68.

CHAPTER 8

Markarian comments: "I Challenge You!" editorial. *The Record,* Nov. 5, 1980, full page ad, p. A-17.

Shapiro quote: "The Corporate Chief's New Class," by Marshall Loeb, *Time,* Apr. 14, 1980, p. 87.

IDC item: Astor file. Management Safeguards, Inc.

Begelman item: Ibid

Drexal Burnham item: Ibid

Lewis item: "Dropping By To Keep His Hand In," *Time,* Mar. 9, 1981, p. 64.

Rifkin item: "The Spreading Danger of Computer Crime," *Business Week,* Apr. 20, 1981, p. 88.

Kraft item: "More Pressure To Prosecute Executive Crime," *Business Week,* Dec. 18, 1978, p. 104.

Schwab item: "Another Black Mark for Corporate Ethics," by Dan Dorfman, *New York,* Mar. 21, 1977, p. 11.

Oklahoma item: "Oklahoma!" *Time,* Oct. 12, 1981, p. 31.

Pitney-Bowes material: "The Pressure To Compromise Personal Ethics," *Business Week,* Jan. 31, 1977, p. 107.

Linowes quote: "The Corporate Conscience," by David F. Linowes (Hawthorn), p. ix.

Hayes quote: "Conscience: The Spirit of the Law," by James L. Hayes, *Management Review,* Jan. 1979, p. 2.

Life quote: "Meet Mr. Matsushita" (sub-section: "An Idea Hit Me—It Was Ridiculous"), by James Mills, *Life,* Sept. 1964, p. 112.

Time quote: "Leaders for the 21st Century," *Time,* Apr. 14, 1980, p. 23.

CHAPTER 9

Masaharu quote: "The Best of Two Worlds," by Steve Ludwig, *International Management,* Nov. 1967, p. 42.

Vogel quote: "Japan as Number 1," by Ezra F. Vogel (Harper & Row, Inc.).

Thurow quote: "Productivity: Japan Has a Better Way," by Lester C. Thurow, *New York Times,* Feb. 8, 1981, p. F2.

Survey item: "Japan's Edge: An Ability To Take a Longer View," *World Business Weekly,* Sept. 14, 1981, p. 36.

Tokyo Sanyo Electric Co. information: "Japan—Where Operations Really Are Strategic," by Steven C. Wheelwright, *Harvard Business Review,* p. 67.

Lee Aspin quote: "Tip O'Neill on the Ropes," *Time,* May 18, 1981, p. 17.

RCA item: "RCA's Whirling Merry-Go-Round," *Business Week,* Feb. 9, 1981, p. 76.

Broadway Hale Store information: "Following the Corporate Legend," *Business Week,* Feb. 11, 1980, p. 62.

Japan survey quote: "Can the Japanese Originate As Well As Adapt?" *World Business Weekly,* Sept. 14, 1981, p. 31.

References 333

Warner-Lambert information: "Warner-Lambert: Reversing Direction To Correct Neglect," *Business Week,* June 15, 1981, p. 65.

Memorex information: "Memorex Tries a Turnaround—Again," *Business Week,* Jan. 19, 1981, p. 78.

Time material: "The Money Chase," *Time,* May 4, 1981, p. 61.

Tinsley quote: "Business Organizations in the Sustainable Society," by Dillard Tinsley, Woodlands Conference paper, 1979, p. 6.

Xerox material: "The New Lean, Mean Xerox," *Business Week,* Oct. 12, 1981, p. 126.

International Paper Co. information: "International Paper Tries Managing for the Long Run," *Business Week,* July 28, 1980, p. 94.

CHAPTER 10

O'Toole material: "Work in an Era of Slow Economic Growth," by James O'Toole, Woodlands Conference, 1979, p. 18.

Volkswagen material: "Employee Pride Is the Goal at a Volkswagen Plant," by Ben A. Franklin, *The New York Times,* Aug. 16, 1981, p. 26.

Thurow quote: "Productivity: Japan Has a Better Way," by Lester C. Thurow, *The New York Times,* Feb. 8, 1981, p. F2.

Kolson quote: "Teaching Thrift to Bureaucrats," by Robert E. Kolson, *The New York Times,* Mar. 29, 1981, p. F3.

Losey information: "Report on: International Study Mission to Japan," sponsored by Technology Transfer Institute, by Michael R. Losey, Dec. 1980.

Sure Fail quote: "Sure Fail—The Art of Mismanagement," by Raymond Dreyfack (distributed by Farnsworth Publishing Co., Inc.), p. 129.

American Can material: "Where Different Styles Have Led Two Canmakers," *Business Week,* July 27, 1981, p. 80.

Xerox material: "The New Lean, Mean Xerox," *Business Week,* Oct. 12, 1981, p. 126.

Drucker quote: "Managing in Turbulent Times," by Peter F. Drucker.

Visa material: "The Iconoclast Who Made Visa No. 1," *Business Week,* Dec. 22, 1980, p. 44.

Flanagan quote: "New Management Style Aimed at Crumbling Image of Bureaucracy," by James Flanagan, *The Los Angeles Times,* Oct. 26, 1980.

Schlitz information: "Brewmaster: Frank J. Sellinger," by Ray Kenney, *The New York Times,* Mar. 1, 1981, p. F8.

CHAPTER 11

Brown quote and Watson statements of philosophy: "A Business and Its Beliefs," by Thomas J. Watson Jr., McKinsey Foundation Lecture Series, Columbia Univ. School of Business, 1963.

Lemelson item: "Inventor's IBM Deal," by Leonard Sloane, *The New York Times,* Nov. 18, 1981, p. D2.

Open Door Policy material: "About Your Company," IBM publication, p. 28.

Hewlett-Packard information: Personal correspondence, plus *Measure* and other HP publications.

Ways quote: "The American Kind of Worker Participation," by Max Ways, *Fortune,* Oct. 1976, p. 180.

Bolling/Bowles quote: "America's Competitive Edge," by Richard Bolling & John Bowles, McGraw-Hill Book Co., p. 130.

Hayes quote: "Dana: Few Rules, Many Sales," by Thomas C. Hayes, *The New York Times,* Oct. 19, 1979.

Kirchner quote: "In Face of 36% Growth Spurt, DEC Sticks to Its Style," by Bert Kirchner, *Electronic Design,* Jan. 4, 1979, p. 236.

WSJ quote: "Digital Equipment Rides Waves of Success From Minicomputers," by David Gumpert, *The Wall Street Journal,* July 18, 1978.

Engstrom quote: "The Digital Mystique," by Theresa Engstrom, *Boston Magazine,* Aug. 1981, p. 140.

Uttal material: "The Gentlemen and the Upstarts Meet in a Great Mini Battle," by Bro Uttal, *Fortune,* Apr. 23, 1979.

O'Toole material: "Work in an Era of Slow Economic Growth," by James O'Toole, Mitchell Prize Award Paper, Woodlands Conference, 1979.

Tandy material: "Tandy a Dandy Success Story," by Pat Remick, *American Business,* Sept. 1981, p. 14.

GM material: Remarks by A.S. Warren at the American Institute of Industrial Engineers, May 18, 1981.

Money references: "Ten Terrific Companies To Work For," *Money,* Nov. 1976.

Hayes material: "The Japanese Way at Quasar," *The New York Times,* by Thomas C. Hayes, Oct. 16, 1981, p. D1.

Motorola ad material: Various issues of *Time.*

Wood material: "Right from the Start," by Robert C. Wood, *Technology,* Nov.-Dec. 1981, p. 77.

Sony information: "How Japan Does It," *Time,* Mar. 30, 1981.

Romine speech: "Developing Solutions: Learning from Other Companies," by Dale Romine, General Motors Quality of Work Life Executive Conference, Apr. 11, 1980.

CHAPTER 12

Time quote: "The Extended Nuclear Family," *Time,* Oct. 26, 1981, p. 20.

Japan Survey material: "Survey: Japan," *World Business Weekly,* Sept. 14, 1981, p. 40.

References

Stephens quote: "Visions: The Rising Sun of Productivity," by Bill Stephens, *Mgr.* (Atlantic Richfield publication) 1981/Two, p. 3.

Losey material: "International Study Mission to Japan" report, by Michael R. Losey, Dec. 1980, p. 59.

Nelson quote: "Business Feels the Heat of U.S. Antibias Laws, *Business Week,* Nov. 23, 1981, p. 58.

Facsimile machine information: "Jápan Takes Over in High-Speed Fax," *Business Week,* Nov. 2, 1981, p. 104.

Auto industry material: "A Dazzling Display in Tokyo," *Time,* Nov. 16, 1981, p. 126.

MITI robot item: "Robots March On," *Parade,* Oct. 11, 1981.

Salzman quote: "Management Issues in Engineering and Manufacturing Automation," by Roy M. Salzman, *Time,* June 8, 1981 (Special advertising section).

Business Week writing team quote: "The Reindustrialization of America," McGraw-Hill book, by the Business Week Team, p. 167.

O'Toole material: "Work in an Era of Slow Economic Growth," by James O'Toole, Mitchell Prize Award paper, 1979 Woodlands Conference on Growth Policy.

Salzman material: See Salzman quote above.

Juran information: "Why Japanese Cars Sell So Well," by Anthony Paul, *Readers Digest,* p. 53.

INDEX

Absenteeism, controlling, 280-286
Adolph Coors Co., 110-111
Adversary system, American free enterprise as, 33-34, 38
Age, of Japanese workforce, 292-293
   (See also Lifetime employment)
American Can Co.
   bureaucracy in, 235-236
   decision making in, 137
American industry
   advantages of, 297-302
   companies exemplifying Japanese management style in, 243-272
   ethos of, 12-13
   managerial changes in recommended for, 71-77
   mandates necessary for transformation of, 303-313
   quality control circles applied to, 133-138
   work restructuring in, 167-171
Anxiety in American industry, 150-152
   elimination of, 156
Apex Electronic Corp., 217
Appliance industry, Japanese advantages in, 28
Assembly workers
   at Kubota, 59
   at Toshiba Corp., 53
Automation, attitude toward, 117-119
   (See also Computer industry; Robots)
Automobile industry, American
   bureaucracy in, 236
   government involvement in, 145-147
   job repetition in, 165
   labor relations in, 140, 141-142
   (See also Ford Motor Co.; General Motors)
Automobile industry, Japanese
   advantages in, 27, 28, 32, 45-46, 287-288
   government involvement in, 144
   organization, 45
   quality in, 227
   self-interest in, 230-231
   technological advances in, 298

Bethlehem Steel, 142
Boredom, 164-165
Bribery, 173-174, 177-182
   (See also Social responsibility)
Broadway Hale Stores, leadership succession in, 204
Bureaucracy
   elimination of, 44-45
   layerism in, 234-236, 260-261
Burnout, 123-124
Butler Manufacturing Company, self-management in, 87-90, 160-164

Canon, 317
Career growth, Japanese concept of, 74
   (See also Job advancement)
Casio Computer Co., 72, 317
Communication, Hewlett-Packard and, 252-253
Communications industry, job repetition in, 165
Compensation, 155
   Delco Remy and, 268-269
   Digital Equipment Corp. and, 264
   Matsutani and, 67-68
   Nissan Motor Co. and, 56
   Suntory Ltd. and, 70-71
   Tokai Bank Ltd. and, 67-68
   Toshiba Corp. and, 53
Computer industry
   American industry's advantage in, 299, 307
   international cooperation in, 321-322
   Japanese competition in, 29, 30
   Japanese government involvement in, 144-145
   long-range planning of innovations in, 208
Computers
   management dehumanization by, 114-116
   worker resentment of, 117-119
Consensus decision making, 42-44, 130-131

computer use with, 117-119
Delta Airlines, 246
Digital Equipment Corp. and, 263-264
disadvantages, 301
evaluating, 99
government and, 77
labor unions and, 77
Panasonic and, 274-275
resources pooled with, 318
Texas Instruments and, 254
(See also Quality circles)
Cooperative management, 42
Customer, needs of, 38

Dam management, Matsushita on, 18-19
Dana Corp., 258-261
job advancement and, 300
Datsun (See Nissan Motor Co., Ltd.)
Decision making
elitist, 137-138
group (See Consensus decision making
Dehumanized management, 109-111
Delco Remy Division, of General Motors, 268-269
Delta Airlines, 243-247
Deming, W. Edwards, 36, 60
Digital Equipment Corp., 261-265
Dishonesty, 173-174, 177-182
(See also Social responsibility)

Education
technology advanced by, 323-324
U.S. advantage in, 301
Elitism, 126-129
competition fostering, 127-128
decision making, 137-138
Employee Participation Groups (EPG) in General Motors, 83, 90-94, 96-97
Employment practices
advantages of sustained in future, 291-293
hiring, 37
insubordination, 155-156
retirement, 113-114, 153
seniority, 154
uniformity of, 69-70

women and, 68, 295-297, 323, 325-326,
(See also Compensation; Fringe benefits; Job advancement; Job rotation; Labor unions; Lifelong employment; People-sensitive management; Recruitment; Training)
Energy, Japanese industry and, 289-290
Ergonomics, 223-231
Ethics (See Social responsibility)
Expectations, of worker, 106-108

Family, corporation as, 73
(See also Group effort)
Firearms industry, Japanese advantages in, 29
Ford Motor Co.
decision making in, 137
leadership succession in, 202
Free enterprise, as adversary system, 33-34, 38
Fringe benefits, 120-122
Kobe Steel, 65-66
Nissan Motor Co., 57
Sharp, 63
Frustration of worker, work restructuring reducing, 223-225
Fujitec, 298
Fujitsu, 323
Fukawa Works plant, of Toshiba Corp., 51-54

Gaines Pet Food, 97-98
Geneen, Harold S., 110
General Foods, 97-98
General Mills, 203
General Motors, 72
decision making in, 136-137
delayering, 268
Delco Remy Division, 268-269
Fleetwood Fisher Body Plant, 269
government involvement in, 145-147
humanistic management at, 268
labor relations in, 146-147
Lordstown operation, 116
National Center for Productivity and Quality of Working Life, 145-146, 147

Index

Quality of Working Life in, 83, 90-94, 96-97, 116, 145-147
Genesco, 202
Goals
 achievement of, 52-53
 Kubota Corp. and, 60
Government
 consensus decision making and, 77
 labor relations with in U.S., 76-77
 necessity of Ministry of International Trade and Industry for the U.S., 310-312
 regulation by, 34, 35, 143, 147
 U.S. technological advantage and, 300
Gross national product, of Japan, 27
Group effort, 125-129
 conditions necessary for, 150
 contests for, 53
 criticism of ethics of, 98-99
 Delco Remy and, 268
 Employee Participation Groups at General Motors, 83, 90-94, 96-97, 98
 goals attained by, 52-53
 Hewlett-Packard and, 252
 loyalty to group, 129-130
 necessity of for U.S. industry transformation, 303-304
 Texas Instruments and, 257
 transference to U.S. industry, 147-148
 values of, 37-39
  (See also Consensus decision making; Quality circles; Work environment)
Growth
 Matsushita on, 18-19
 planning for long-term, 32-33, 308-309

Harley-Davidson Motor Co., 29, 32
Harvard Business School, "Chair of Leadership" established at, 9
Hewlett-Packard, 249-253
Hiring policies (See Recruitment)
Hitachi, 145
 research and development and, 321
 software subsidiary of, 323

technology and, 298
Third World and, 317
Honda, 32
Human Enterprise, The, 176
Human relationships, Matsushita on, 15-16
Humility, necessity of for corporation long-range planning, 212-215

IBM, 240, 247-249
 Japanese competition, 39
 Japanese products marketed by, 317
Idemitsu Kosan, 76, 120, 128
Inbreeding, in Japanese industry, 293-295
"Indicative Planning Process," 35
Individuality, Japanese industry squelching, 294
 (See also Elitism)
Inland Steel Co., 142
Innovation, Japanese striving in, 322
 (See also Technology)
Internationalization, Japanese industry and, 319
International Paper Co., 214-215
Inventory management, 46

Japanese industry
 in America, 272-280
 problems in for future, 288-293
 requirements for in future, 314-327
 as role model for American industry, 305-306
 success of (See Success of Japanese management)
 vulnerabilities in, 75-76, 293-295
Job advancement, 153-155, 300
 career growth, 74
 Panasonic, 274
 U.S. industry and, 300
Job attrition, 325
Job rotation, 40, 165-167, 226
 at Delta Airlines, 246
 at Panasonic, 274
 at Toshiba Corp., 52
Job security (See Lifetime employment)
Johnson & Johnson, 215
Jones & Laughlin, 143

Kaiser Steel, 266-267
Kanban System, 231-233
Knowledge
    Japanese manager and, 31
    Matsushita on, 20-22
Kobe Steel, 64-66
Kubota, Ltd., Tsukuba plant, 58-61

Labor relations, 139-143
    automation and, 299-300
    government and, 76-77
    Kobe Steel, 64-65
    necessity of Ministry of International Trade and Industry for in the U.S., 310-312
    Sharp and, 62-63, 64
    Toshiba Corp. and, 54
Labor strikes, 35
    Japanese attitude toward, 77
Labor unions, 33, 34-35, 57-58
    consensus decision making and, 77
    Matsushita on, 17-18
    Nissan Motor Co. and, 58
    Quality of Working Life and, 95-97
    Toshiba Corp. and, 54
Layerism, 234-236, 260-261
Lawyers, in Japan, 125-126
Layoffs, 112-113
Leadership, grooming for, 197, 201-204
Leisure, effect of on Japanese productivity, 291
Lifetime employment, 39, 40, 65, 74-75, 112-114, 153
    Delta Airlines and, 246
    Digital Equipment Corp. and, 263
    job change and, 294-295
    technology versus, 324-325
Long-range planning
    Delta Airlines and, 245-246
    Digital Equipment Corp. and, 264-265
    humility along with, 212-215
    IBM and, 249
    Japanese method of, 199-201
    leadership grooming and, 197, 201-204
    managerial support of, 215-218
    for plant modernization, 198
    Procter & Gamble and, 271

short-term planning compared with, 197, 198-199, 208-212
in technology and research and development, 198, 204-212
Texas Instruments and, 255-256
training, 198
for U.S. industry transformation, 73-74, 307-308

McGregor, Douglas, 157-158
McLuhan, Marshall, 116
MacMillan Jardine, 31
Management by objectives, of Hewlett-Packard, 250-251
Manager
    Japanese style of, 30-31
    Matsutani's ideas on, 16-17, 66-67
    as noncreative conformists, 75
Manufacturing productivity, of Japan, 27-28
Mark Controls Corp., 217
Matrix Management, 42
Matsushita, Konosuke, 7-9
    on compensation, 67-68
    on leadership succession, 197
    on manager, 66-67
    Matsushita School, 8-9, 194-196
    philosophy of management of, 14-23, 106
    PHP, 8, 193-194
    PHP Institute, 191-193
    popularity of, 179
    on social responsibility, 190-196
Matsushita Electric Industrial Co., Inc., 8
    Harvard "Chair of Leadership" established by, 9
    insubordination dealt with in, 155-156
    Panasonic Corp. as subsidiary of, 272-276
    philosophy of management of, 14
    planning in, 73
    Quasar Electronics Co. as subsidiary of, 276-278
    research and development of, 75, 321

Index

social responsibility of, 190-191
technology of, 297-298
uniqueness of, 76
Matsushita School of Government and Management, 8-9, 194-196
Matsutani, 67-68
Memorex Corp., 210
Ministry of International Trade and Industry (MITI), 76-77, 145, 298
    goals of, 318
    necessity of for U.S. industry, 309-312
    research and development and, 205, 206, 207, 208, 319-322
    software development and, 322-323
    Third World involvement, 316-317
    yen flow and, 319-320
Motivation, 167-168
    productivity increased by, 50
    quality as source of, 226-227
Motorcycle industry, Japanese advantages in, 29, 32
Motorola, 276-278
Murata Kikai, 30

National Center for Productivity and Quality of Working Life, 145-146, 147
National Semi-Conductor Corp., 138
National Steel Corp., 142
Natural laws, Matsushita on, 14-15
Natural resources, American industry advantage in, 301
Needs of workers, work environment restructuring according to, 225-226
Nippon Electric Co., 317
Nippon Steel, 74
Nippon Telegraph and Telephone Public Corp., 319, 322
Nissan Motor Manufacturing Corp., 55-58, 73
    technology and, 298
    U.S. division, 148-149, 279
Nuclear energy, for Japanese industry, 289-290

Office works, Quality of Working Life and, 99

Openmindedness, manager's need for, 22
Operation Outreach, 315-316
Organization (See Bureaucracy)
Owens-Illinois, Inc., 236-237
Panasonic Company, 272-276
Participative management, 259-260
Partnerships, between American and Japanese companies, 317
People-sensitive management, 39-41, 51, 105-106
    computer use along with, 114-119
    dehumanized management compared with, 109-111, 117-119
    positive self-perception fostered by, 123-124
    profits-centered management compared with, 119-120
    social entitlements of workers, 111-112
    worker expectations, 106-108
    (See also Employment practices)
Philosophy of management
    American (See Quality of Working Life)
    of Matsushita, 14-23
    need for, 23
    role of, 9-13
PHP, 8, 193-194
PHP Institute, 191-193
Pitney-Bowes, Inc., 184-185
Planning (See Long-range planning)
Plant modernization, 41-42
Procter & Gamble Co., 269-271
Productivity
    ability of Japanese workers to sustain pace of, 290-293
    bureaucratic leanness and, 234-236
    efficiency through economy of operation, 233-239
    employee placement for, 239
    improvements made in, 236-238
    Japanese advantage in, 220-223
    motivation for, 50
    optimization of in Kanban System, 231-233

theories on, 49-50
work environment restructuring and, 223-231
Productivity growth rate, Japan's compared to other countries, 27
Profits
    inappropriate, 38
    long-term planning for necessary in U.S. industry, 307-309
    management focusing on, 119-120
    Matsushita on, 19-20
    preoccupation with, 208-212
Profit sharing, Texas Instruments and, 254-255
Protectionism, Japanese industry and, 290

Quality
    Japanese industry achievement of, 35-37
    motivation associated with, 226-227, 228
    necessity of for U.S. industry transformation, 306-307
Quality circles, 131-133
    application to American industry, 133-138
    definition, 132
    Employee Participation Groups and, 83, 90-94, 96-97, 98
    initiation of, 131
    Kubota Corp. and, 60-61
    loyalty to, 129-130
    Nissan Motor Co. and, 56-57, 279
    Quality of Working Life and, 84
    Quasar and, 277
    Sharp and, 62
    Suntory Ltd. and, 69
    Texas Instruments and, 254
    Tokai Bank Ltd. and, 68-69
    Toshiba and, 53-54
    working group suggestions from, 322
Quality control
    American industry improvement in, 72
    Kobe Steel and, 66
    Toshiba and, 279
    (See also Quality circles)

Quality of Working Life (QWL), 79-81
    acceptance of, 97-98
    assessment of, 92-94
    definition, 82, 83-84, 85-86
    dishonesty and, 176
    establishment of for smaller companies, 100-104
    in General Motors, 83, 90-94, 96-97, 98, 116, 145-147
    interest in, 287-288
    labor unions and, 95-97
    limitations, 84-85, 98-100
    need for, 81-82
    self-management in, 87-90
    social responsibility and, 184
    training for, 94-95
    trust as foundation of, 86-90
Quasar Electronic Co., 276-278
QWL (See Quality of Working Life)

Radio Shack, 267
RCA, 203
Recruitment, 37, 40, 152
    Nissan Motor Co., 55
    Panasonic, 274
Research and Development (See Technology)
Restructuring the work environment, 167-171, 223-231
Retirement, 113-114, 153, 292-293
Rigid Paper Tube Corporation, 216
Robots, 118, 156-157
    Japanese advances in, 30, 298
    jobs displaced by, 324-325
    in Nissan Motor Co., 55
    research and development in, 321
Rockwell Manufacturing, 202

Scanlon Plan, 260, 304
Schlitz Brewing Co., Jos., 237
Sears, Roebuck & Co., 234-235
Security in employment, 74-75
    (See also Lifetime employment)
Self-interest of workers, productivity fostered by, 228-231
Self-management, 156-160
    Butler Manufacturing Co., 87-90, 160-164
    evaluation of, 98, 99
Self-perception, people-centered management fostering positive, 123-124

Index

Seniority system, 154
Sharp Electronics Corp., 61-64, 137, 279, 317
Siemens Co., 166-167
Social responsibility, 173-176
    corporate response to, 184-186
    dimensions of, 186-190
    dishonesty, 173-174, 177-182
    for employees, 33
    Matsushita on, 190-196
    pressure for, 182-184
        (See also Employment practices)
Software development, Ministry of International Trade and Industry and, 322-323
    (See also Computer industry)
Sony
    absenteeism controlled at, 280, 281-282, 285-286
    U.S. division, 279-280
Specialization, job rotation compared with, 165-166
Sporting arms industry, Japanese advantages in, 29
Steel industry, labor relations in, 142-143
Story City experiment, in self-management, 87-90, 160-164
Stress (See Anxiety)
Strikes (See Labor strikes)
Success of Japanese management, 25-26, 31-32, 46-47
    bureaucratic channels eliminated from, 44-45
    consensus decision making, 42-44
    cost advantages in, 45-46
    efficiency of operations, 26-28
    government regulation of, 34, 35
    group sales in, 37-39
    industry success in, 28-30
    labor relations and, 33, 34-35
    managerial personality and, 30-31
    people-sensitive management, 39-41
    planning for long-term growth and, 32-33
    plant modernization, 41-42
    quality achieved by, 35-37
Sunao spirit, Matsushita on, 22

Suntory, Ltd., 69-71
    Katsura Brewery, 69
Supplier, as part of team, 38-39

Tandem Computers, Inc., 265-266
Tandy Corp., 267
Teamwork (See Group effort)
Technology
    American industry's advantage in, 297-300
    education advancing, 323-324
    long-range planning in, 198, 204-212
    3M, 271
Technology Transfer Institute, 35
Texas Instruments, Inc., 253-257
Theory X, 157-159
Theory Y, 158
Third World, Japanese industry involvement in, 316-317, 318
3M, 271-272
    absenteeism controlled at, 280-285, 286
    Japanese products marketed by, 317
Time clocks, 87
Tokai Bank, Ltd., 66-69
Tokyo Sanyo Electric Co., 201
Toshiba Corp., 279
    Fukawa Works plant, 51-54
    research and development and, 321
Toyota, 32, 45, 46, 72, 73, 298
Trade policies, Japanese industry and, 290
Training, 152-153
    Kobe Steel, 65
    Kubota Corp., 60
    leadership grooming and, 202
    Nissan Motor Co., 55-56
    Quality of Working Life and, 94-95
    Tokai Bank Ltd., 67
    Toshiba, 52
Trust, 71-72
    Digital Equipment Corp. and, 261-262
    Hewlett-Packard and, 251-252
    necessity of for American industry transformation, 303-305
    Procter & Gamble and, 270
    productivity increased by, 86-87
    3M and, 271

Tsukuba plant, of Kubota, 58-59

U.S. industry (See American industry)

Visa International, 239-240

Warner-Lambert Co., 209-210
White collar crime, 173-174, 177-182
   (See also Social responsibility)
Women, 295-297
   in American companies, 295-297
   in Japanese companies, 68, 323, 325-326
Work effort, Kanban system and, 231-233
Work environment, 149-150, 223-231
   boredom, 164-165
   improvements in, 304-305
   stress elimination, 156
   U.S. industry, 150-152, 153
   work restructuring, 167-171
      (See also Employment practices; Quality of Working Life)
Work restructuring, 167-171, 223-231
Worker expectations, 106-108

Xerox Corp., 312
   long-range planning in, 213-214
   productivity improvement in, 238

Yen, flow of, 319-320

Zero Defects (ZD) movement, 37, 131